A Baker's Tale

The Story behind Oliver Adams Bakery from its Beginnings in 1856

Jane Evans

Northampton Bakeries Ltd.

Published in 2000 by
Northampton Bakeries Ltd
Dallington Fields Bakery
Gladstone Road
Northampton NN5 7AJ

ISBN: 0 9539 716-0-0

© Jane Evans 2000

The rights of Jane Evans to be identified as the
Author of this work have been asserted by her in accordance with the
Copyright Designs and Patents Act 1988

All rights reserved. No part of this publication may be reproduced,
stored in a retrieval system or transmitted in any form or by any means,
electronic, mechanical, photocopying, recording or otherwise,
without the prior permission in writing of the Publisher.

Front cover illustration:
Thomas and Elizabeth Adams, ca. 1860

Printed in Great Britain by Stanley L. Hunt (Printers) Ltd., Midland Road,
Rushden, Northamptonshire

Contents

List of Illustrations
Acknowledgements
Foreword

Chapter 1 -	Thomas Adams, Journeyman Baker - Baking in Victorian Times and Earlier	1
Chapter 2 -	The Search for Thomas' Ancestors and a Connection with John Adams, the 3rd American President	33
Chapter 3 -	Thomas Adams, Master Baker 1856-1890	44
Chapter 4 -	'Land for the People!'	69
Chapter 5 -	The Radical Rebellion	91
Chapter 6 -	On Council Business	105
Chapter 7 -	Branching Out	114
Chapter 8 -	Tea-rooms and Bakeries	131
Chapter 9 -	'The Best Thing since Sliced Bread'	148
Chapter 10 -	Mayor of Northampton - 70 Years On	167
Chapter 11 -	The Boom Years	176
Chapter 12 -	Full Circle	189

Bibliography
Index

List of Illustrations

Page

Cover: Thomas and Elizabeth Adams, ca. 1860
1. A London baker convicted of selling underweight loaves in the Middle Ages (from *Assisa Paris* 1266, Corp. of London Records Office) 2
2. The Amos bakery at 12 Sutton Street, Flore, before renovation, ca. 1975 3
3. Richard Amos taking the last loaf out of the oven at Sutton Street (1960) 5
4. Medieval bakers 7
5. Medieval bakery stall 9
6. Dough trough 22
7. A brake for kneading dough (from F. Vine's *Biscuits for Bakers* 1896) 27
8. The former Quaker meeting house at Flore 35
9. The family tree of President John Adams (from J.B.Gardner's *Henry Adams of Somersetshire, England and Braintree, Massachusetts* 1927) 38
10. The Adams memorial in the church of Barton St. David, Somerset (source as for 9) 41
11. The Northampton Post Office on the corner of the Drapery, ca. 1850 45
12. Rev. John Bennett, Minister at Castle Hill 1833 - 1859 (from T.Gascoigne's *A History of Castle Hill Church* 1674-1895) 46
13. Castle Hill Congregationalist Chapel 1852 (source as for 12) 47
14. Elizabeth Oliver, Thomas' second wife 49
15. Wooden peels for feeding loaves into the oven 54
16. Section of an Eagle coal-fired range (from C.Herman Senn's *New 20th Century Cookery Book,* 5th ed. 1913) 57
17. Victorian loaves 60
18. The 1881 directors of the Northampton Building Society 79
19. The Building Society estates built between 1860 and 1923 81
20. Plan of the East Park estate - 1884 85
21. The Building Society's earlier headquarters at 11 Abington Square 87
22. The new head office on Abington Square, acquired in 1923 89
23. Clock given by Charles Bradlaugh to Thomas Adams 92
24. The statue of Charles Bradlaugh on Abington Square 93
25. Charles Bradlaugh 97
26. Joseph Gurney 99
27. The Northampton Racecourse, ca. 1896 (from *Racing Illustrated 1896*) 107

28.	The River Nene at the site of Becket's Park, ca. 1880	109
29.	Crime on Midsummer Meadow, 1885	111
30.	Walter Quincey Adams	117
31.	Horse and cart	118
32.	A double deck oven (from E.Dare's *Thoughts of a Journeyman Baker*)	119
33.	Pork pie advert	122
34.	W.Q.Adams' cart	123
35.	Cross section of a grain of wheat (courtesy of Flour Advisory Bureau)	127
36.	Brax brown bread advert	129
37.	Frank Adams' parents-in-law, Daniel and Elizabeth Rigby	132
38.	Frank and his family	133
39.	Billing Road from Northampton General Hospital, ca. 1900	135
40.	Thomas Rigby Adams with his fellow students, ca. 1895	140
41.	Thomas Rigby's bakery on West Street	144
42.	Kettering Road from Abington Square end, ca. 1910	145
43.	Edgar's bakery on the corner of Wellingborough Road and Allen Road	146
44.	National Mark flour advert	149
45.	Poster: 'The kitchen is the key to victory' (1916)	150
46.	Poster: 'Eat more bread' (ca.1930)	151
47.	The Kingsthorpe bakery, ca. 1940	153
48.	Poster: Bread into battle (1944)	154
49.	The Wedgwood Café in Abington Street	156
50.	The Corner House Café on Wood Hill	158
51.	One of Osborne Robinson's curved window paintings in The Clipper	159
52.	Another painting in The Clipper (the New York skyline)	160
53.	The board of directors, ca. 1950	161
54.	Aerial view of King's Heath and the new bakery, ca. 1956	162
55.	The huge dough bowls in the new bakery plant (1950s)	163
56.	The automatic bread slicing and wrapping machine (1950s)	165
57.	Percy and Barbara Adams as Mayor and Mayoress	170
58.	Barbara Adams outside the Pickwick Café	172
59.	Abington Street decorated for the coronation of Elizabeth II	174
60.	The horse-drawn cart and hand-cart from the Derby Road bakery	177
61.	The Adams carnival float (1956)	178
62.	One of the familiar Adams delivery vans at King's Heath (1950s)	179
63.	The crumpet machine (1960)	180
64.	An elaborate iced cake made by Adams in 1960	181
65.	Cartoon about white sliced bread (1974)	182
66.	Theobald's, Kettering (1950s)	184
67.	Lawrence's, St. Giles Street, Northampton	186
68.	A Northampton bus from 1947 advertising Adams bread	191

69.	An Adams shop window	193
70.	Tom Adams in the bakery (1981)	194
71.	An automatic 'travelling' oven at King's Heath bakery (1960)	197

Picture credits

My thanks go to the following for permission to use their photographs:
The Adams family for 14, 20, 23, 30, 34, 37, 38, 40, 41, 43, 50, 53 - 57, 60- 64, 66, 67, 69, 71
Richard Amos for 2 and 3
Business & Commerce Digest for 70
East Pennine T.C., R. Marshall Collection for 68
Nationwide Building Society for 18, 19, 21, 22, 26, 59
Northampton Independent and Chronicle & Echo for 8, 11, 24, 25, 47, 49, 58
Talent Pastimes Ltd. Stamps, Postcards and Cigarette Card Dealers for 42

Abbreviations used

C&E - Chronicle and Echo
N. I. - Northampton Independent
N.M. - Northampton Mercury

Acknowledgements

I gratefully acknowledge the help given me by Philip and Tom Adams and many members of staff at Oliver Adams bakery, both past and present, in particular Iris Vickers, Richard Patching, the late Ted Frost and his wife Ann, Bert Masters and Ann Reed; also the members of the public who came forward with reminiscences about the bakery and the shops. Other members of the family have been very helpful with their memories and contributions, in particular the late Edna Bodily, Peter Robinson and Pam Cooper.

I must also express my thanks to the staff of the Northamptonshire Studies Collection, Central Library Northampton, the staff of the Northamptonshire Record Office, the Nationwide Archives and the Black Country Museum, and John Smith of the Flore Heritage Society.

Finally, thank you to my husband Nick for his support and comments on the text and to Stanley Hunt (Printers) Ltd. for their advice and help in the design of the book.

Foreword

My ancestors and some of the less scrupulous bakers of the early 19th century shared one raw material in common - ground bones. In that long ago period flour was liable to be adulterated by adding bones to increase the bulk of a sack of flour. Meanwhile Josiah Spode was experimenting with the addition of bone to china clay in order to produce brilliant white bone china. Whereas Church's China still sell this today, we can rest assured that Adams are selling more wholesome bread than some of the bakers of the previous century did. Bone-free, wholesome buns from Lawrence's make up my daily lunch.

Any story of Northampton cannot miss the contribution made by Thomas Adams and his family. The importance of social conscience, Liberal politics and Non-Conformist religion are at the heart of this family story. Thomas Adams took the lead where other families, such as my own, followed. Many Northamptonshire families will share these common threads to our history, and we can read this book and think of our own ancestors, their work, their religion and their involvement in the local community.

When I was Mayor, the present Tom Adams showed me a fabulous Ormolou clock that the Radical Liberal MP Charles Bradlaugh gave to his great-great-grandfather, Thomas Adams, as a token of thanks for Thomas' support given during the parliamentary campaigns. Church's China's only known link with Bradlaugh is an engraving illustrating riots outside the Mercury offices on the Market Square following some adverse comments the paper made about him. Our windows appear as badly smashed as the newspaper offices next door. Sadly the reaction of my great-great grandfather is not recorded, nor what he may have said to Councillor Adams.

Our families' involvement in the Council is separated by a gap of over 30 years - from the time when Percy Adams was Mayor and the last Liberal Councillor in the 1950s, to my own election and the return of the Liberals to the Council in 1983. Still today the Adams family continues its tradition of quality service in our town. When it comes to discussion about the future of Northampton, it is good to know that members of the Adams family, whether as politicians or local business people, are there with something to say. Long may that continue to be so.

Richard Church
Mayor of Northampton 1997/98

Chapter 1

THOMAS ADAMS, JOURNEYMAN BAKER

Baking in Victorian times and earlier

You could be forgiven for thinking that the life of a baker in medieval England was easy - a job without pressure, answerable to no one, dependent merely on the harvest and the local miller. Even in Victorian times we tend to think of bakers happily serving their local community from their bakehouse on the corner, cooking their customers' Sunday dinners in the capacious ovens and producing wholesome bread made from flour stoneground at the local mill.

However, in reality the picture was different. From the Middle Ages right up to the Victorian period bakers were burdened by strict laws establishing what was called the Assize of Bread - an assessment which determined the weight and price of a loaf. In the 14th century a baker who sold underweight bread would have it hung round his neck, be tied to a board harnessed to two horses and then drawn through the streets as a public humiliation for his offence. And as late as the middle of the 19th century, far from wholesome loaves being baked on every street corner, government inspectors were liable to find black beetles and cobwebs falling into impure dough as it was kneaded in the hot and smelly bakehouses, staffed by exhausted young men working 18 hour shifts.

By the time the young man, Thomas Adams of the village of Flore in Northamptonshire, decided to learn the baking trade and become a journeyman baker in 1847, punishments of public humiliation for illegal practice were of course no longer used, and the Assize of Bread had been finally abolished in 1822, but the conditions under which a young apprentice had to work in the baking trade were very hard. Since the abolition of the Assize, competition had become intense, and the quality of bread had deteriorated in many cases.

Thomas' story is a fascinating one, for he came from humble beginnings to be the founder of a baking business that would eventually establish

Thomas Adams, Journeyman Baker

A London baker in the Middle Ages convicted of selling underweight loaves is drawn on a hurdle through the streets

itself as the leading bakery in Northamptonshire, known familiarly in the latter half of the 20th century as Oliver Adams the Baker. His sons left diaries and letters that have made it possible to gain insight into the life of a baker in the late Victorian and Edwardian period, but to set the young Thomas' experience in context there are interviews and reports made by government inspectors of the baking trade in the mid 19th century. These tell of the extraordinary working conditions which a journeyman baker might encounter, particularly in a major city. Thomas was lucky – Northampton was still comparatively small with a population of 27,000 in 1851, and in his earliest years he learnt the trade from a country baker in Flore for whom conditions would have been much pleasanter than in a town.

He was born on December 1st 1831 at the village of Drayton near Daventry. His father, William, was a labourer and a tenant of William Balderson, a shoe manufacturer. William Adams had married Betsey, a young woman from Chapel Brampton, and their first son, William, was born in 1826. Samuel, their third son, was born in 1835. The 1851 census reveals that when the sons grew up, William found employment as an agricultural labourer, while Samuel worked as a servant. Thomas, the second son, decided to become a baker.

It is known from Thomas' own personal reminiscences that he was brought up in the Congregationalist church – a Puritan movement whose founder, Robert Browne, was for 40 years rector in the Northamptonshire village of Achurch in the early 17th century, and was buried in St. Giles' churchyard, Northampton.

Thomas' parents may well have been strict and puritanical. It would certainly seem that his father was very strong-minded and ambitious. A minor incident mentioned in the papers of a Daventry solicitor reveal that William was arrested after being accused by his landlord, William Balderson, of pulling down two pigsties, allegedly the landlord's property. William refused to pay the fine demanded of him by the Justice of the Peace, and so in the winter of 1833 when Thomas was only one year old, his father was taken away to do hard labour for two months. On his release, William was determined to stand up for himself and employed the Northampton attorney, Augustus Yeates, to clear his name. Unfortunately, the outcome of the affair is not known.

William is said to have gone on to become a shopkeeper at the nearby village of Weedon – a notable rise from being an agricultural labourer and a reflection of the kind of determination which led to his attempt to clear his name and of the ambition that he must have harboured for himself and his family. In the 1851 census for Weedon there were no less than 19 grocers in the village. Weedon was home to the large army barracks that is still visible today beside the Grand Union canal, and so local retailers would have enjoyed the business provided by such a large number of soldiers.

Even the baker, Edward Amos, a few miles away at Flore, benefited from the custom of Weedon barracks. This was the man who would befriend Thomas a few years later and begin to teach him the craft of baking.

The Amos Bakery at 12 Sutton St., Flore, before renovation (1975)

While living at Weedon Thomas began attending the Church Charity School in Dodford. The schoolmaster there was Thomas Linnell, a man of about 40, who noted his young pupil's quick intelligence and was later to become a great friend.

The Adams family moved to Flore during the 1840s, probably to the cottage at 42 Sutton Street, Mead's Yard, for that is where they are recorded in the 1851 census. By 1851 the eldest son, William, had a wife, Mary, and a daughter of 2 months, Jane Ann. Thomas' father had probably died as there is no record of him in the 1851 censuses. Perhaps it was his death that had precipitated the family's move to Flore.

Living at Flore meant an extra 3 miles' walk to school for Thomas, but he is said to have learnt his lessons well, and in the evening would go to the house of Mr. Amos, the baker, to help the Amos children with their schoolwork.

The Amos bakery was at no. 12 Sutton Street, on the same lane as the Adams' cottage. When the opportunity arose, Thomas would slip into the bakehouse and try his hand at moulding dough. This seems to have helped decide his career, for on leaving school he was accepted by Mr. Amos as an apprentice and worked there for several years.

It is thought that the bakery was built in about 1800. Before the Amos family acquired it, it had belonged to a Richard Clark Smith who had bought it in 1816 for his son, Robert. Robert died in 1834 and his widow then married their apprentice, Edward Amos. Edward's family continued to run the bakery until 1960, when trade began to decline. The Amos family still live locally, and Richard Amos bought a hotel in Weedon which he expanded and made into the Crossroads Hotel. It is still possible to see the old bakehouse oven from no. 12 Sutton Street, for it was transferred to the Crossroads to provide an interesting interior feature. Its preservation illustrates the great interest which the Amos family have in their history, and it is ironic that the descendants of Edward Amos' young apprentice, Thomas Adams, should have been the bakers who agreed to take over the bread rounds from the Amos family in 1960.

When Thomas worked for Edward Amos, the business did not rely on Flore for its trade. Edward used to take bread to Fosters Booth in the 1830s to sell to the coach passengers breaking their journey along the Watling Street (now the A5). He used to fall asleep, to be woken by the coach drivers banging on the roof of his van with their whips. If he fell asleep on his way back, the horse would find its own way home. Thomas probably helped in delivering the bread to the local inns and the barracks. As has already been mentioned, Weedon barracks was an important source of custom, particularly during the Crimean War, and the business was very prosperous when Edward died in 1879. The run-down in military personnel at Weedon, culminating in the closure of the Ordnance depot in 1965, led to the rapid decline in the demand for bread in the area, which in turn led to the closure of the Amos bakery.

When Thomas reached the age of 16 in the year 1847, he must have realised that there was no future for him in Flore. He would have to go to seek work in Northampton. Later on in his life he used to enjoy relating the story of how he rolled up the whole of his wardrobe in a bundle under his arm, put into his pocket his patrimony of four pence (the inheritance from his father), and set off along the rough road to town.

He could not afford to go by carrier, which would have taken only 2 hours. He had no pony and trap, so he walked. In winter the by-lanes would be inches deep in mud. The turnpike roads were better, being paved with stones, but

Thomas Adams, Journeyman Baker

*Richard Amos taking the last loaf out of the oven at
12 Sutton Street, Flore (1960)*

the mud still built up, and roadmen were employed to use long scrapers to move the mud from the centre of the road into heaps at the side. If it had turned dark, there was no compulsory lighting of highways – oil or tallow candle lanterns being used, but Thomas probably made sure that he completed the ten mile walk before nightfall. He may have had nowhere to stay.

Possibly he was given an introduction to a former Flore inhabitant residing in 117 Bath Street in the old St. Katherine's district west of All Saints' church, for in the 1851 census Thomas was living at the home of George Jeffery, a maltster born at Flore. The houses were not large in that district, so it is interesting to note that the Jeffery household consisted of 2 adults, 5 children, 1 servant and 2 lodgers, of whom Thomas was one. The other lodger was another young journeyman baker, John Hines from Kislingbury, and the 3 oldest sons were a shoe factor, a tailor and another baker.

Thomas did not waste time in looking for employment. He heard that the Williams bakery in College Street needed assistance and went in to offer his services. He had to answer a few questions put to him by Mr. Williams, and was then straightway told to leave his bundle in the bakehouse, run after one of the journeymen and help push a handcart that had just left the shop laden with loaves. From then on until his retirement 33 years later Thomas was never out of work.

His arrival in Northampton, friendless and virtually penniless, conjures up an image of the portrait of the young David Copperfield in Charles Dickens' novel. It is however the fairy tale of 'Dick Whittington' that most resembles the life story of Thomas Adams, for he rose to become Mayor of Northampton twice, in 1884 and 1885, and his death in 1890 brought together countless mourners from all walks of life. There is no more convincing way of highlighting his life story than to quote from the Northampton Mercury's description of his funeral on February 15th 1890:

'All that was mortal of Alderman Thomas Adams, J.P., twice Mayor of Northampton, was interred in the Northampton General Cemetery on Thursday afternoon, in the presence of a vast crowd of his fellow townspeople and amid myriad signs of deep, true mourning. Seldom, indeed, in Northampton's long history has been seen so spontaneous and universal an expression of fullest esteem and most reverent respect. Literally, the town sorrowed for the loss of one of her noblest and best sons, and publicly exhibited her sympathy with an irreparably bereaved family. Thomas Adams lived among us so long and so well that we had come to regard him as almost inseparable from the life of our municipality. So long had he worked for and with us that each seems to have lost a close friend and co-labourer for the common-weal. He came to us a poor lad; by his indomitable courage and tenacity of purpose, by his keen intelligence and his rugged honesty, he rose to the highest honours we could corporately confer. By the sheer force of his personality and the distinct worth of his administrative ability, he drew to himself the admiration of even his strongest political opponents...'

Thomas' home was then one of the villas on Colwyn Road, overlooking the Racecourse. Amid an almost oppressive silence his coffin was placed on the open coach, drawn by four black horses.

'At many houses en route blinds were drawn or shutters up, whilst at others the windows were filled by the faces of the women and children, anxious to get a glimpse of the passing cortège. Many expressions of intense grief, curiously intermingled with irrepressible admiration for the grand array of wreaths, were heard at intervals. At most factories the men turned out and watched the hearse and coaches pass, with sombre aspect. Each street passed added its contingent to the ever-increasing but wonderfully orderly mass of moving humanity, which reached right from the Infirmary to Messrs. Cove and West's factory, and must have comprised at least 10,000 persons.'

However, in 1847 Thomas was only beginning his rise to fame. Forty three years were yet to pass in which he would not only establish an important bakery business, but support and befriend the Radical M.P., Charles Bradlaugh, and take a leading role in one of the earliest building societies in the town, which later became known as the Nationwide. He soon gained a great deal of experience in the baking trade by working for many of the leading bakeries in the town – Jeffery's of Bath Street, Hemming's (possibly on Regent Square),

Smith's in Gold Street, Hooton's in Cow Lane (now Swan Street behind the Derngate theatre), Reeve's on Abington Square, Brawn's in Leicester Street (off the Barrack Road). Within nine years he was able to establish himself as an independent Master Baker with his own bakery on Union Street (now under Marks and Spencer).

In 1845 there were as many as 43 bakers in the town – an indication of the importance of the trade in the life of a local community. Apart from providing every household with their staple food, it was the custom for bakers to cook Sunday joints for the local people, and there are many memoirs of the 19th century and even well into the 20th that tell of the way in which families took their Sunday dinners along to the local baker's before attending Church or chapel.

By 1858 the number of bakers had risen to 58, all within the circle roughly formed by the line running between the bottom of Bridge Street, St. Edmund's church near Abington Square, the Racecourse and St. Andrews Road near Castle Station. The proliferation of bakers is evidenced by the fact that there were three on Newland (now under the Grosvenor Centre), two on Gold Street, four on Bridge Street, three on the Upper Mounts.

Before continuing Thomas' story it is interesting to include the background to what life could have been like for a journeyman baker in the middle of the 19th century. As mentioned before, conditions had been made very hard by the increase in competition brought about by the decline and final abolition of the Assize of Bread. Older bakers in the first part of the 19th century tended to look back on the days of the Assize as relatively good times. The Assize may not have been popular among all bakers, but it at least served to regulate the trade and the level of competition, and to protect the customers from unfair practices.

Medieval bakers

Thomas Adams, Journeyman Baker

A Brief History of Baking from 1200 - 1800

To understand these relatively good times it is as well to begin at the beginning: As early as 1202 in the reign of King John, laws were formulated to regulate the price of bread and fix the amount of profit allowed to a baker. The Assize of Bread (and incidentally also of beer) was established in 1266 during the closing years of the reign of Henry III. It was a franchise conferred on the lords of the manor, and in later centuries on the local magistrates, and was designed to regulate the weight of a penny loaf according to the prevailing price of wheat and grade of flour used. The pillory was the authorised punishment to be given to any baker found selling an underweight loaf. Prosecutions were frequent.

The actual workings of the Assize in the Middle Ages is brought to life by a book written by the celebrated Richard Whittington, Lord Mayor of London and inspiration for the fairy tale. The book is called Liber Albus (the White Book) and was compiled in 1419 for the instruction and guidance of Whittington's successors, detailing the customs and social conditions in the City of London in the 13th and 14th century.

As far as the bakers were concerned, four general meetings were held for them every year and the Assize was to be worked out by 'four discreet men'. To decide on the price of bread these men had to follow the following procedure:

'The four men so sworn as aforesaid are to buy three quarters of corn; one, namely upon the pavement in Chepe, one at Greschirche or at Billyngesgate, and a third at Queen-Hythe; of which corn they are to make wastel (2d quality), light bread, and brown; and after, with great diligence, they shall have baked such loaves they shall present them, when hot, to both the mayor and aldermen at the Guildhall, and there, while so hot, such loaves shall be weighed.'

Loaves were known by their price – the penny loaf, for example, and there then followed the process of determining the weight to be sold for a penny, which weight was to vary with the price of corn. There was one expensive kind of loaf called demesne bread or Panis Dominicus, made of the very finest flour and with an effigy of Jesus Christ impressed upon it. This halfpenny loaf was to weigh the same as the farthing loaf of wastel, which was presumably made from an inferior flour.

The profit which was allowed the baker was based on the principle that the price charged for the bread made from a quarter of wheat (8 bushels) should allow the baker to have 4d for himself, two loaves for his own use, and the remaining bran. Also, the profit should allow ½d for three servants, ½d for two boys, ½d for salt, ½d for kneading, ½d for candles, 2d for wood, and 1½d for bolting (sieving).

Thomas Adams, Journeyman Baker

A century later in 1497, when the best wheat was now sold for 7s a quarter, a baker was allowed a correspondingly larger amount of profit - 7d for himself, his horse, his wife, his dog and his cat, 6d for furnace and wood, 4d for the miller, 5d for two journeymen and his apprentices, and 2d for salt, yeast, candles and sack bands. The bran he could also keep 'to his advantage'.

Both the mode of setting the Assize and the principle on which the price of bread was determined appear to have remained unchanged by legislation from those early periods until the time of Queen Anne. By then bakers had begun to feel that the complex system was unjust and oppressive because the weights were constantly changing, as the price of wheat changed.

At any time a penny loaf would have three different weights: firstly, the so-called white loaf made from flour that was as finely bolted as was then possible; secondly, the wheaten loaf made from coarsely bolted meal, (this was half as heavy again as the white loaf); and thirdly, household bread – the largest and heaviest, made from unbolted meal, or what we would call wholemeal flour.

As an example of the complex weight regulations which a baker had to observe: in 1329 the price of wheat was 6s a quarter, so the penny white loaf was to weigh 3lb 13oz, the penny wheaten loaf, 5lb 12oz, and the penny household, 7lb 11oz. Today a standard large loaf weighs only 800g (1lb 12oz). The lesser weight in demand today reflects how much smaller households are and that we consume less bread now.

Even today it is still difficult to calculate precisely the final weight of a loaf, so it must have been a great burden on bakers to conform to the strict regulations of the Assize. In 1976 a baker publicly asserted 'that the final weight of a loaf of bread is in God's hands as much as the baker's', and this is in an age when bread flours are submitted to rigorous quality tests before they leave the mill, the amount of water they absorb is a known factor, and the temperature of the ovens is uniform.

Medieval bakery stall

Under the Assize, bakers would have felt obliged to bake overweight loaves to stay on the safe side of the law, and this in turn resulted in a reduction in the already modest profit legally allowed them.

As an aside, there is one interesting feature which is worth noting in the history of baking before the 17th century, for it is often assumed that bread in olden times was always purely wholemeal: there were in fact brown-bread bakers and white-bread bakers, and the former were not allowed to impinge on the province of the latter. The coarse bread baked by the brown-bread bakers was said to be for 'the hind servants'. These bakers also made pease-meal bread for horses. It was baked in very large loaves and usually consisted of different proportions of oats, rye and pease (a pea-plant).

During the Middle Ages it is important to remember that the bakers did not allow themselves to be merely passively subjected to government regulation. They organised themselves into guilds. Bakers and many other tradesmen saw the advantage of uniting together, for they achieved a form of monopoly and control of their particular trade in their own locality.

By the end of the 15th century the Liber Custumarum of Northampton (a book describing the affairs of the Borough Council) shows that bakers were among the traders organised into guilds in the town. Town councils saw a financial advantage in these associations because they could regulate them and exact fines as punishment, even when the offences were not recognised by statute law or even local bye-laws. Half of the fine would go to the common purse of the town.

The Origin of the Phrase, 'a Baker's Dozen'

In the 16th century hucksters were itinerant tradesmen selling bakers' loaves. Bye-laws were passed to determine the huckster's profit of one loaf in thirteen:

'It is ordained that the bakers of this borough for the time being shall sell bread to the hucksters – 13 loaves for 12, as before has been accustomed, upon pain of forfeiting for every default 40s to the Chamber and his body to prison during the Mayor's pleasure.'

Constitution of the Town of Bedford

The power of the bakers is indicated by the following reference in the Liber Custumarum. In the middle of the 16th century it is revealed that the number of bakers had been increasing in Northampton and that they were supplying customers in the country as well as in Northampton. On market days they were buying so much grain that they were inflating the price. To prevent this from happening, bakers were forbidden to take out of town over 2 horse-loads of grain when the price of wheat was between 6s 8d and 12s a quarter. If wheat was over 12s a quarter, only 1 horse-load could be taken out by each baker. The Town Assembly did not want a high price to be charged for grain as this would make it necessary for the Assize to set a high price for bread.

Bakers found the Assize system oppressive. Prices of wheat varied throughout the country and fluctuated from month to month. The legally required weights might change every 3 months, or whenever the local magistrates thought fit to set an Assize. Even minor changes in the price of wheat affected the weight required. The range was 6d to £5.

It was not just geographical variations in the price of wheat that gave the bakers cause to feel aggrieved. By the 17th century bakers were not even buying their wheat direct from the farmers, but from the millers who would of course charge a different price from the farmers because they were selling flour, not wheat.

Assize Bread (1813)

The Peck loaf wheaten to weigh	17lb	6oz	*and sold for 4s 6d*
Ditto Household	17	6	4s 1d
Half-peck loaf	8	11	2s 3d
Ditto household	8	11	2s ½d
Quartern loaf	4	5	1s 1½d
Ditto household	4	5	1s ½d
Half-quartern loaf	2	2	6 ¾d
Ditto household	2	2	6 ¼d

No other sort of bread, or loaves of any other price are allowed to be made or sold within the said town.

Wm. Brown, Mayor

N.M. 30.10.1813

Thomas Adams, Journeyman Baker

In the Middle Ages when the Assize of Bread was first established, the bakers bought their wheat direct from the farmers, paid a miller to grind it and bolted it themselves, the law allowing them to keep the bran for their own profit and use. Milling had slowly developed into a separate trade and bakers began to buy ready-milled flour direct from the millers or through a 'factor' or middleman. It was no longer realistic to calculate the weight of bread according to the price of wheat. It would have been more realistic to base the calculations on the price of milled flour. By the end of the reign of Elizabeth I in 1603 the Assize had become unworkable, but a whole century passed before the obsolete laws on bread were changed and the new system in common practice was recognised as legal.

In 1709 the laws established two distinct systems of selling bread. Bakers could either follow a modified version of the old system and sell by weight changeable according to the price of flour, or they could bake their bread to standard weights, a price being set according to the weight of loaf. The first system was still called Assize Bread and the second, Priced Bread. Bakers had to opt for one or the other.

The most common size of Priced Bread was the quartern (or quarter-peck) loaf weighing 4lb 5½ oz. This was the weight of bread officially calculated to be the yield from a quarter-peck (3½lb) of flour. Peck loaves weighed an amazing 17lb 6oz, and half-peck loaves, 8lb 11oz.

It is popular to criticise the amount of bureaucratic paperwork involved in commerce nowadays, but 200 years ago the Assize of Bread led to a considerable amount of record-keeping on behalf of bakers, millers and corn merchants, as the following item in the Northampton Mercury (Vol. 93, p.107) reveals:

'To the Town of Northampton. To wit.
Notice is hereby given, that by virtue of an Act of Parliament … an Assize of Bread is intended to be set for the Town of Northampton, and all Cornfactors, Millers, Mealmen, Bakers … are hereby required on Friday in each week till further notice to make returns … of the true quantities of all wheat and wheaten flour respectively …which shall have been bought or sold by them, within seven days preceding in each week, and the true and exact prices for which such wheat or wheaten flour shall have been respectively bought or sold, and the names and residences of the persons of whom bought, or to whom sold, and which returns are to be signed by the party making the same. And all persons required by this notice to make any such returns, who shall neglect or refuse to make the same, or who shall make any false returns, will be liable to a penalty for each offence not exceeding the sum of ten pounds.

Signed, DANIEL DILLEY,
Receiver of Assize Returns for the Town of Northampton   18th September, 1813.

> ### Priced Bread (1800)
>
> The Assize of Bread set the 30th day of August 1800 for Northampton, to take place Monday next, the 1st of September and to be in force 7 days for the said town of Northampton.
>
> | | |
> |---|---|
> | The Sixpenny Loaf, Wheaten, is to weigh | 1lb 3oz 0dr |
> | Ditto, Household | 1lb 9oz 3dr |
> | The Twelvepenny Loaf, Wheaten | 2lb 6oz 0dr |
> | Ditto, Household | 3lb 10oz 6dr |
>
> George Osborn, Mayor
>
> N.M. 30.8.1800

Depending on these local prices the magistrates would decide on the prices of the various loaves.

Throughout the 18th century there were frequent complaints about the unfairness of the pricing system, as different modes of setting the Assize were adopted in different parts of the country. Some places, for instance, only considered the price of flour, not the price of wheat. A baker was supposed to be able to make 20 peck loaves, or 80 quartern loaves from a sack of 280lbs of flour. In reality, with good flour, it was possible to make more than 80 quarterns. The surplus plus the allowance for his expenses gave the baker a good profit and the customer, a fair and equitable price.

By the early 19th century, with the Industrial Revolution well underway, the urban population had greatly increased, leading to a corresponding expansion in the baking trade. It was finally admitted that the original Assize system was obsolete, and in 1815 the 1266 Assize laws were repealed. The standard weight of loaf remained, but without any price control. Further acts in 1822 and 1836 abolished even the standard weights and allowed the baker to sell by any weight, so long as it was clearly stated and was weighed in front of the customer if required. The 1822 Act also made the old peck weights illegal; all weights were now to be expressed by the avoirdupois system of 16 ounces in the pound. The habit of referring to quartern and half-quartern loaves persisted into the early part of the 20th century, but they now meant 4lb or 2lb loaves.

> **An Ordinary Cake to eat with Butter**
>
> *Take two pounds of flour, and rub into it half a pound of butter; then put to it some spice, a little salt, a quarter and half of sugar, half a pound of raisins stones, and half a pound of currants; make these into a cake, with half a pint of ale-yeast, four eggs and as much warm milk as you see convenient; mix it well together; an hour and half will bake it. This cake is good to eat with butter for breakfast.*
>
> E.Smith, The Compleat Housewife (1727)

A Brief History of Baking from 1800 – 1860

So what did the new freedom for the bakers bring? What kind of business environment awaited the young Thomas Adams when he chose to enter the baking trade?

Underselling

In 1863 the beadle of the Bakers' Company, Mr. Rice of Harp Lane in London, reported to the government that the abolition of the Assize had completely altered the character of the baking trade:

'*I entered the baking trade as an apprentice in 1811, and became a master baker in 1815 …When I first was in business for myself there were only three master bakers in the City who sold bread below the rates fixed by the Assize. A class of bakers very soon sprang up, who sold bread at a price much below what bread made of good and genuine flour could be sold for. They drew off the custom from the shops that continued to sell the best article, and have been gradually superseding them all over London.*

Many of these 'undersellers', no doubt, supply pure bread of an inferior quality at a lower price than the best bread, and they are content with a lower rate of profit than was allowed during the existence of the Assize; but a large class has come into existence who sell bread under them again, the 'cutting trade', and these are supplied by the millers with flour mixed with various sorts

of meal, and also adulterated with alum; so they sell bread at a price much below the other branches of the trade.'
>> Reprints of British Parliamentary Papers: Industrial Revolution, Factories Vol. 3: Reports from H.S. Tremenheere on Journeymen Bakers and the Bakehouses Act with Appendices. (I.U.P., 1969)

Potato Bread

'Lovers of toast and butter will be much pleased with this kind of bread. The potato is not here added with a view to economy, but to increase the lightness of the bread, in which state it will imbibe the butter with more freedom…'
>> Dr. A. Hunter, *Receipts in Modern Cookery, with a Medical Commentary* (1805)

Ingredients:
To 450g (1lb) of white flour use 120g (¼lb) of potato, mashed very smoothly, completely dry, and still warm.
15g (½oz) of yeast
½ pint (280g) of milk and water mixed
minimum of 20g (¾ oz) of salt
Tin size: 28cm by 10 cm by 8cm deep, with a capacity of 1.5 litres (2 ½ to 3 pints)

Have the flour and salt ready in a bowl, the yeast creamed with a little water, and the milk and water warm in a jug.
When the potatoes are cooked, peeled, sieved and weighed, mix them with the flour as if you were rubbing in fat. Then add the yeast and the warm milk and water. Mix the dough as for ordinary bread.
Leave it until it is well risen, which will take rather longer than usual – up to 2 hours. Break it down, knead lightly, shape, and put into a 1.5 litre tin. Cover it with a damp cloth and leave until the dough reaches the top of the tin.
Bake in a moderately hot oven, 425F, 220C, gas no. 7, for about 45 minutes, taking care not to let the crust get too browned or hard.
>> Elizabeth David, *English Bread and Yeast Cookery* (1977)

Intense competition had thus entered the trade. It is a familiar factor in business now, and the introduction of cheap sliced bread sold in supermarkets in the 1960s caused a similar debate among the baking trade to that to which Mr. Rice refers. The practice of selling 'cheap bread' had in fact already got underway before the end of the 18th century - (cheap, meaning below the price fixed by the Assize). When the practice had once begun, it was found to be profitable and became widespread. Baking was a popular trade to go into because it required only a small amount of skill and little capital.

The Master of the Bakers' Company stated to a government committee in 1815 that there had been a rapid increase in the number of bakers in London – 200 new bakers in one space of 5 years, and 'underselling' was rapidly increasing. One witness before the committee, a Mr. Harvey, said how easy it was to set up as a baker. When starting out he himself had been prepared to do the work of two or three men. By the middle of the century it was still easy to set up in the trade, but the competition continued to be very fierce and the effect was felt in the harsh working conditions of the journeymen bakers and in the quality of bread. The government inspection of 1863 led by H.S. Tremenheere, which has been quoted above, was designed to remedy this situation and to investigate the complaints made by the journeymen in 1848.

It had been thought that the abolition of the Assize would actually reduce the number of bakers by 'causing the trade to fall into the hands of capitalists', but this did not prove to be the case. It was too easy for a small investment to furnish one individual with a relatively profitable business. Virtually all that was needed was money to buy a sack of flour, some brewers' yeast, and of course an oven. A large capitalist enterprise would find it difficult to compete, for a large concern could not extract from the workmen 18 hours work for 12 hours pay. Also it was inconvenient for the public to be served by large bakers. People wanted a baker working on their own street corner. Capitalism could have diminished the waste of labour and consequently increased the profit available, but it was not till well into the next century that large-scale bakeries really began to develop. This was probably due to the vast mechanisation and improved transportation of the 20th century, which made the bakeries able to reach a much wider market. In the middle of the 19th century the majority of bakers still baked under 10 sacks of flour a week. To have a turnover based on 12 sacks was considered good business and only required the use of one to two ovens. A large bakery would bake 100 sacks a week.

So the new freedom for bakers brought with it an intensely competitive business environment and a consequent worsening of the conditions in which the apprentices and journeymen bakers were required to work.

In 1848 (the year in fact after Thomas Adams had started as an apprentice) the journeymen bakers handed in a list of complaints to the government in an attempt to ameliorate their working conditions. In 1854 an investigation was begun into the state of the trade and H.S. Tremenheere produced his report in 1863. It includes the actual evidence supplied by various members of the baking trade and thus provides a vivid picture of the hard life that was involved in being a baker.

The government inspector made the following pronouncement:

'There is probably no branch of trade supplying a vast and constant demand which has so completely remained in its primitive condition of ministering to that demand from a multitude of small and insulated sources, as the baking trade.'

The state of the baking trade in England was so notoriously bad that it was discussed by Karl Marx in 'Das Kapital', where he mentions the report produced by the government in 1863.

It is probable that the large amount of surplus labour in the trade served to delay demands for an improvement in working conditions. Mr. Tremenheere stated that the surplus labour arose from several circumstances:

'...the principal being that the trade is very easily learnt; that being a sickly trade there are many out of work, who when convalescent are anxious to get employment again on any terms; that the bakers of Scotland and the west of England, who employ chiefly apprentices, dismiss them as soon as they are out of their apprenticeship, upon which large numbers of them come to seek work in London; also that, as I understand, there is a great influx of Germans into the trade, who are content to work at first for low wages. This surplus of labour, by creating a great competition for work, renders it possible for the masters to maintain their system of long hours at low wages, in every case where they think the interests of their trade require it.'

Although the baking trade was not effected by capitalism to any great extent at this period, the influence of 'big business' can still be seen to have played a part in its development – big business in this case being the millers. The millers rose to a position of power during the 18th century.

The butcher he will cheat you until he makes you stare,
The poulterer will sell you an old rabbit for a hare,
The grocer sands his sugar and sells sloe leaves for tea,
And then the dusty miller who's a bigger rogue than he?
And they're all a cheating cheat, cheat, cheating,
And they're all a cheating in country and town.

Popular Song about adulteration

Previously the baker bought his wheat from the farmer, had it ground by the miller, but dressed it himself according to the bread to be made. Gradually during the 18th century the miller became the purchaser. Not being subject to the Assize law, his profits became considerable.

Soon millers were able to employ corn-factors (middle-men or 'flour agents') whose work also served to raise the price of flour. They acted as a kind of wholesaler to the baker. Towards the end of the 18th century millers also started becoming proprietors of baker's shops, employing journeymen as their agents and allowing them a small commission of 5-7s (25-35p) per sack of flour sold.

The millers increased their outlets by establishing the custom of sending out much of the bread baked in their own shops to chandlers' (grocery) shops. Here it was possible for them to sell at a rate below the Assize because of the profits they had accumulated from the cornfactors and their journeymen bakers.

The influence of the millers was significant and it is interesting that about 150 years later in the 1960s bakers were again facing the interference of the millers. History could indeed be said to be repeating itself.

Nightworking

The cheap bread stimulated demand and led to the millers' bakeries producing an additional 1 or 2 batches per day. This was only made possible by the practice of night working.

This practice became more and more prevalent. Journeymen bakers working in a miller's bakery used to ask their employees, who were often friends, to bake another batch of bread for some extra pay or a free dinner. Usually these journeymen eventually became the proprietors of the bakehouse – at the cost of a considerable debt. Obviously they could not afford to buy the bakehouse outright and had to commit themselves to buying their flour from the miller or his cornfactor until the debt had been discharged. The price of their flour would be raised by the miller so that they had little chance of ever getting out of debt completely. These new proprietors, therefore, found it necessary to demand from their workers extra hours (night working) as a right. The increased output was essential to help them discharge their debt.

As with most things, the practice of night working began in London. It appears that country bakers did not need to do work such inconvenient hours. Lack of fierce competition would have made a baker's life much easier. However, by the end of the 19th century night working existed even in towns the size of Northampton.

In order to find out what kind of hours were worked by a journeyman baker in the centuries prior to the Victorian period it is possible to refer to the Statute of 1562 in the reign of Elizabeth I. This followed many statutes on the working conditions of labourers since the first Statute of Labourers in 1349 in the reign of Edward III. (Unfortunately the Great Fire of London of 1666 destroyed the records of the Bakers' Company.) The Statute shows that in comparison with the night-working expected of bakers in Victorian times, life in previous centuries was quite easy.

In 1562 the hours of labourers, including bakers, were as follows: between mid-March and mid-September – 5am to 7 or 8pm with 2½ hours allowed for meals; from mid-September to mid-March – dawn to dusk. The 2½ hours included half an hour for breakfast, half an hour for drinking, one hour for dinner and half an hour for sleep when it was allowed (from mid-May to mid-August). Any labourers, servants and apprentices not at work at the appropriate times were to lose one penny for every hour's absence.

(Another interesting point about earlier working conditions is the strict wages policy in operation in the 16th century. All wages were assessed by the Justices of the Peace after the Easter Sessions. On being allowed by the Lord Chancellor and certified to the Sheriffs, the wages were proclaimed on market days before Michaelmas. The punishment for giving or taking higher wages than those appointed was ten days' imprisonment. It is known that under the Statute of Labourers under Edward III and Henry VI punishment was even meted out for taking 'unreasonable' wages, and regulations even existed for matters such as diet and clothing.)

Pumpkin Bread

A Recipe to make Bread that will keep moist and good very long

Slice a pompion, and boil it in fair water, till the water grows clammy, or somewhat thick; then strain it through a fine cloth, or sieve, and with this make your Bread, well kneading the dough; and it will not only encrease the quantity of it, but make it keep moist and sweet a month longer than Bread wetted with fair water only.

The Family Magazine (London, 1741)

To return to the new practice of selling cheap bread: When Philip Adams of Oliver Adams bakery recalled life in the baking trade in the 1960s, he described how the supermarkets and millers began to encroach on the market previously provided for by small bakers, and explains what an abrupt shock it was to encounter the fierce competition which ensued.

About 150 years previously, a Mr. John Dwarber of Fetter Lane, Fleet Street, was relating a similar situation to the Government Inspector of the baking trade – only his words and emotions were more dramatic:

'Such competition naturally engendered much animosity in the trade, and the old style of men, in the bitterness of their hearts, stigmatised the new men as "undersellers"... The public supported some of these shops to such an extent that enormous amounts of trade were done... The undersellers so effectually staggered the "full-price bakers" that, so far as the trade went, they got it nearly half into their own hands. This was the first step towards that which has all but rendered the full-price bakers a traditionary class... The trade, after a very few years, entered into another transition period. The undersellers, in their turn, had to meet an increase of competition they never calculated on. Population increasing rapidly, new neighbourhoods arising as if by magic, shops accumulating in large numbers – this indeed was an era for the baking trade of an insanity of competition unexampled in any other trade. I say unexampled, because a baker sells but one article, and if he sell too low, or is compelled to sell at a loss, ruin would soon stare him in the face. Many other purveyors, selling miscellaneous stock, can and do often ticket a leading article at a low figure, under a hope of drawing notice to other things, and often find a profit on the general stock by so doing. This increase of bakers' shops very soon over-ran the demand for them...

But has this ordeal through which the trade has passed been beneficial to anybody? Substantially I think not. Better bread was never made in London than under the old full-price regime. I need not say to you, sir, that while healthy and honest competition elevates those who practise it, unfair and dishonest competition necessarily enervates and degrades all within the pale of its influence. Among the evils consequent on reckless trading we may name that craving of the general public for low-priced articles miscalled cheap. Bankrupt and insolvent courts, their respective staffs and accessories, have fattened by it; many thousands have been pauperised by it, tens of thousands of tradesmen's children have been thrown on the world to win the right to live, through it; and those traders who maintain a foothold in this Babel are they respected? Often are their names associated with some trickery in trade, some dereliction of duty, that however fashionable and politic it may be in trades to wink at, or worse, pretend ignorance of, leaves each destitute of the richest treasures of life – the *confidence and respect of their fellow man - the very food they eat often embittered by the conviction that they live on "sufferance".'*

The quality of the bread was said to be inferior in the 'underselling' bakeries, and some bakers went to astonishing lengths to reduce the cost of their baking by replacing some of their flour with cheaper ingredients – chalk and ground stone being just two examples. First of all, however, it was not just inferior bread which was being sold – underweight loaves were also put on sale to cheat the customer of a few pennies.

The government report recorded one traditional (or full-priced) baker's view:

'Much has been said in the evidence about the working classes being often cheated in the weight of their loaf at the chandlers' shops, which are so numerous in the trade. I believe that is quite true. In the full-priced trade we weigh our dough, 4lbs 6oz to 4lbs 8oz for the 4lb loaf, and we bake it close upon two hours. In the under-priced and 'cutting' trade the dough is weighed, 4lbs 4oz to 4lbs 6oz to the 4lb loaf, and it is baked an hour and a quarter; sometimes more, sometimes even less. Where the bread, on being served over the counter, is weighed to the customer, the full weight of 4lbs is made up with every loaf; but a large proportion of the bread sold to the working classes at the chandlers' shops is not weighed to them, and they lose accordingly one or two ounces of bread with every loaf.'

Conditions for a Journeyman Baker in the mid 19th century

Hours of Work

So the underselling of bread was well underway by the time Thomas Adams was entering the trade as a journeyman baker. The competition it brought with it led to a worsening of the working conditions in a bakehouse at a time when no laws existed to protect those employed in the baking trade.

The first Factory Act had been passed in 1833 and it had made improvements in working conditions, such as banning night work for under-18 year olds in factories. However, bakehouses were not included in legislation covering factories or even workshops, and it was only in 1863 (after the publication of the government report quoted above) that the Bakehouse Regulation Act was passed.

The Act failed to address the problem of the long night hours worked – one of the main complaints made by journeymen bakers to the government in 1848.

Thomas Adams, Journeyman Baker

So what was life like for a journeyman baker? What kind of conditions might Thomas Adams have encountered when he set out to learn the trade in Northampton? The report claims that conditions in London were the same as those in many cities such as Bristol, Nottingham and Birmingham. Northampton was a smaller town, having only 58 bakeries in 1858 compared with about 100 in Nottingham, 200 in Bristol, and 430 in Birmingham, but the situation may have been somewhat similar, and in any event the report is worth considering for the fascinating picture it presents of conditions in one of the most important trades in the mid 19th century.

In the dry language of the government inspector, Hugh Seymour Tremenheere, we learn the not so dry facts that the work of a London journeyman baker usually began at 11pm. He would make the dough for 30 to 45 minutes, lie down on the kneading board, which also served as the covering of the trough in which dough was made, and with a sack under him and another rolled up as a pillow, sleep for about two hours.

The great niece of a London baker recounted to me how she could recall the way of life in a bakery in the early part of the 20th century: the family upstairs would know when it was 2 o'clock in the morning because of the loud clatter as the sleeping journeyman baker fell off his kneading board. As the dough rose, the board was lifted up and the innocent sleeper would tumble to the floor.

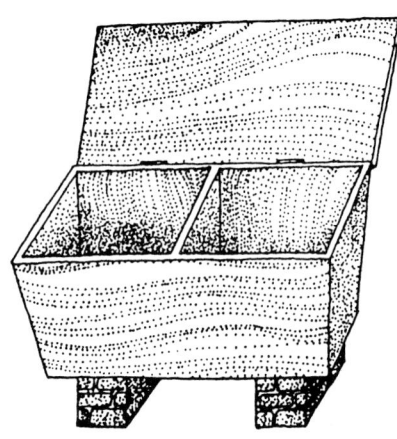

A dough trough
(Trough was pronounced 'trow' to rhyme with dough)

Five hours of hard work would follow – throwing, moulding and baking the dough, making rolls and fancy bread, and then taking it up to the shop. In London where space was at a premium, bread was made in what would usually be the coal-hole and the front kitchen. The flour would be kept in the back kitchen. The oven was usually under the street. Sometimes the space under the street was used for storing the flour and making the dough, in which case the oven would be at the back of the house. The temperature of a bakehouse would be between 75 to 90 degrees F, the smaller ones usually being 90 degrees.

The broken sleep pattern and the hard and continuous work in such hot temperatures were believed to undermine the constitution of the young men and render them liable to various diseases. The average life of a journeyman baker was 42. Many master bakers felt that under-18 year olds should not do night work, and that abnormal hours of work had a 'very bad effect upon their morals'.

After baking, the next phase of work involved the distribution, which was equally hard as it involved carrying baskets, perhaps on the head, or wheeling hand-carts. The working day might finish between 1 and 6pm, some bakers bringing out more batches of bread until late afternoon.

The Muffin-Man, 1851

'I did not hear of any street-seller who made the muffins or crumpets he vended. Indeed, he could not make the small quantity required, so as to be remunerative. The muffins are bought off the bakers, and at prices to leave a profit of 4d in 1s ... The muffin-man carries his delicacies in a basket, well swathed in flannel, to retain the heat ... An old man told me, "My best customers is genteel houses, 'cause I sells a genteel thing. I like wet days best, 'cause there's werry respectable ladies what don't keep a servant, and they buys to save themselves going out. We're a great convenience to the ladies sir – a great convenience to them as like a slap-up tea."'

Henry Mayhew, *London Labour and the London Poor* (1851)

It was pointed out in the government report that delivering bread to private houses was an attractive part of the work for some journeyman bakers because they could increase their wage from about 18s to as much as 30s by dishonest means. They would enter more bread in their account books than was actually asked for, demand an excessive price, and pocket the sum covering the non-existent loaf or loaves. A Mr. Chalice, clerk of Mr. Spiking of Dover Street, wrote in one pamphlet that 9 out of 10 heads of small families paid for a half-quarter (800g) loaf per week more than their household had actually consumed. Of course the collusion of servants was often necessary and the dishonest profit shared accordingly.

In this period (1860) a baker's wages varied from 14s to 32s, excluding free bread, flour and lodging.

Many journeymen started under the age of 18, usually at 16 (as in the case of Thomas Adams), and often as early as 15. The unsocial and unhealthy hours of work were felt to be particularly bad for young men under the age of 18, and it was suggested that no youth under 18 should work in a bakehouse later than 9pm or before 5am. The 1851 Census reveals that in all of Great Britain there were about 50,000 bakers and confectioners, of whom about 14,000 were aged 15 to 20. 8,500 of these would probably be 18 years old or less.

One baker bringing evidence to the government inspector on the unhealthy working hours recalled:

'When I was a journeyman, I have been at times so exhausted by the long hours that I could not walk upstairs to my bed, but have been obliged to crawl on my hands and knees; and after three hours in bed have been obliged to get up again. I consider that I owe the preservation of my health to temperate habits and a strong constitution.'

The argument for the long hours was based on customer demand for early bread and on the convenience of those accepting deliveries. A Mr. Mules reported to the inspector that:

'The labouring classes will have hot bread for all their meals as a general rule; they say their children like it best, and it serves them as a hot meal, and it is more satisfying. Thousands of them cannot afford the time to cook if they had the means.'

Regarding the wealthier customers, a Mrs. Jones of Belgrave Square claimed:

'It is indispensable in this part of the town that the bread should be delivered as much as possible before one o'clock. After that it would be very inconvenient to the servants, and would not be liked by our customers. The housekeepers have other duties after the servants' dinner hour, and at many houses the area gate is locked at one o'clock.'

Other bakers, however, reported that the public generally consumed the bread of the day before anyway. Day-old bread, being drier, goes further because less is eaten.

Mr. Tremenheere was overwhelmed by the tales of hardship told by individual bakers summoned to the inspection. John Wells' tale is just one example:

Thomas Adams, Journeyman Baker

'I began work as a journeyman baker at 13, my hours were from 11pm to 3pm the next day. I continued at this for many years. I am 36 years of age, and have always worked in London, except for a few months. I had to leave the bakery business for 4 or 5 years in consequence of its having injured my health ... I have known and still know scores of men who began as early as myself and worked those long hours, and I have known great numbers who have been injured in consequence.

I have worked at harder places for several years; I have worked continuously from Thursday night up to 11pm on Saturday night; I have done that for months together until I was worn out.

I have a cousin who is about 20, who I don't think has more than 10 years more life in him; he began at about 12, and has continued at the night and day work ever since. Young men who come out of the country at about 17 to 18 soon begin to suffer for their night work.'

The journeymen's initial complaints were made in 1848. Eventually the government report published in 1863 led to the Bakehouses Regulation Act of 1863. It covered all towns having a population of over 5,000 and laid down rules for the inspection and regulation of bakehouses, the abolition of night-working for under-18 year olds, and the restriction of Sunday baking. Unfortunately there was no regulation made to restrict the long hours or night-working for adults.

A subsequent government report reviewing bakehouses outside London noted that circumstances were similar in other parts of the country, but it is interesting to note that there were very few bakehouses in the North of England. Here it was a well established custom to bake bread at home.

To complete the picture of the government regulation of bakeries in the mid 19th century - in 1875 the report from the Select Committee on the Factory and Workshops Act showed that local authorities were not enforcing the provisions of the Act of 1863.

'In certain great bakery works they employ the boys from 30 to 36 hours, sometimes straight away. We have no means of preventing that ... At present nobody visits them at all.'

C.S.Hall, the certifying factory surgeon at Carlisle, reported to the committee that bakehouses ought to be covered by the Workshops Act, for the Bakehouse Act did not cover length of hours worked - *'very young children being employed amongst the hot ovens for almost unlimited hours'*. Mr. Hall went on to add that compared with the Factories Act, the Workshops Act was little known, largely ignored, and little enforced.

In the year 1875 a Mr. Wood was the Sub-Inspector for Northampton for the Factories and Workshops Act, and unfortunately he made no reference to the town's bakeries in his report to the Select Committee. He just made a significant remark on the effect of the Education Act in Northampton, saying that it had not had much effect upon school attendance in his district. Legislation was clearly not the whole answer to a problem. It needed to be backed up by adequate enforcement.

Standards of Cleanliness

Back in 1863 Hugh Tremenheere did not only report on the hours worked by journeymen bakers, he made recommendations on the second aspect of the inspection - the cleanliness of bakehouses. The picture of Victorian baking that is created by some of his reports is a fascinating study of what life could be like in a world as yet unconcerned about hygiene and a healthy working environment. We have no way of knowing what conditions were like for the young Thomas Adams when he worked for various bakeries in Northampton before setting up on his own, but if he experienced only a little of the life depicted in the government's report, he would have had a very different experience from what would be expected in the 20th century.

Mr. Tremenheere described the conditions in the following way:

'*One of the principal complaints of the journeymen relates to the injury done to their health by the absence of all proper arrangements for ventilation and cleanliness in the great majority of bakehouses. It was stated to me by the first witness examined, Mr. John Bennett, the Secretary of the London Operative Bakers' Association, that "very many bakehouses in London are in a shockingly filthy state, arising from imperfect sewerage and bad ventilation and neglect; and the bread must, during the process of fermentation, get impregnated with the noxious gases surrounding it. Many journeymen bakers also in London sleep under the pavement, in the bakehouses. The sleeping places, especially in the East End of London, and some at the West End also, are of the worst description, frequently in the basement of the building and under the stairs; plenty of them have no beds except in the bakehouse itself."*

The next witness stated that "the places where he had worked had almost always been arches under the ground, with no means of ventilation, except through the doors. They are generally, therefore, fearfully hot, and many of them infested with vermin, etc. The bakehouses are also often so close to the drains that they smell very bad. It is a common practice to lock the bakehouses at night, while the men are at work; consequently where there is no ventilation except through the doors, it is very stifling, and very apt to ruin men's health altogether." Mr. Nevill stated, "I have known many bakehouses in a shocking state as places of work, and most injurious to the men, and so infested with rats, beetles, cockroaches, etc. and so full of noxious smells that it must infect the bread."'

*A brake for kneading dough (The pole was loose enough
to allow free working up and down and from side to side)*

One inspector, a Mr. James Mills reports on the comment made to him by one of the bakers visited:

'One of the men stated that in breaking up the sponge by hand in the old way, it was a common thing for him to be obliged to lift up his head from hanging over the trough, being almost suffocated by the gas (carbonic acid*).'*

The evidence is also given of one man, now a foreman in the trade, who had experienced work in some of the worst examples of bakehouses:

'There are very few bakehouses not overrun with black beetles in great numbers, and it is almost impossible to keep them out of the bread. You could gather a quart pot full in ten minutes.'

Crickets might also be flying about, as these memories of Edwin Dare in an article entitled 'Thoughts of a Journeyman Baker' relate:

'My thoughts often drift back to a German baker I knew who always insisted on taking a cricket in a matchbox from one bakehouse to another whenever he changed premises. He reckoned it brought him luck – but those crickets were always hard to find because they hid themselves in cracks around the oven. They were poor specimens compared with the "flying torpedoes" which terrorised the staff in an underground bakehouse in which I worked in Greenwich. These were crickets which had inbred, cross-bred and multiplied to become armour-plated and almost lethal. As though signalled to do so they would suddenly take flight and zoom around the bakehouse. We would sail into action against them (a lump of dough as our weapon) but it was a losing battle until, one week-end, a pest destruction expert with a smelly candle put paid to them all and solved our troubles.

Underground bakehouses were gruelling places to work in and only became prohibited premises a comparatively few years ago after over half-a-century of campaigning against them. They really were underground, often with just one window opening to give access to a pavement grating, and the only natural light, of which there was never enough to work by, came from glass bricks let into the pavement. Apart from the energy sapping heat and airlessness, every loaf had to be taken leg-achingly upstairs to the shop (on heavily loaded wooden trays carried on the head) or to the barrows or vans ready for delivery.'

History Workshop Issue 3, (Spring 1977)

Another witness at the inspection described the way in which cobwebs frequently festooned a bakehouse. As people walked on the floor above, the floorboards would shake and the cobwebs fall, and the unfortunate journeyman found himself kneading them into the dough.

In amassing evidence for his case against the existing state of the baking trade, Mr. Tremenheere included the medical report of a Dr. William Guy of King's College Hospital:

'I am a physician to King's College Hospital. In prescribing for the out-patients of the hospital, I have been in the habit of making inquiries respecting their occupations, and have also minutely examined into the health of particular classes of men. My attention was very forcibly called to the state of the journeymen bakers, by the cases of several patients who followed that business.

…The facts were briefly these: - It was shown that a large proportion of the journeymen in the baking trade began their work at 11 at night, and continued at work, with certain intermissions, for from 18 to 20 hours; that the great majority of their places of work were unwholesome, being very close, very dirty, very damp, and very offensive.; that the heat in which they work, by exhausting them, renders them liable to inflammatory affections, colds, and rheumatism; that the flour dust, and the gusts from the oven (consisting of carbonic acid, alcohol, and sulphurous acid gas from the coal) irritate their lungs, and predisposes to consumption; that the severe exertion leads to palpitation, diseases of the heart, ruptures of blood vessels, and apoplectic seizures; and that as, on a reasonable estimate, upwards of one fourth are under twenty years of age, the early age at which they have to encounter these trials to their constitution tends greatly to undermine it. I stated also, as the result of my own inquiries, confirmed by the authority of Mr. Neison, that the expectation of life among the journeymen bakers was lower than that of most other trades.

…I am able to say that rheumatic fever, inflammation of the lungs, and consumption, but especially the last two, colds, indigestion, bowel complaints, skin diseases, spitting of blood, bleeding at the nose, and ruptures, are the prevailing complaints to which the bakers are subject; and that no class of men, excepting perhaps the grinders of Sheffield, are so liable to severe and fatal *diseases of the chest as the bakers. They are four times as liable to those diseases as compositors, whose low state of health I had previously ascertained. Their average age at death presents the low figure of 42 years.*

I attribute their superior liability to disease to long hours of work, great muscular efforts, exposure to heat, the inhalation of the particles of flour and of noxious gases, and to the close underground places in which they work.'

The final recommendations of Hugh Tremenheere included the inspection of bakehouses to examine the ventilation, drainage and cleanliness, the limewashing of the interior every six months, and ventilated and separate sleeping quarters for the men.

Adulteration of Flour

The hardships undergone by some journeymen bakers are not the only factor to be considered in any description of the baking trade in the middle of the 19th century.

The kind of bread which was produced sometimes contained the most alarming bulk additives to keep the cost down. These loaves were known as 'adulterated bread'. They make concerns about additives in the late 20th century seem paltry by comparison. Just as the bakers' long hours are said to have started at the end of the 18th century, so is the adulteration of bread.

It was highly unlikely that bread would be adulterated in the Middle Ages. It was the custom for each baker to mark his loaves with his own imprint. The Liber Albus mentioned previously quotes a law made in about 1320:

'That each baker shall have his own seal, as well for brown bread as for white bread; that so it may be better known whose bread it is. And that each alderman shall view the seals of the bakers in his ward and that each baker shall show his seal at each wardmote, that so it may be known.'

In the reign of Queen Anne in the beginning of the 18th century the law also required

'that every common baker shall fairly imprint or mark on every loaf the sort, price, and weight of every such loaf ... and if any bread shall be wanting in the due weight, or shall not be duly marked according to directions of this act, it shall be lawful to seize and take the bread so found.'

One of the main benefits of the Assize was that nothing could be added to the bread by the baker. Only grain appointed by the Assize could be used. (However, one writer in 1839 suggests that adulteration began as early as the middle of the 18th century, some time before the final abolition of the Assize.)

After abolition the practice began of selling low-price bread which was made to appear like the best bread, but was in fact impure and deficient in weight. One witness before the government inspector, a Mr. Francis Crisp, listed the ingredients used to adulterate bread: alum (which is a crystalline double sulphate of aluminium and potassium), pearlash (potassium carbonate), soap which creates a strong fermentation and whitens bad flour, 'stone flour' (which is made of Derbyshire stone), carbonate of magnesia, chalk, clay and sulphate of lime.

He said that the practice of adulteration was widespread in London, especially regarding alum. Large quantities of 'Baker's Stuff' were being sold, consisting of alum, ground fine, both pure and mixed with salt. A Dr. Hassall in a recent analysis of 32 specimens of bread found that 17 contained alum. Rice was also widely used, necessitating the use of more alum to bind the dough.

Alum is very harmful when taken daily, even in small quantities, and especially in the young and weak. Although the Act for Preventing the Adulteration of Articles of Food and Drink was passed in 1860, inadequate funding meant that bakeries were not inspected regularly enough to deter bakers from adulterating their loaves, even in the 1860s. According to the government report alum causes severe gastric irritation and can lead to the ulceration of the bowels, also causing frequent constipation, headaches, liver derangements and diarrhoea.

> *'Observe, brown bread is often recommended by medical men. When used as a matter of health, almost the only chance of succeeding, is by procuring the undressed meal, and making the bread at home. If bakers are applied to for brown bread they generally produce it by merely taking a portion of the regular dough, and sprinkling among it as much bran as will bring it to the colour required.'*
>
> Esther Copley, *The Complete Cottage Cookery* (1849)

The situation was found to be the same in other parts of the country. In fact in 1848 in Leeds a company called the People's Flour Mill had been formed, largely through the efforts of working class people, to ensure that their flour was unadulterated. Similar societies existed elsewhere in the North – a reflection of the fact that the vast majority of Northerners baked their own bread and would therefore want pure flour.

Other meals were also used to adulterate the bread, for example, the husks of wheat, barley, oats, rye and rice, in none of which is there any nutritional value. They merely served to add bulk and make the flour go further, enabling the baker to sell at a low price and undercut his competitors.

Mr. Rice, beadle of the Bakers' Company, gave evidence to the inspection that some millers were also responsible for supplying adulterated flour to these low-price bakers.

'This lowness of price much attracts the public, who are always looking out for "cheapness" in everything. And however low a man of this class may advertise his bread, there is pretty sure to be someone near him who will, for a time, advertise it lower. This leads each, in turn, to apply to the millers for flour at a lower price; it must necessarily be more adulterated; and thus the public is constantly getting mixtures, sold as flour, which are as much adulterated as it is possible for them to be, and still to be able to be made into bread.'

As in any free market situation, the customer is also liable to be blamed for purchasing the product in the first place. Matthew Bramble, although merely a fictional character in Smollett's novel, 'Humphrey Clinker', makes a wise assertion when he says:

'the bread in London is a deleterious paste, mixed up with chalk, alum and bone-ashes; insipid to the taste and injurious to the constitution... The good people are not ignorant of this adulteration, but they prefer it to the wholesome bread because it is whiter than the meal of corn. Thus they sacrifice their taste and their health ... and the miller or the baker is obliged to poison them and their families, in order to live by his profession.'

> **'Without wishing in the slightest degree to disparage the skill and labour of breadmakers by trade, truth compels us to assert our conviction of the superior wholesomeness of bread made in our own homes.'**
>
> Eliza Acton, *Modern Cookery* (1855 ed.)

Although there is no record of the young Thomas Adams' experiences as an apprentice and later as a journeyman baker, we do know that even in 1880 the bakers of Northampton were still underselling one another and causing hardship in the trade. At the 25th annual dinner of the Master Bakers' Society at the Swan Inn (at which Thomas' son, Frank, was present) a revealing speech was made by Mr. Purser:

'Prior to 20 years ago the state of the baking trade in Northampton was in a deplorable state, and if that condition of things had continued very much longer, many honest, hard-working men, who were straightforward and doing their best to pay twenty shillings in the pound, would have had to do one of two *things. If a man had a little money he must have lost it, and if he had no money he must have got into debt, and never could have paid his creditors. That was a state of things no honest man would desire to see, and it was that which led to the establishment of this society.'*

N.M. 15.5.1880 Suppl. p.1

The report of the government inspector in 1863 illustrates not only the extremely competitive business environment which characterised the baking trade in the mid 19th century, it also provides evidence of the harsh hours and the dirty and unhealthy surroundings that a young man was liable to encounter who chose to embark on such a career. Last but not least, the report reveals the kind of bread which the 'underselling' bakers were producing, containing as it did appalling bulk additives and offering the customer a cheap but unhealthy alternative to the wholesome bread of the more traditional bakers.

In the late 20th century in the face of the competition presented by the sliced white loaf of the supermarkets, the descendants of Thomas Adams decided to concentrate on producing 'traditional bread' – the kind of natural and wholesome loaves which would make their bread distinctive. The sliced white of today cannot of course be compared with the strange mixture of flour, alum, soap, ground stone and clay which might be presented as bread flour in the mid 19th century, but it may well be that like his descendants in the late 20th century Thomas had to make a decision in favour of 'traditional' baking.

In 1856 he took a major step in his career when he became a Master Baker and acquired his own bakehouse on Union Street, in the very centre of Northampton. Against all odds he made a success of his small business. Traditional quality was as important then as it is now.

Chapter 2

THE SEARCH FOR THOMAS' ANCESTORS AND A CONNECTION WITH JOHN ADAMS, THE 3rd AMERICAN PRESIDENT

In the middle of the 19th century Americans began to take an interest in their ancestral roots in England. For many, 200 years had passed since their ancestors had set foot in New England, and life had been such a struggle that two centuries had elapsed before they had found the leisure and inclination to research their past.

Northamptonshire prides itself on being the ancestral county of two famous Americans – George Washington, the first President of the United States, whose family came from Sulgrave and Brington, and Benjamin Franklin, a statesman and scientist at the time of the American War of Independence, whose father emigrated from Ecton. A third figure is often also linked with the county – John Adams, the third President. Since about 1900 the idea has been put forward that his ancestors came from Flore, the village near Daventry where Thomas Adams' family settled in about 1845.

From the mid 20th century onwards Thomas Adams' descendants have been intrigued at the possibility that their ancestor, connected as he was with Flore, might have been descended from the Adams family who were the forefathers of the third President of the United States.

A journalist writing for the Northampton Independent in 1910 publicised the little known fact that President John Adams' grandfather was said to lie buried in the garden of the former Quaker Meeting House now known as Adams' Cottage. The house still stands in an alley off King's Lane and there are extensive records showing that many Quakers with the name Adams lived in or near Flore during the 17th and 18th century. He concluded his article with the words:

'There is no doubt that if patriotic Americans saw what appears to be such sacrilege of sacred ground, they would endeavour to raise as fitting a memorial to John Adams' ancestor as they have done at Ecton to the forebears of Franklin.'

N.I. 2.7.1910

The Search for Thomas' Ancestors

In that same year Sulgrave Manor was bought by the Sulgrave Institution to preserve the ancestral home of the first American president and to make a mecca for American visitors to Britain. Arthur Branscombe, a Washington historian, heard about the supposed American connection with Flore and brought it to the attention of the American branch of the Sulgrave Institution. Their chairman, John Stewart, called the editor of the Northampton Independent, W.H. Holloway, asking for him to take steps to purchase Adams' Cottage, and this was duly arranged.

'It is now the intention of our American friends to restore the old building to something like its original appearance as an old Quaker meeting house. Fortunately many of its ancient features are preserved, including the cupboard where the Quakers kept their Bibles and hymn books. The Sulgrave Institution now appeals through this journal for the loan or purchase of the old Quaker stools, forms or books, particularly those belonging to the Adams family, many of which are known to be in existence in this county or in the United States. They also intend to lay out the garden reverently as a cemetery – a real God's acre – and erect a memorial tablet recording the names and dates of death of all the thirty five buried here.'

N.I. 27.10.1923

The link was further cemented by the visit of John Adams' great-grandson, Brooks Adams, who was visiting England in November 1923. Brooks was of course extremely interested to discover this connection with his forebears and promised to make a handsome contribution to the endowment fund of Adams' Cottage.

It was explained to Brooks that one of the descendants of John Adams' ancestors was a Quaker called Richard Adams who married a Quakeress, Dorcas, in about 1730. This lady had a silver spoon marked with her initials DA, which was passed down the family, and it was an exciting moment when Brooks held the spoon in his own hands, believing it had belonged to one of his distant cousins.

Richard and Dorcas had had a daughter, Mary, who married John Capell in 1772, and it was John and Mary's son, Thomas, who bought Adams' Cottage in 1853.

Margaret Capell Wykes (now Mrs. Harrold), Richard and Dorcas' great-, great-, great-granddaughter, wrote an interesting article in the family history magazine, Footprints (January 1985), in which she explained how one of the Adams from Flore – Henry – emigrated to New England in 1638. It was one of his descendants who became President John Adams. The records of the Northamptonshire Quaker births, marriages and burials dating back to 1647 still exist, and there are many Adams who lived in Flore, Upper Heyford, Nether Heyford and Bugbrooke. Margaret Harrold believes, based on tales handed down through the generations, that Henry was the great-uncle of Richard and Dorcas, and thus her great-, great-, great-, great-, great-uncle.

She claims that the Henry Adams who emigrated was the son of a Thomas Adams who later helped establish the Quaker meeting house at Flore which was set up in 1668. Thomas is said to have been an Anglican clergyman who was ejected from the Church of England in 1662 for his Non-Conformist principles, and who later became chaplain to Lady Clare at Heyford. There is no written evidence establishing Thomas as the father of Henry, although Thomas may have been one of the trustees who administered the Quaker meeting house after it was bought as a barn in 1678. Records show that the first trustees were John Tibbs of Bugbrooke, yeoman, William Sharp of Flore, tailor, Richard Bradshaw of Flore, shoemaker, William Geneway of Muscott, husbandman, Thomas French of Nether Heyford, cooper, and Thomas Langton Junior of Whilton, yeoman. Several Adams appear in the list of trustees on the deed for 1741 – Richard Adams of Flore, gentleman, Joseph Adams the younger of Bugbrooke, gentleman, Richard Adams of Nether Heyford, gentleman, and

The former Quaker Meeting House at Flore

The Search for Thomas' Ancestors

William Adams the younger of Upper Heyford. No less than 21 Adams are listed as having been buried in the garden of the meeting house between 1660 and 1813. The Quaker records only started in 1647 for Northamptonshire, and nothing is found there to establish definitely that Thomas or Henry were the ancestors of Richard and Dorcas. The only mention of this married couple is that they had four children between 1730 and 1751, the last of whom was the Mary who married John Capell, and that they were buried in the garden of the meeting house – Richard in 1787 and Dorcas in 1789.

Margaret Harrold believes that Richard and Dorcas are directly descended from Henry Adams' brother, Richard, who was married to a Dorothy and lived in Upper Heyford. Richard is believed to have bought land in Pennsylvania from William Penn, the famous Quaker who gave his name to that state. This must have been after 1681, for that is the year when Penn obtained the land in settlement of a debt owed by King Charles II to his father. There is in fact reference to a Richard and Dorothy of Upper Heyford in the Quaker records – for the birth of their son, Joseph, is recorded in 1678, and also Joseph's marriage in 1703. However, once again it is only stories passed down through the Capell family that establish a link between Richard and Dorothy back to Henry the emigrant, and forwards to Richard and Dorcas.

It was an exciting task to try to trace the ancestors of the Thomas Adams who grew up to become a baker. There were and still are so many Adams in the area around Flore that it would surely be possible to find some links. It would be even more exciting if the link could be traced back to the many Quaker Adams who used to live in and near Flore in the 17th and 18th century, and perhaps even to one of the Quakers said to be an ancestor of the third American president.

A little was known about Thomas' father, William, and how his family finally moved to Flore from Drayton, but where did William come from? Unfortunately, the baptisms of his children merely recorded that he resided in Drayton. It is not known when he died and there is no record of his marriage to Betty of Chapel Brampton - perhaps because, being a Congregationalist, he was not married in the Church of England.

The parish registers for Daventry, which includes Drayton, show that there were several William Adams baptised in the parish in the latter half of the 18th century, but no definite connections could be claimed as long as Thomas' father's place of birth was unknown. So after a great deal of investigation, the search had to be abandoned.

Perhaps it would be possible to trace a link to the celebrated Quaker Adams of Flore by following the line forward through the Quaker records. It soon became clear that although family units were very clear for the period between about 1660 and 1780, lines then petered out as Quakerism lost its appeal

The Search for Thomas' Ancestors

and members of the family became baptised in the Church of England. (There is one touching piece of evidence of a Joseph Adams born in 1718 in Upper Heyford who renounced Quakerism in the year of his death, 1794, perhaps on his deathbed.)

Whether going backwards from 1825 or forwards from 1647, there seemed to be a brick wall barring any further investigation. Perhaps Thomas Adams' descendants would never know if they were related to the third President of the United States. Yet the trail leading back to the Henry Adams who emigrated to New England in 1638 and became the forefather of John Adams, was intriguing. It became more intriguing still when the Secretary of the Flore Heritage Society, John Smith, heard about the search and dismissed the assumption that there was a link between Flore and the American Adams. He denied any such connection existed and suggested that the source of the story might be the vivid imagination of Thomas Capell who bought Adams' Cottage in 1853.

A village history written in 1899 by Daniel Robinson is the first known written record mentioning the link, but there is no primary evidence known to the Flore Heritage Society. Perhaps Thomas Capell, knowing the stories his mother told him of his Quaker ancestors, Richard and Dorcas and Richard and Dorothy, and knowing of the recent lives of John Adams and his son, John Quincey, (who became the sixth President), pieced the names together and suggested a theory that later became known as fact. He may have been encouraged in his theorising by distant family memories of a Richard Adams of Northampton who is recorded as having sailed to New England to settle in Salem, Massachusetts in the period 1620 to 1650, the very time when Henry Adams is said to have emigrated.

John Smith quotes a family history published in New York in 1927 which traced the President's ancestors to a Henry Adams of Barton St. David, Somerset. It is a little known volume entitled 'Henry Adams of Somersetshire, England and Braintree, Massachusetts: his English Ancestry and Some of his Descendants' compiled by J. Gardner Bartlett and Col. Charles Edward Banks. The book can be found in the Northamptonshire Studies collection of Northampton Central Library, and it is a very thoroughly researched history of the President's ancestors back to a Henry Adams who arrived in Massachusetts in 1638 with his wife and family of eight children. The Americans seem to have taken great pains to preserve their local documents and so it is possible to follow the whole family saga of births, marriages, deaths, land purchases and fights with the Indians, as the colony developed in the days before the War of Independence. The family history contains for example the sad details of one of Henry's grown-up children being killed in the doorway of his home as his village was raided by the Indians. His wife lay wounded inside, dying from an accidental gunshot that had been fired through the floor of her bedroom.

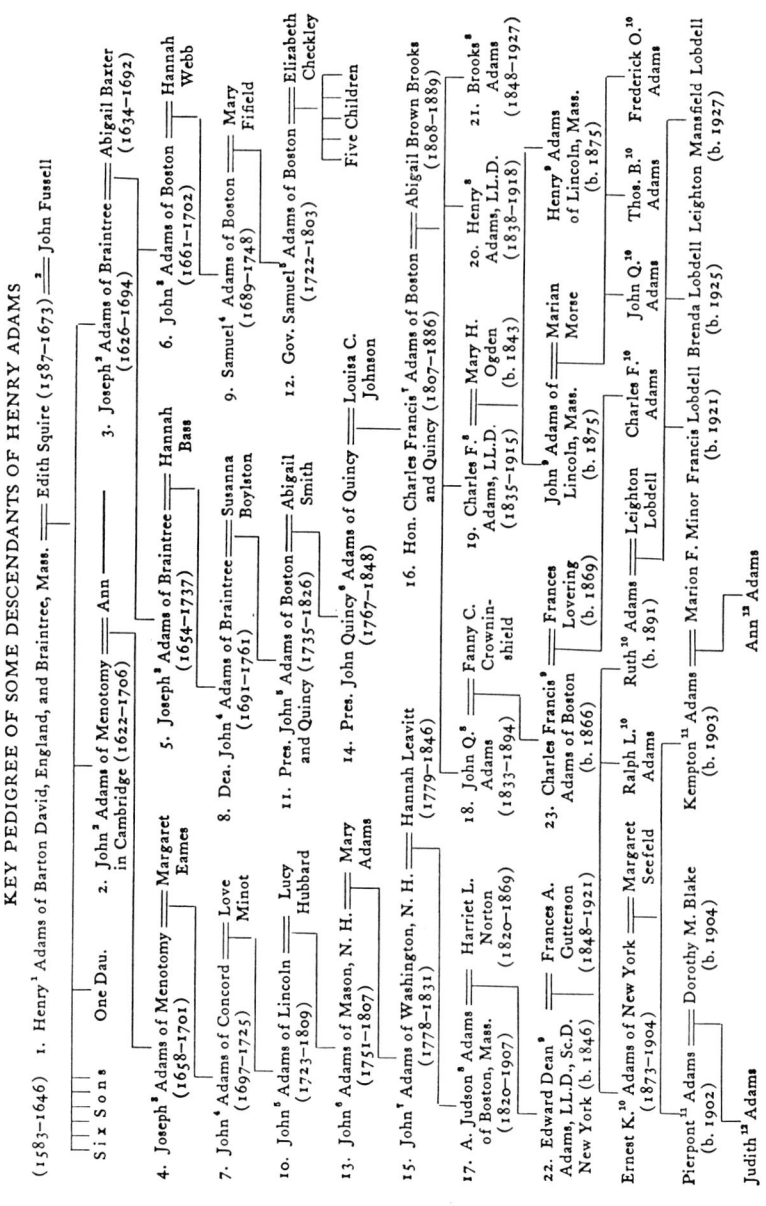

The Search for Thomas' Ancestors

KEY PEDIGREE OF SOME DESCENDANTS OF HENRY ADAMS

(1583–1646) 1. Henry¹ Adams of Barton David, England, and Braintree, Mass. = Edith Squire (1587–1673) = ?John Fussell

Six Sons — One Dau. — 2. John² Adams of Menotomy in Cambridge (1622–1706) = Ann — 3. Joseph² Adams of Braintree (1626–1694) = Abigail Baxter (1634–1692)

4. Joseph³ Adams of Menotomy (1658–1701) = Margaret Eames
5. Joseph³ Adams of Braintree (1654–1737) = Hannah Bass
6. John³ Adams of Boston (1661–1702) = Hannah Webb

7. John⁴ Adams of Concord (1697–1725) = Love Minot
8. Dea. John⁴ Adams of Braintree (1691–1761) = Susanna Boylston
9. Samuel⁴ Adams of Boston (1689–1748) = Mary Fifield

10. John⁵ Adams of Lincoln (1723–1809) = Lucy Hubbard
11. Pres. John⁵ Adams of Boston and Quincy (1735–1826) = Abigail Smith
12. Gov. Samuel⁵ Adams of Boston (1722–1803) = Elizabeth Checkley — Five Children

13. John⁶ Adams of Mason, N. H. (1751–1807) = Mary Adams
14. Pres. John Quincy⁶ Adams of Quincy (1767–1848) = Louisa C. Johnson

15. John⁷ Adams of Washington, N. H. (1778–1831) = Hannah Leavitt
16. Hon. Charles Francis⁷ Adams of Boston and Quincy (1807–1886) = Abigail Brown Brooks (1808–1889)

17. A. Judson⁸ Adams of Boston, Mass. (1820–1907) = Harriet L. Norton (1820–1869)
18. John Q.⁸ Adams (1833–1894) = Fanny C. Crownin-shield
19. Charles F.⁸ Adams, LL.D. (1835–1915) = Mary H. Ogden (b. 1843)
20. Henry⁸ Adams, LL.D. (1838–1918)
21. Brooks⁸ Adams (1848–1927)

22. Edward Dean⁹ Adams, LL.D., Sc.D. New York (b. 1846) = Frances A. Gutterson (1848–1921)
23. Charles Francis⁹ Adams of Boston (b. 1866) = Frances Lovering (b. 1869)
John⁹ Adams of Lincoln, Mass. (b. 1875) = Marian Morse
Henry⁹ Adams of Lincoln, Mass. (b. 1875)

Ernest K.¹⁰ Adams of New York (1873–1904) = Margaret Seefeld
Ralph L.¹⁰ Adams
Ruth¹⁰ Adams (b. 1891)
Charles F.¹⁰ Adams = Leighton Lobdell
John Q.¹⁰ Adams
Thos. B.¹⁰ Adams
Frederick O.¹⁰ Adams

Pierpont¹¹ Adams (b. 1902) = Dorothy M. Blake (b. 1904)
Kempton¹¹ Adams (b. 1903)
Marion F. Minor Francis Lobdell Brenda Lobdell Leighton Mansfield Lobdell (b. 1921) (b. 1925) (b. 1927)

Judith¹² Adams
Ann¹² Adams

The Family Tree of President John Adams

The Search for Thomas' Ancestors

The American half of the genealogy was written by J. Gardner Bartlett who was the author of a dozen volumes of genealogies of New England settlers. Educated as an architect, he had found genealogical research so interesting that he had eventually become one of the best-equipped students of early New England family history and had spent seven years studying original records in England. His claim that President John Adams was descended from a Henry Adams who arrived in New England in 1638, is based on historical evidence.

Yet the first half of the genealogy follows the English line back from the year 1638, back from a Henry Adams of Barton St. David, Somerset who had mysteriously disappeared from the parish records in about the year 1630. The link was suggested and then become accepted as fact, that these two Henry Adams were one and the same people. Thus the famous American Adams family were said to come not from Flore, but from Somerset.

The English half of the book was written by Charles Banks, who 'had visited all the counties of England and spent months of work as secretary in the Public Record Office, London'.

His work on the genealogy of the Adams family from Barton St. David was again very carefully researched and documented, but the claim made in the chapter linking the two families could not fail to arouse a certain feeling of scepticism. How could the writers be sure Henry Adams came from Somerset when others were equally convinced he came from Flore? The book even discussed another claim that had been made concerning Henry's origins - in 1853 a long pedigree had been published setting forth the descent from a landed family at Fenn in Stoke-Gabriel, Devon. Several years later 'it was shown that the alleged connection ... was false and rested on forged evidences'.

The Northamptonshire claim was also discussed. The story behind the Sulgrave Institution's purchase of Adams' Cottage was explained, providing further evidence of the intriguing story behind the search for the origins of John Adams:

'In November 1923, an old farm cottage at Flore in Northamptonshire was announced as the ancestral home of Henry Adams, in a syndicated newspaper article published in America by the Sulgrave Institution. This organisation had unfortunately been induced to purchase this Flore cottage as an Anglo-American shrine, on the mistaken representations of two English journalists who erroneously claimed it was the ancestral home of Henry Adams.'

So the Sulgrave Institution sold the cottage at a loss in 1925, having owned it for a period of only two years.

Philip Adams, the oldest surviving descendant of the Oliver Adams bakery family, was determined to pursue research into the validity of the Somerset claim. If it could be discounted, the romantic idea of a third famous American connection with Northamptonshire would remain alive, and the

The Search for Thomas' Ancestors

possibility that Thomas Adams was related to the Henry Adams who became the forefather of John Adams. On the other hand, if the claim was found to be reliable, another of Northamptonshire's myths would be dispelled.

Between 1620 (the year when the Mayflower landed at Plymouth, Massachusetts), and 1641 (the beginning of the English Civil War) about 25,000 English emigrants crossed the Atlantic to New England. The voyages were organised by various companies, ranging from small ones such as the Dorchester Adventurers run by the Rev. John White to the large Massachusetts Bay Company.

It would seem logical that Henry Adams of Somerset experienced a conversion to Puritanism which led him to brave the dangerous crossing of the Atlantic ocean. No such conversion is recorded. It is only known that Henry Adams of Barton St. David married Edith Squire of Charlton Mackrell in 1609 and moved to the nearby village of Kingweston. Edith's sister, Ann, sailed to New England in 1632 with her husband, Aquila Purchase. Henry's sister-in-law's emigration could have been the inspiration for him to take his own family to the New World.

The link between the two Henry Adams (of Somerset and Massachusetts) is not helped by the fact that there are recorded baptisms for only three of the children in Somerset – Thomas (1612) in Barton St. David, and John (1622) and Edward (1629) in Kingweston, whereas his party on arrival in New England consisted of 'ten heads'. The Massachusetts Henry made a will in 1646 naming six of his children: Peter, John, Joseph, Edward, Ursula and Samuel, and other documents suggest that he also had three more sons – Thomas, Henry and Jonathan. So for six of his children there is no record of baptism in Somerset.

As there is no actual documentary evidence proving that Henry came from Somerset, perhaps the mystery could be solved by evidence relating to his wife. If she could be proved to have originated from Kingweston, then the truth of the link would be firmly established. Again there is no documentary evidence, but there does exist very convincing circumstantial evidence – namely the movements of two young men, Jonathan and John Adams.

A Jonathan Adams emigrated to New England in 1651 to live near his mother, Edith, who had been widowed and subsequently married John Fussell. (Henry Adams died in 1646.) Jonathan is recorded as having been working on the farm known to belong to Edith Adams' grandfather in Kingweston. Other documents describe this Jonathan as the brother of Edward and Peter Adams. This Edith Fussell is therefore very likely the widow of Henry Adams, and her connection with Kingweston strongly suggests that she is the Edith Squire who married Henry of Barton St. David. It would be an amazing coincidence if this were not the case.

> TO THE GLORY OF GOD
> IN HONOUR OF ST. DAVID
> AND
> IN MEMORY OF
>
> ## HENRY ADAMS
>
> BORN IN THIS PARISH ABOUT 1583
> AND A FOUNDER
> OF NEW ENGLAND 1638
> ANCESTOR OF TWO PRESIDENTS
> OF THE UNITED STATES
> OF AMERICA
> JOHN ADAMS AND JOHN QUINCY ADAMS
> WHOSE EXALTED SERVICES
> TO THEIR COUNTRY
> EVOKE
> A TESTIMONY OF RESPECT FOR
> THEIR ANCESTRAL HOME
> THIS MEMORIAL HAS BEEN ERECTED
> BY
> EDWARD DEAN ADAMS
> A.D. 1926

Adams Memorial in the Church of Barton St. David, Somerset

The Search for Thomas' Ancestors

The movements of a John Adams of Concord, Massachusetts, serve also as evidence of the truth of the story: *'On 25 Dec. 1649 John Shepheard of Braintree in New England, carpenter, husband of Margaret, the daughter of Henry Squire late of Kinweston neere Somerton in Somersetshire, granted a lettre of Atturney to John Adams of Concord to receive etc. all rents due for lands now or late in the tenure and occupation of Jonathan Adams living neere Baltonsborough in Somersetshire…'* It is known that the American Henry Adams' son, John, went to live in Concord. It is therefore highly likely that Margaret was John's aunt – which would explain why she entrusted him with the task of collecting her rents in England. This provides the second piece of circumstantial evidence linking Henry Adams' wife with Kingweston.

If anyone wants to understand more fully the family history of Henry Adams' family of Braintree, Massachusetts, J. G. Bartlett's book is strongly recommended. It has only been possible to summarise his findings here very briefly.

It seemed that President John Adams' origins were in fact in Somerset, not Flore. It would have been satisfying to have seen firm evidence in the form of a passenger list showing the home towns of the immigrants to New England in 1638, but after enquiries of the Record Offices in Somerset and Devon, the Public Record Office, and the American National Archives, it was clear that they either no longer existed or if they did, would have been found by the avid researchers of the period between 1910 and 1930 who were investigating the ancestry of American families from New England.

J. G. Bartlett had obviously made thorough searches of the American local documents. Charles E. Banks is quoted as having spent months of work in the P.R.O. in London prior to compiling his 'Topographical Dictionary of 2885 English Emigrants to New England 1620 – 1650' (ca.1930). John Camden Hotten's book 'The State Papers Domestic in the P.R.O., covering emigration from Great Britain to the American plantations from 1600 – 1700' makes no mention of a Henry Adams, only a Hester Adams from Taunton. Wickenden's book 'Emigration from Taunton to New England' is based on 'vital records of Massachusetts and Colonial State and Trade Papers for America and the West Indies' (1931), held in the P.R.O. He does in fact refer to Henry Adams of Barton St. David, but as his book was published four years after J. G. Bartlett's, his source may have been secondary, and not the original emigration papers.

So even though Flore is denied its place alongside Sulgrave, Brington and Ecton as the home of the ancestors of an illustrious American, it was undoubtedly the home of several Quaker families who attended the meeting house now called Adams' Cottage, between 1668 and 1791.

William Adams (Thomas the baker's father) may well have been descended from a Quaker family because of his membership of the

The Search for Thomas' Ancestors

Congregational Church, whose strict puritanism is akin to the faith of the Quakers.

There were many Quaker families in his area during the previous one and a half centuries, and many families named Adams as well. For example, in Drayton at the time when William brought up his family there, there lived a John and Elizabeth Adams with a large family. In Weedon in the 1840s and 50s a grocer's shop was owned by a Thomas, then a Robert Adams. In Flore in the 1840s were two men with the Adams surname – one a butcher and the other a farmer. A William Adams married a Mary Clarke in Drayton in 1712. Perhaps William was a family name and this William was Thomas' father's grandfather. Sadly we shall never know.

What does seem likely is that the Thomas Adams who is said to have helped found the Quaker meeting house and who subsequently gave his name to the cottage, was remembered by Mary Adams and John Capell at the end of the 18th century through family stories handed down from generation to generation, and was then made the centre of a wonderful story about his Puritan son, Henry, emigrating to New England to become the great-great-grandfather of President John Adams. Perhaps the confusion occurred because of the distant memory of the Richard Adams who is recorded as emigrating from Northampton to Salem, Massachusetts in the first half of the 17th century.

Whatever the reason for the story, the apparent myth became an acknowledged truth, and since the latter half of the 19th century has become a mistaken, but cherished part of local history for many Northamptonians.

Chapter 3

THOMAS ADAMS, MASTER BAKER 1856–1890

By 1856 Thomas had spent nine years as a journeyman baker. Including his apprenticeship at Flore he had been in the trade for eleven years, so he was well prepared to branch out on his own and set up as a Master Baker.

While working at James Smith's bakery on 25 Gold Street in 1853, he had married Sarah Rogers. They had set up home in nearby Woolmonger Street which is now beneath the new St. Peter's shopping centre. Town centre demolition and development was going on even in the late 19th century, for this residential area was built over as shops expanded down Gold Street. For instance, in the 1890s the furniture shop called Jeffery's was extended at the back directly over the site of some of these terraced houses.

Thomas and Sarah's home was close to the edge of town - in the 1850s the population of Northampton was only 27,000 and only a few houses had been built beyond West Bridge. An area of aristocratic houses with gardens sloping down to the river was situated to the south of St. Peter's church; no houses at all existed beyond Bridge Street station, the only station in the town; the Workhouse (later St. Edmund's Hospital) was in the country, and the only houses between the General and St. Andrew's Hospitals were Nine Springs Villa and Beaumont Villa on Cliftonville.

Not far from Woolmonger Street, on the Drapery, the vegetable stalls would be erected on market days, for the Market Square itself overflowed, stalls being set up on Sheep Street, Regent Square, Campbell Square, Horsemarket and Marefair. Also on the Drapery, on the corner at Mercers Row was the Main Post Office. In order to buy a stamp customers had to rap on a little door about a foot square and the stamps would be cut off a sheet with scissors. The commercial heart of the town was close to a variety of residential areas - trees grew in Lady's Lane and there were beautiful gardens behind the houses in Sheep Street.

Thomas and Sarah might have visited the theatre in Marefair or the circuses that used to perform in a field called Mannings Close on the site

Thomas Adams, Master Baker 1856-1890

The Northampton Post Office on the corner of the Drapery and Mercers' Row, ca. 1850

of Hazelwood Road. For a time the only public room in the town was the Assembly Room at the George Hotel by All Saints' Church. Entertainment here included the great showman, Barnum, and the famous dwarf, General Tom Thumb, but the Milton Hall on Newland was built at about this period and competed with the Assembly Room with exhibits of waxworks and a visit by a strange tribe of Africans called the Hottentots. As far as Victorians were concerned, Thomas and Sarah had a great array of entertainment virtually on their doorstep.

Sarah must have been quite well educated for she ran a Dame school. Thomas also had received a good education for someone from his economic background. He must have been a thoughtful young man for he is said to have been influenced early in his life by the poetry of Robert Burns and the American Quaker, John Greenleaf Whittier. Robert Burns is well known for his passionately independent spirit, and John Whittier was fired by his strong sense of social justice to campaign for the abolition of slavery. Many of Whittier's poems were set to music as hymns, the most famous one today being 'Dear Lord and Father of Mankind'.

Knowing Thomas' fervent radical politics in his later years when he came under the influence of Charles Bradlaugh, it is interesting to see how concerned he was with social justice even in the early part of his life. At this

Thomas Adams, Master Baker 1856-1890

*Rev. John Bennett
Minister at Castle Hill 1833 - 1859*

time he was also a committed Christian, but his faith was not to last as long as his sense of justice, for while supporting Bradlaugh he became a Secularist, or humanitarian.

    On Woolmonger Street Thomas and Sarah did not live far from the Congregationalist Chapel, Castle Hill, situated on Chalk Lane near Castle Station. Soon after his arrival in Northampton, Thomas became a Sunday School teacher there during the ministry of the Rev. John Bennett from 1833 to 1859 . Bennett was vociferous in his political dissent – a fact which must have appealed to the young Thomas, knowing his political interests. Church membership had numbered only 106 on the minister's arrival but grew to 160 during the next twenty five years. It is said that *'his large and loving heart,*

his sociability and his fidelity as a friend attracted and attached the aged and the young.'
   T.Gascoigne, *A History of Castle Hill Church and its Pastorate 1674 -1895*

Eloquent in exposing corrupt politicians and deeply interested in the rights of the working class, he had come from Somerset, a county where there was a great deal of poverty:

'Three times a day the people had potatoes and bread, with now and then a little bit of bacon... 15 out of 20 never tasted any other kind of food, and their clothing was equally coarse and poor.'

Bennett was not an academic man, but clearly a fervent preacher. In 1851 when he organised the celebrations for the centenary of the death of Philip Doddridge, the important Non-Conformist Minister of 18th century Northampton, he found that they led to a revival in Castle Hill Chapel and an increase in the number of young people attending Sunday School. Thomas would have been a part of that revival.

Castle Hill Congregationalist Chapel 1852

Thomas Adams, Master Baker 1856-1890

Setting up as a Master Baker entailed a move to Union Street, which was situated on the site of the present Marks and Spencer, and it was quite natural for Thomas to change his church membership to Princes Street Chapel nearer his new home. Here he continued his Sunday School teaching. Congregationalism, as with Methodism, was growing rapidly in popularity in the Victorian era with a corresponding proliferation of new chapels.

Thomas would have left Castle Hill Chapel (renamed Doddridge) before the arrival of Thomas Arnold, another famous minister who served there from 1860 to 1882. His ministry was so powerful that the congregation soon grew too large for the Chapel. The building was enlarged twice; schools were built, and the Primrose Hill branch was opened in St. James End, first in a cottage used as a preaching station. By 1879 the membership of Doddridge Chapel was 289.

It is interesting to bear in mind Thomas Adams' early experience of this Non-Conformist revival when his later years of Secularism are considered.

The time at Union Street was made hard by the death of Sarah after only a few months of living in their new home. Thomas lost not only a wife, but also a helpmate in his new business. At least he had no children to worry about, and within the space of a few months he married again – his new wife was Elizabeth Oliver from West Haddon.

On the 18th of January 1858 Thomas and Elizabeth had their first child – Walter Quincey. Family tradition has it that the strange second name was given to Walter as a sign of his kinship to John Quincey Adams who was President of the U.S.A. from 1825-29 and son of President John Adams. If this is the case, it would suggest that as early as the 1850s the American connection with Flore was being talked about outside the confines of the family who were living in Adams' Cottage.

During the years of running his own bakery on Union Street Thomas had an experience which was to affect him deeply. He and his wife were renting their small bakehouse and must have been going through all the excitement and problems encountered in running their first business. After only a short time the owner of the property sold the premises over Thomas' head to a rival baker who took almost immediate possession. Thomas and his wife were thus turned out of their home. They would obviously have felt keenly the disadvantage of not owning their own property - an experience which was doubtless at the back of Thomas' mind when he later espoused the cause of the building societies and worked hard to enable people to become home owners.

Forced to vacate his first bakehouse, Thomas moved to a small property on Kerr Street, which is on the site of the new Magistrates Court.

Thomas Adams, Master Baker 1856-1890

Elizabeth Oliver, Thomas' second wife

Thomas Adams, Master Baker 1856-1890

His business must have prospered because he decided to expand. On the 8th of November 1862 the Northampton Mercury reported that a complaint was received by a Mrs. Castle of the Mounts that Mr. Adams' newly built bakehouse in the adjacent house was a nuisance. Perhaps the noise created by night working was the cause of the complaint (although the premises had already been occupied by a bakery). The trouble Thomas caused by altering his bakehouse may well have brought to his mind his father's experience on pulling down a couple of pigsties. In Thomas' case he did not have to go to prison and it is known that the complaint was not acted upon. The Survey and Building Committee of the Town Council ruled that the bakehouse was not 'a public nuisance' although it might be 'a private injury'.

Three more children were born to Thomas and Elizabeth at Kerr Street – Frank Oliver in 1859, Arthur William in 1860 and Jane in 1862.

By 1864 business had grown so much that Thomas decided to move into bigger premises. This time they chose an old brewhouse on 39 Lower Mounts (near the site of the present Chronicle and Echo offices). From the details of the auction of the property across the road at no. 40, Thomas' new home probably included (apart from the bakehouse itself) a coal house, flour rooms, stable, loft, manure vault, yard and covered gateway to the street, over which was an extra large flour room. The growth of industrialisation and population in Northampton meant that there was a steady increase in trade in general. Terraced houses began to spread round the outskirts of town. In 1845 there were 43 bakeries listed and by 1858 the number had increased by about one third to 58, with the edge of the town now extending eastwards to the Workhouse on the Wellingborough Road and the Racecourse and westwards to St. Andrews Road.

The growth of population is only one of the factors causing the increase in trade for a baker such as Thomas Adams, the other being that fewer and fewer housewives were baking bread in their own homes. The old style of dome-shaped brick oven fitted into the wall of the kitchen was no longer being built, now replaced by the coal-fired iron range. The iron range's oven space was much more limited, and its construction and design did not produce such good bread as the brick oven, so progress in the name of kitchen design brought an indirect benefit to the commercial baker.

What do they mean?

To scuffle - to wipe the floor of the oven with a wet sack tied to a long pole

Sole - the floor of the oven

Peel - a tool for putting the loaves in the oven, up to 10 feet long with a long handle of ash wood and a kind of oar blade made of beech.

Slip - similar to the peel, but used for putting in rolls, the blade being 5" wide with a rounded underside. The knack to be mastered was the twist and sliding motion that would leave the pieces of dough neatly spaced on the hot sole.

Upset - a metal container about 2' long, 1' high and 3 or 4" wide. It was partially filled with ashes and strategically placed in the oven to protect the baking bread from any 'hot spots'.

Domestic Baking in the mid 19th Century

Thomas would have used a large version of the brick oven. They were of extraordinarily skilled construction, the bricks precisely placed to form the arched crown, the floor or 'sole' sometimes of small glazed bricks, sometimes of large flagstones. In districts where there was plenty of scrubwood, gorse or blackthorn from the hedges, heating such an oven cost very little. The wood had to be collected and bundled into faggots and stored in a dry place. There is a first-hand account by a commercial baker trading in the 19th century, Fred Lester, which describes the work involved:

'The wood we used was house faggots. These were put whole into the oven – an awful struggle generally to get them through the door. One was laid straight across the back of the oven and one down either side – three altogether. These were put in the oven overnight so that they got nice and dry, otherwise they did not burn when lighted in the morning. Very often the whole place would be filled with choking, eye-smarting smoke in which atmosphere we had to work.

When three faggots were burnt down and the hot ashes spread over the bottom of the oven, another faggot was burnt in the mouth of the oven to make an even heat. After that the ashes were all raked out and taken in buckets to be emptied outside. Then a pail of water would stand on the floor in front of the oven and a long pole with a swinging sack tied on the end of it, this being called a "scuffle". The sack was soaked in the pail, put in the oven and swung round and round until all the oven bottom was quite cleared of ashes. This made the oven ready for setting the bread in...

I have forgotten to mention the very unpleasant job of getting the ashes out. The one doing that would be stripped except for trousers and unbuttoned shirt. These ashes would be scorching hot, and as the wood oven was close to the back door, which had to be kept open during the operation, if it happened to be a wet windy day, what with the smoke and fumes the man doing this did not have a very enjoyable time. Sometimes the whirling "scuffle" would fetch out a hot coal which would go down inside the man's shirt. Then there were fireworks and language.'

Fred Lester, *Looking Back*, (Mayfield, 1951)

The design of the brick oven was important in producing the characteristic crust. The heat radiated from the arched roof of the oven on to the surface of the bread while the bottom of the loaf was heated by direct contact with the floor of the oven, producing a compact bottom crust and a darker bubble-bearing top crust. The Victorian writer, W. Mattieu Williams, describes the workings of the oven:

'The old-fashioned oven ...is an arched cavity of brick with a flat brick floor. This cavity is closed by a suitable door, which in its primitive, and perhaps best form, was a flat tile pressed against the opening and luted round with clay ...Baked clay is an excellent radiator, and therefore the surface of bricks forming the arched roof of the oven radiates vigorously upon its contents below, which are thus heated at top by radiation from the roof, and at bottom by direct contact with the floor of the oven.'

W. Mattieu Williams, *The Chemistry of Cookery*, (1885)

Various methods were used to help determine whether the temperature was high enough for baking. The 'watch and tell-tale' was a small pebble specially selected from the fields, which changed colour with variations of temperature. It could be built into the oven. When it became fiery red, the oven was ready. Another method involved throwing lightly against the side of the oven a handful of flour. If it burned up with a blaze of sparks, the required temperature had been reached. Similarly a stick could be struck against the floor of the oven and if sparks flew, the oven was ready.

In 'Lady Bountiful's Legacy', edited by John Timbs in 1868, a fourth method is described:

Thomas Adams, Master Baker 1856-1890

'The oven is known to be properly heated to receive bread, when a little of the newest flour, thrown in on its floor, blackens without taking fire: old flour will not suit the test.'

Esther Copley in 'The Complete Cottage Cookery' (1849) gives detailed advice on how to fire an oven:

'The fuel for heating an oven should be very dry, and such as will heat through quickly. The stalky part of furze, and the brush-wood of faggots answer the purpose best. If larger wood is used (such as beech spokes and billets) they should be split in pieces about the thickness of a spade handle. Coals are altogether improper; so also are all knotty roots or greenwood. From one hour to an hour and a half is the time required for heating an oven; nothing but experience can give aptitude and exactness in determining the proper heat; when this is attained, everything should be placed quite ready, that the business now to be proceeded with may be accomplished in the least possible time. Take out the fire, sweep the oven very clean, by means of a rag mop fastened to a long handle. Put in the loaves with a peel, that is, a flat shovel with a long handle; it must be dusted with flour, between each time of putting in a loaf. Yet the whole operation of taking out the fire, cleaning the oven, putting in the bread, and shutting the door, should not take up five minutes; as much less as possible.'

Once the required temperature had been reached and the embers cleared out with a long handled iron tool curved at the end into a half-circle, the oven floor had to be swabbed out. The floor of the oven needed to be damp to create the atmosphere of steam so important to the successful baking of bread. 'Douting' of the glowing cinders might be done with a long pole to which was attached a short length of chain and a piece of sacking dipped in water.

Before the oven was fired, the dough would have been put to rise first thing in the morning. During the kneading process, lumps of dough were torn off and flung upon the scales. It was surprising how frequently an experienced baker could remove exactly the amount to make a loaf. To make a cottage loaf – one of the most popular in Victorian times – the lump was divided into one large and one small piece. After further kneading, the smaller portion was put on top of the larger and a final dig given with the knuckles to produce the depression always found in the centre of the top.

The loaves were introduced into the oven by means of long-handled wooden spades known as peels, and were removed by the same means.

There are memoirs that record with nostalgia the delights of home-baking in a brick oven, but the descriptions do not deny the hot, hard labour that was involved, taken as a matter of course by the mistress of the house or cook:

Thomas Adams, Master Baker 1856-1890

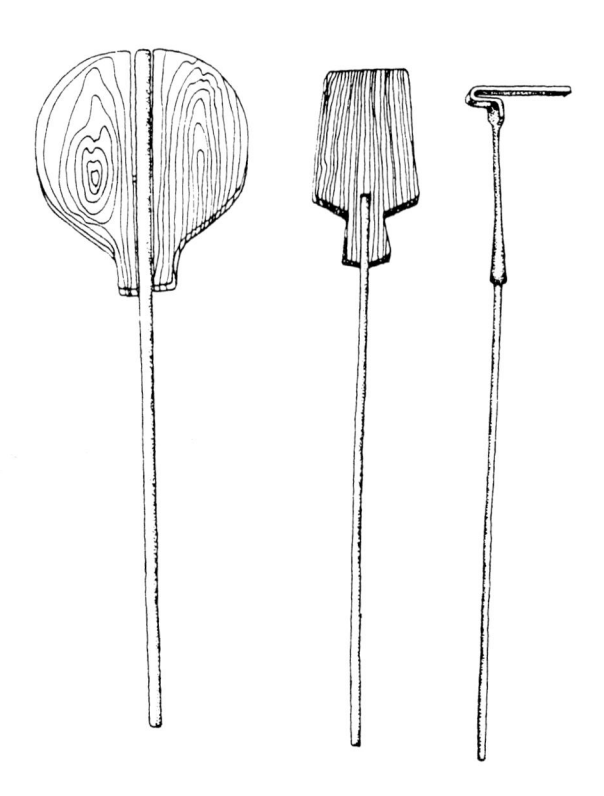

*Wooden peels for feeding loaves into the oven.
On the right is a rake for clearing out the ashes.*

'On baking day the cook filled a huge red pan with enough flour to make a week's bread for a household of sixteen. This was stood in a warm corner by the kitchen stove. Plenty of salt was sifted in. Three pennyworth of yeast, brought in a tin can from the small brewery in the next parish, was ready, but it was often unsatisfactory, dark coloured and bitter. The good housewife carefully doctored it with sugar and other things, for bad bread at every meal for a week could not be risked. The dough was well mixed, and kneaded several times by the stalwart armed cook. Meanwhile the great cavern of an oven in the chimney corner of the back kitchen was filled with gorse and hazel faggots till it roared up the huge chimney, from which quite a piece of sky could be seen as you stood below... When the flames died down the glowing embers were shovelled out with a long-handled iron peel. A bundle of green broom was dipped in water, and the oven floor swept hastily. Then the loaves were placed in one by one on a still longer, clean-scrubbed wooden peel and the iron door was shut.

The whole must have been hot, hard work for a woman, but it was taken as a matter of course in all old farm houses...When the loaves were baked, and lifted on to the old oak dresser to cool, the whole house was filled with the sweet wholesome odour that told it was baking day.'
Maude Robinson, *The Daily Bread of Old-time Sussex,* (Sussex County Magazine, Oct.1940)

The hard work involved meant that a week's supply of bread was baked at one go. However nostalgic the descriptions of home-baking, the bread must have sometimes been quite stale and dry.

The yeast was obtained from a brewery. It was called barm and would keep in a cool earthenware jar for up to six months without going sour. Sometimes the brewer's yeast was unsatisfactory, as Maude Robinson recalls, and it would have to be improved with sugar.

George Ewart Evans' account of home-baking in 'Ask the Fellows Who Cut the Hay' (1956) is a perfect example of nostalgia for bygone days with no regard for the drawbacks. In this case he enthuses over the bits of charcoal which adhered to the bread:

'*Small pieces of charcoal – the embers left from the fuel – often adhered to the loaves of bread that had not been baked in tins. These bits of charcoal gave an extra flavour to the bread according to the old people who are generally very critical of modern shop-bread. They say that no bread has the flavour of the home-baked bread. It was made from stone-ground flour with all the goodness of the wheat grains left in it; and, therefore, it was much more sustaining than the present day bread. It needed to be, for a meal in these days would often consist – apart from a hunk of cheese – almost entirely of bread, and before the coming of breakfast cereals many country children started their day with a "mess of bread and hot skimmed milk".'*

For all the efficiency of these domed brick ovens, they occasionally needed repairing. In 'Five Miles from Bunkum' (1972) Christopher Ketteridge and Spike Mays give a graphic account of the ordeal involved:
'*Periodically a very necessary but highly uncomfortable task was performed for the baker, the renewing of the lining of his furnace. Old fire lumps had to be cut and replaced with new ones, and in addition a man would often have to work inside the oven renewing brick paving in the floor. The oven was no more than eighteen inches from floor to crown and the terrific heat prevented him from staying inside more than a minute at a time, after which he would come out quickly, streaming with sweat and gasping for air. In he would go*

again, lying prone to do his work, his body blocking out the light and his legs protruding from the oven door. The heat precluded the use of a candle. This work was done in between baking times, but even at weekends when there was not baking the oven could not be cooled sufficiently to make conditions bearable. Whenever Chris repaired furnace and oven, which he has done several times, usually a severe cold followed the ordeal.'

Despite its virtues the brick oven clearly had its drawbacks, and new kitchen design introduced the coal-fired iron range to the modern Victorian home. Cooking habits were radically altered as houses were no longer built with an open hearth fire in the kitchen with a spit in front and a separate bread oven in the wall at the side. In her book 'English Bread and Yeast Cookery (1977)' Elizabeth David claims:

'Spit-roasting and bread baking were the two basic traditions doomed by the accelerating changes of the late 18th and early 19th centuries... In newly built farm cottages, just as in smaller town dwellings, cooking facilities were often limited to the combined kitchen-living-room stoves or "kitcheners", consisting of a hob, a little barred grate and an oven so small that it is difficult to see of what practical use it can have been to a family with growing children to be fed. These ovens were, it is true, fairly deep, so that the small openings are deceptive, but even making allowances for this point, bread-baking would not have been a very practical proposition in cottage kitcheners. In those days of large families and severely restricted diet, bread was the staple food. Coal, unlike the wood for the old ovens, was expensive. It was scarcely worth while stoking up the oven to the necessary heat just to bake a day or two's supply of bread at a time.'

Eliza Acton, in her book 'Modern Cookery' (1855 edition), commented that the new iron ovens were not well suited for baking bread, as the surface of a loaf would become hardened and browned long before the heat had sufficiently penetrated to the centre of the dough.

Gas and electric ovens were also criticized. They were said to be too drying on account of the draught of air necessary for the proper combustion of the gas. In the 1906 edition of 'Mrs. Beeton's Book of Household Management', Herman Senn explains the unsatisfactory nature of the modern oven for bread-baking:

'The unsuitability of the modern oven is principally due to thinness of the sides and the fact that it is not airtight; consequently all the steam escapes, rendering the bread dry and the crust hard and chippy, and not moist and crisp like baker's bread or bread baked in a large brick-built oven. For it should be remembered that it is absolutely necessary to keep all the steam in the oven when baking bread, for the vapour assists the crust to assume the brightness and gloss seen on new bread, known as "bloom".'

Section of an Eagle coal-fired range

Faced with the difficulties of domestic bread baking, inexperienced housewives were not even always given adequate advice in the various books available on house management. The instructions could be extraordinarily vague:

'The oven should be well heated and sufficiently large to bake the quantity of dough you make at one time.'
Alexis Sayer, *Shilling Cookery for the People* (1855)

or

'Heat your oven to a satisfactory degree of heat with a sufficient quantity of dry small wood faggots.'

Charles Francatelli, *A Plain Cookery Book for the Working Classes* (1862)

When confronted with a coal-fired iron range, it is not surprising that more and more people decided to stop baking bread at home and buy from their local baker. This was particularly convenient because there were bakers on virtually every street corner. By the 1880s customers could even have their bread delivered to their door.

Thomas Adams, Master Baker 1856-1890

Thomas Adams was not slow to take advantage of the boom in the baking trade, when he moved into the old brewhouse on the Lower Mounts. He allowed the beer license to lapse and turned the business into a bakery. Here he remained until his retirement in 1880 when he had a new house built at 77 High Street, overlooking the Racecourse (now Colwyn Road). The house was pulled down in about 1991 to make way for a garage, but it was one of the elegant Victorian villas, some of which still overlook the southern side of the Racecourse. Grand as they seem to the eyes of someone in the 21st century, there was apparently a class distinction discernible in the 19th century in the size and style of the villas being built in this area. Philip, Thomas' great-grandson, recalls:

'They were not the same class as the villas on East Park Parade, where the manufacturers lived. The tradesmen lived in Colwyn Road.'

From 1880 to 1888 Thomas' eldest son, Walter, ran the business, at some point in that period installing a new coal-fired oven with a side flue. He must have acquired the premises next door, for the address at this period becomes 39-41 Lower Mounts.

While living on the Mounts, Thomas and Elizabeth had five more children in the space of eleven years – Edgar (1864), Wallace (1866), Annie (1868), Herbert (1872) and Ethel (1875). Ethel died while still a baby. The six sons all grew up and entered the baking trade at some point in their careers.

With eight growing children and a bakehouse to run, Thomas and Elizabeth's house must have been a noisy lively place. Fortunately, Thomas was a robust man who was careful of his health, being a non-smoker and an advocate of temperance, although not a strict tee-totaller. Twice, however, he fell victim to rheumatic fever – a disease common in cold, damp conditions, and which may cause damage to the heart. Bakers were particularly prone to these kind of diseases on account of the dangers of moving from a very hot atmosphere into the cold of the air outside the bakery. Thomas' work in the bakery was also interrupted by an injury he incurred when he fell through a trapdoor in the floor. Apart from this, however, he was renowned for hardly ever taking a break from work, and could only be persuaded to take one, or at the most two days off work at a time for a holiday.

New Inventions in Baking

Thomas' natural ambition probably gave him an interest in all the latest inventions that were being discussed in the baking trade. Victorians loved inventions and by the mid 19th century there were several new ideas to improve the life of a baker and the quality of his product.

One invention was a dough-making machine designed by a Mr. Stevens. It was basically a closed trough with a handle to turn to mix the dough. Following on from all the evidence about bakers being susceptible to lung disease, it was a much healthier method of making dough, for the flour dust was contained within the trough. The bread produced was said to be much better as well, being more nutritious, and less was lost by fermentation. The bread kept moist for longer, had a thinner crust, and was less liable to crumble. The other great advantage from a commercial point of view was that more loaves could be produced from one batch of flour, as less flour dust was dispersed. An extra three 4lb loaves could be made from one sack of flour – a saving which vividly illustrates the huge amount of dust which must have been in the air and in the bakers' lungs.

The government inspection of bakeries in the 1860s was in favour of the machine from the health point of view alone:

'Even in clean, cool, well-ventilated bakehouses, the method of mixing the dough means men's perspiration is mixed in with the dough. They plunge their arms into the liquid prepared as the ferment, and subsequently into the semi-liquid mass in the trough where they mix water and half the flour with the ferment. Sweat is inevitable from the heat, the severe work, the disadvantageous posture. The other disadvantage is that during the 30 to 45 minute process of making the dough, the men inhale the flour dust and the carbonic acid generated by the fermentation. This is a major cause of their being so liable to lung disease.'

Reprints of Brit. Parl. Papers Vols. 3, 4, 5 (I.U.P., 1969)

On a national scale the 3% gain in the amount of flour used had huge implications for saving in the national consumption of flour. Less grain would need to be imported.

A second invention that was being talked about in the 1860s was 'Mr. Dauglish's aerated bread'. The process involved in making this bread reduced the making time to less than two hours and would, it was said, *'take baking out of the unhealthy handcraft to a manufacture which capitalists could then be encouraged to invest in. This would lead to the improved prosperity and well-being of the workmen.'* (op.cit.)

Dr. Dauglish's system depended on the use of fizzy water in the dough. The dough was enclosed in a container and aerated under pressure with highly carbonated water. His bread began to be sold in 1859 and achieved a certain amount of commercial success. The making time was reduced to less than two hours because no fermentation was required. Fermented bread and the kneading which it requires, takes 8 to 12 hours for each batch.

Thomas Adams, Master Baker 1856-1890

Apart from the time saving, Dr. Dauglish's invention was another one to claim significant savings on flour used. This was because all of the grain could be used except for the coarsest bran. Dr. Dauglish calculated that if all the bread in England was made by his process, a saving of 50,000 sacks of flour per annum was possible.

At this period not all of the grain was used in the baking of bread. Flour was normally bolted or sieved to remove the bran (13% of the grain's content) in order to produce a white flour suited to the popular taste. Dr. Dauglish's process made it possible to use virtually all the grain and still produce the white bread that would please the customer. The lack of fermentation meant that the dark brown colour did not develop, and the bread remained white.

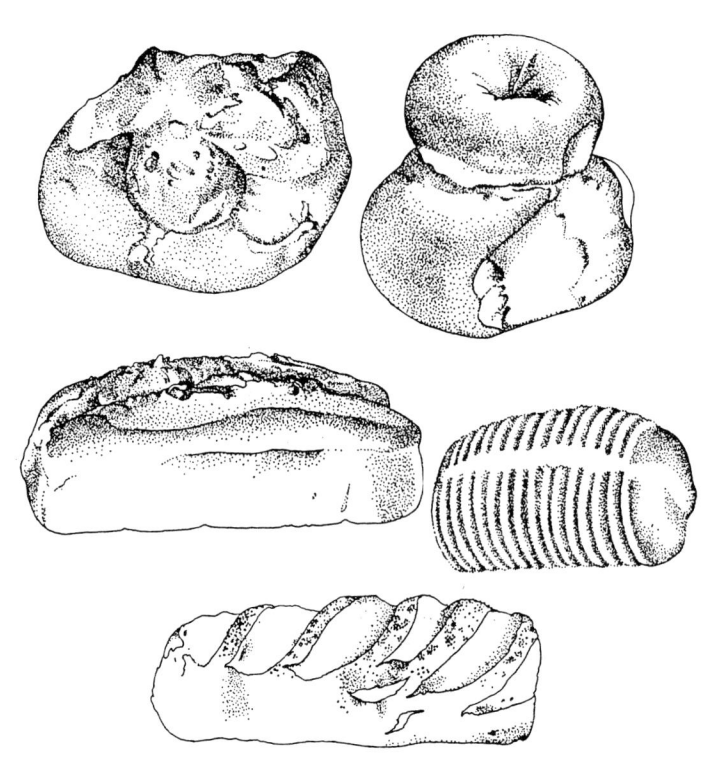

From top left clockwise: coburg, cottage, crinkled or musket (baked in a double cylindrical mould), bloomer and split tin

Thomas Adams, Master Baker 1856-1890

Loaves and Buns in Victorian times

So what kind of bread were bakers like Thomas Adams producing? Nowadays, with the present trend to healthier eating, bread made from stoneground wholemeal flour is assumed to be what was eaten in 'the good old days' when food was more 'natural' and made in the 'traditional' way.

It is surprising therefore that from medieval times to the mid 19th century, white bread with the bran sifted out of the flour was preferred. In the Middle Ages it was a luxury of the rich. A medical book published in 1542 states:

'Bread having too much bran in it is not laudable.'

Andrew Boorde, *Dyetary of Health* (1542)

This seems to have been very much the general opinion for at least 300 years. Even during the years of grain shortage in the early 19th century when one might have expected people to include bran in their bread flour in order to make it go further, it was popular practice to boil the bran, use the water from it – called bran tea – to improve the flavour of the bread dough, and still use the bran for the horses or pigs. People were of course only able to determine what went into their bread dough because flour was sifted at home, the bran being given to the animals.

Henry Mayhew wrote a famous book on the 19th century working classes in which he describes the popular feeling about brown bread:

'One of my elder informants remembered his father telling him that in 1800 George III had set the example of eating brown bread at his one o'clock dinner, but he was sometimes assailed as he passed in his carriage, with the reproachful epithet of "Brown George". This feeling continues, for the poor people, and even the more intelligent working men, if cockneys, have still a notion that only "white" bread is fit for consumption.'

Henry Mayhew, *London Labour and the London Poor* (1851)

Even the cookery writer, Eliza Acton, regarded wholemeal bread with caution:

'It may possibly not suit all eaters equally, but it seems at least worthy of a trial.'

Eliza Acton, *The English Bread Book* (1857)

The public demand for white bread seemed based solely on colour rather than texture or taste, for even when a machine was invented that could create the equivalent of what we know as wheatmeal flour (with the husk and bran only partially removed), the resulting bread was looked on with distaste because it was brown in colour, not white. This bread was 'invented' in about 1846 by an American, Mr. Bentz, who designed a machine for removing the outer seed-coat of the wheat grain prior to grinding, and without injuring the grain itself. By this means he preserved the highly nutritious portion of the internal coat of the grain which normally adheres to the bran and is torn away in the process of grinding, thus being lost to human consumption.

'The invention was brought to the attention of the Emperor of France who caused some experiments to be done. When this flour was subjected to the ordinary process of fermentation, and made into bread, much to the astonishment of the parties conducting the experiments and of the inventor himself, the bread was brown instead of white. The consequence of course has been that the invention has never been brought into practical operation.'

Reprints of British Parliamentary Papers, Vol.3 (IUP, 1869)

Although the Victorians were using white flour, which is known not to have as much taste as wholemeal, the flavour of their bread was in fact much enhanced by the kind of yeast which they used – the other vital ingredient in bread. Originally bakers used brewer's yeast. Brewing beer used to take two or three days because the yeast fermented very slowly. Bakers would go and collect two or three gallons of brewer's yeast in a bucket, and when they put it in their dough, the dough also fermented very slowly. The slow fermentation brought about changes in the development of lactic acids and other elements in the dough, and it is this which gave the dough its flavour. The slow fermentation process is therefore an important part in what we now call the 'traditional' loaf.

Despite the widespread preference for whiter and whiter bread, in about 1870 some people, led by medical writers, were starting to become perturbed by the deterioration in the nutritional content of their daily bread. Bakers started selling a type of bread made from a brown wheatmeal (about 90% pure, rather than 100% pure wholemeal). It is thought that the term 'farmhouse loaf' was coined at this time. A farmhouse loaf was made in a rather wider, shallower tin than the normal ones, and it seems possible that even in the Victorian era the term 'farmhouse' was used to evoke the idea of healthier living.

All loaves baked without tins were crusty. The most characteristic and distinctive shape among English breads, probably unique to this country, is the cottage loaf – two round loaves baked one on top of the other, the top one always being smaller than the bottom one. Eliza Acton says that in the mid 19th century, when she was writing, the cottage loaf was the commonest of bakery loaves. It is extremely difficult to reproduce it in modern bakery ovens or domestic cookers. It is hard to achieve the right shape and texture, crust and crumb. Elizabeth David makes the interesting point that although it has all but disappeared,

> 'to the English the cottage loaf remains the basic symbol of homely, wholesome bread. The shape would still be clearly recognised by any Englishman anywhere, even had he never set eyes on the real thing. As a racial memory it will die hard.' (op.cit.)

One of the most common of crusty breads was the Coburg – a round loaf with cuts in the crust. If there was just one cut, it was sometimes called a Danish. No baker seems able to account for the origin of the name Coburg. Although it is tempting, it cannot be assumed that it was first used in the 19th century as a compliment to Queen Victoria's consort, Albert of Saxe-Coburg-Gotha. Coburg was already used as the name of a fabric woven from mixed and rather coarse yarns. So the Coburg loaf, which is nothing more than a variation of the basic round loaf made for centuries, may well have been one made from mixed and coarsely ground flours. Or it may owe its name to one of the many German bakers who settled in London during the latter decades of the 19th century, and since it was also sometimes known as the Brunswick loaf, this seems the most probable answer.

Another crusty loaf still popular today is the bloomer – a long plump loaf with squarish ends and evenly spaced diagonal cuts on the whole crust surface. Again there seems to be no certain explanation of the name. 'Bloom' is a word much used in the baking trade to describe the particular sheen on good crumb and good flour. At one time it was understood that the bloomer loaf was of a special quality, made from high-grade flour and enriched with milk and butter or lard.

Bread baked in tins was a late development during the 19th century, although tins were known to be in use for baking in the early 18th century. It is strange that Britain and Holland were the only European countries widely to adopt the use of tins for baking bread. In France only soft sandwich loaves and rusk bread are baked in tins. All other French loaves are fashioned by hand or special dough-moulding machines.

When iron ranges became the norm in the English kitchen rather than an open fire combined with a bread oven, the use of tins became more widespread for baking bread because tins improved the texture of the bread and crust. The tin served to protect the loaf from the all-round radiation of heat. Also, in the small confined space of an iron range, the use of tins made it possible to bake more loaves, as they did not have to spread out. Perhaps as tin loaves became more popular in home baking, commercial bakers also started including them in their range of bread.

Different seasons would bring different tasks for the baker. Hot cross buns used only to be sold on Good Friday:

'Perhaps no cry – though it is only for one morning- is more familiar to the ears of a Londoner, than that of "One a penny, two a penny, hot cross buns" on Good Friday.'

Henry Mayhew, *London Labour and the London Poor*, (1857)

The original of the hot cross bun was the spiced fruit bun. They first became popular in Tudor times and were made from a spiced, butter-enriched fruit dough. For a long time bakers were permitted to offer these buns for sale only on special occasions, as is shown by the following decree, issued in 1592 by the London Clerk of the Markets:

'That no bakers, etc, at any time or times hereafter make, utter, or sell by retail, within or without their houses, unto any of the Queen's subjects any spice cakes, buns, biscuits, or other spice bread (being bread out of size and not by law allowed) except it be at burials, or on Friday before Easter, or at Christmas, upon pain of forfeiture of all such spiced bread to the poor.'

<u>Good Friday rhyme</u>

***One for the poker,
Two for the tongs,
Three for the dust-pan,
Hot Cross Buns!***

A few decades later in the time of James I it became impossible to enforce the laws to prevent bakers from making spiced breads and buns throughout the year. However, as recently as the 1960s bakers were following the custom of only producing them for the one day – Good Friday. Nowadays hot cross buns are sold for several months of the year around Easter time.

At Harvest Festivals it was traditional for bakers to make special loaves for the church service of thanksgiving. The loaves were considerable works of art, being moulded to resemble ears of corn or a complete sheaf of wheat.

Mince pies were also made by bakers, at Christmas time. Doughnuts were said to have their season as well, being sold on Shrove Tuesday before Lent, and muffins and crumpets were a traditional treat for tea in winter.

Bakers would bake the muffins and sell them to the muffin men who would ring their bell and utter their cry around the streets. There was a muffin man ringing his bell in Primrose Hill, London as late as the 1930s, always at weekends and in the afternoons in time for tea. Muffins and crumpets are among the most famous of English specialities, although more talked about now than actually experienced. It is only in about 1700 that cookery books start to include recipes for them, but they probably originated before the 18th century.

> ## *Muffins*
>
> *Take two eggs, 2 spoonfuls of new yeast, and a little salt. Mix a little warm new milk and water into a quart of flour. Beat all well together, and let it stand to rise. Bake them for about 20 minutes, until of a light brown, either on a hot iron, or in shallow tin pans in a Dutch oven. When to be brought to table, toast them slightly on both sides, but not in the middle: then notch them round the centre, and pull them open with your fingers, without using a knife, and butter them.'*
>
> Emma Roberts in the revised edition of Mrs. Rundell's
> *New System of Domestic Cookery* (1841)

Another English institution that dates from the early 18th century, if not before, is the small, soft, sweet, fermented cake called the Chelsea bun. Sugary, spicy, sticky, square and coiled like a Swiss roll, the Chelsea bun is one of the most popular sweet buns. It is not known how much of this type of confectionery was sold at the Lower Mounts shop in Thomas' time, but it is likely that once the bread had been baked, the oven would be used for what was called 'morning goods'.

Thomas Adams, Master Baker 1856-1890

It is interesting to note that the Chelsea bun originated at a famous Bun House in Chelsea which was a bakery, pastry cook's and refreshment shop combined. The Bun House was situated near Sloane Square in the Pimlico Road within easy reach of the river, and patrons could sit down at tables to eat their buns fresh from the oven. In its early days the Bun House was renowned chiefly for its hot cross buns, sold in massive quantities on Good Fridays and during Easter when great crowds flocked to Chelsea expressly to visit the Bun House. Even the wife of George II, Queen Caroline of Ansbach, would frequently visit there, arriving by boat and sometimes bringing the King and her family. The Bun House was still flourishing in the early 19th century, but was demolished in 1839.

The Growth of Cafés

In Northampton Thomas' bakery was just a shop, but the warmth of the place on a cold day would have made it an attractive place to call in, as all bakeries would have been in those days:

'There was no place quite so welcome on a cold day as the bakehouse; it was always warm and cosy in there. Local people often stopped during a shower to take refuge in the stables, but if it was really cold weather, many of those who would claim any sort of acquaintance with Father, turned off the road and went into the bakehouse to enjoy the warmth and have a chat before continuing their journey.'

H.S.Joyce, *I was Born in the Country* (1946)

Although Thomas' second son, Frank, would later venture into running a café as well as a bakery, Thomas continued to concentrate on the baking of bread. The attitude towards cafés was changing during this period. With the prevalence of public houses on the corners of the new terraced streets, prominent people of Northampton saw the need to encourage cafés as an alternative place of refreshment. Other towns had adopted similar policies and they were found to be very successful. The drunkenness always associated with public houses was condemned by many Victorians, and in Northampton in 1883 the Mayor gave a speech in which he stated that 8 out of 10 crimes were caused by this particular vice.

Consequently, the Mayor, other councillors, the Vicar of All Saints' and other eminent people of the town set up 'the Northampton People's Café Company' in 1878.

Thomas Adams, Master Baker 1856-1890

'The object of this Company is to provide, in Northampton, Houses for the supply of such Refreshments as Cocoa, Coffee, Tea, and Eatables of various kinds.

The great need of such a provision in this town and neighbourhood has long been felt and generally acknowledged.

It is proposed to fit up the Houses in such a manner as shall prove conducive to the comfort and convenience of the customers, and to supply at any hour of the day, Tea, Coffee, and Cocoa, or other refreshments at very moderate prices.

The Rooms will be furnished with tables and seats, where those who wish can take the dinners they bring with them, or the refreshments they may purchase on the premises.

Newspapers will be provided for the use of the customers.

The Houses will be opened at five o'clock in the Morning, so that the early workman or traveller may be readily supplied.'

N.M. 4.5.1878, p.5

The first temperance café was opened on Gold Street in 1878, the second four years later on Abington Square, and cafés began to increase in the town as the idea caught on with the general public. Perhaps the Adams' bakery helped supply the one nearby on Abington Square. Certainly the café started by Frank on Marefair became very successful and marked the beginning of a new type of enterprise for the Adams bakery business.

By 1880 Thomas had been a Master Baker for 24 years and had brought up eight children. He was only 49, but he made the decision to hand on the business to his eldest son, Walter Quincey, who was then 22 years old. His second son, Frank, had already been working as an apprentice to several bakers in the town, and had started his own business two years previously in Cow Lane, which still runs down beside the Derngate theatre and has since been renamed Swan Street. Thomas had been active in various fields for the past twenty years – local and national politics, the Freehold Land Society (now the Nationwide Building Society) and the Master Bakers' Association. He was ready now to retire to the villa on Colwyn Road. He would continue to play an active part in local affairs, but his son was now in charge of the bakery.

Although Thomas handed on a successful business, times had not always been easy in his period as a Master Baker. The practice of underselling, which was so much discussed in the government inspection of 1863, still existed. From the speech made in 1880 at the 25th annual dinner of the Master Bakers' Association, and which has already been quoted in chapter 1, it is possible to discern how the practice of underselling was reducing the profitability of the baking trade.

Relationships between local customers and the baker on their street corner cannot have been that close, for cheap prices could still lure people away from their regular baker. Sadly it is clear that for all the importance of the baking trade in providing a much needed service on the corner of almost every street in town, customer loyalty was not guaranteed, and underselling meant that prices had to be reduced and profits cut in order to stay in business.

At the relatively young age of 49, Thomas was presumably glad to retire. It was up to Walter to take the business forward into the twentieth century. Thomas would now continue his interest in local affairs and play an increasingly important role in the life of Northampton.

Chapter 4

'LAND FOR THE PEOPLE!'

Nowadays owning one's own home is considered the norm and a goal to which everyone is entitled. Decent sanitation and a clean water supply are taken for granted as part of living in a civilised society, and it is universally assumed that the right to vote should not depend on whether or not one owns a house.

In the early years of Thomas Adams' life no such rights existed, and the state of the housing for the vast majority of working people was cramped and unhealthy. In 1848 there was founded the Northampton Town and County Freehold Land Association – one of the first building societies, which later became known as the Anglia and eventually merged in 1987 to become the Nationwide. In Thomas' later years he became increasingly involved with working for this society, inspired by his deeply felt social conscience and political radicalism. His line of thought and that of many like-minded individuals was simple: the working classes were poorly housed and poorly provided for. Social legislation was required but there were few Members of Parliament who made this a priority as their supporters were the middle and upper classes (who were the only class to own property and therefore vote). Universal suffrage was required, but as a first step towards this, working class people needed to be able to borrow money to buy their own property and thereby acquire the right to vote.

Freehold Land Societies, as they were first called, enabled people to save and have the chance to borrow enough money to buy a plot of land. If the movement was successful, the register of voters could undergo an enormous change and more M.P.s could be elected who would represent the working class.

The 1840s were a significant decade known as 'The Hungry Forties'. 1848 was a year of revolution in Europe, a protest against the old order of oppression. In England the writers, Charles Dickens, Kingsley and Reade were awakening the public's social conscience. It is interesting that in Britain our form of revolutionary change came more peacefully – partly through the founding of various Freehold Land Societies, which were to have such a dramatic effect on the constituencies of Parliament.

Land for the People!

> *It is a lamentable fact that the humbler classes, the industrious millions, know little or nothing of the practical power of the term "FREEHOLD", and its political relationship to the Suffrage! The idea that a Mechanic or Labourer could possess a "Freehold", scarce entered their mind. This Society, however, submits a plan for obtaining "Land for the people", thus conferring on working men the power of possessing "FREEHOLD QUALIFICATIONS AS COUNTY VOTERS!"*
>
> Rules of the NTCFLS adopted 1848

During the latter part of the 18th century and early part of the 19th people were leaving the villages to go and make a living in the towns, and the increase in urban population led of course to a shortage of suitable housing. The background to this population movement was the new wave of Enclosure which occurred between 1760 and 1820. Enclosure of land to replace the open field system of agriculture had begun in the 14th century and become widespread in the 15th and 16th centuries, but a second wave took place in the mid 18th century and reduced many small independent farmers to agricultural labourers or else drove them off the land entirely. Industrialisation provided jobs in town for these people, but housing provision was inadequate. In Northampton the boot and shoe industry provided country people with regular and better paid employment. Thomas Adams, in his migration from the village of Flore to the town of Northampton was part of this demographic change.

As mentioned in chapter 3, he would have had first-hand experience of the injustice to which the working class could be subject when they were living in rented accommodation, liable to eviction at any time. In Thomas' case he was deprived of his livelihood when he was forced to leave his first bakehouse on Union Street. Thomas would also have been well aware of the state of many houses and streets in his home town. The need for houses was coupled with the need for social legislation to ensure the hygienic conditions of the new estates – drainage, for instance, was appalling.

The first Vice-President of the Northampton Town and County Freehold Land Society, Mr. Grundy, spoke against the unhygienic conditions that prevailed at this time. As the Society laid out its first estate of houses,
'he trusted that drainage had been attended to on the land they had purchased, warned as they ought to be by the miserable state of their own town in that respect – a state which reduced it to the condition of the very worst parts of London, and which had caused the sacrifice of no less than 180 lives in the course of the year just ended.' N.M. 18.1.1851

A report on the sanitary state of Northampton, published by the Medical Department of the Privy Council as late as 1871, revealed that the state of the housing being built on the fringes of the growing town was still appalling. It can have been no better in the 1840s and explains the revolutionary fervour with which the Northampton Town and County Freehold Land Society (NTCFLS) planned to organise their own new estates.

---

*The **FREEHOLD LAND SOCIETY** as a depository for future requirements, as a stepping-stone to an honourable independence, as offering the means for a noble resistance to the invitation of the Poorhouse, and as a machine to effect man's political redemption, is without a parallel in the history of this great empire...*

Rules of the NTCFLS adopted 1848

Dr. Buchanan, the writer of the 1871 report, described the situation in vivid detail:
'The suburban parts of Northampton which lie within the new limits of the Parliamentary borough but outside the municipal boundary are in a

miserably neglected state: houses built on waterlogged sites, without plan, with indifferent roads, filthy accumulations, and (except where the Company furnishes the supply) with execrable water. Their story is the common one of town suburbs growing up without town government...

St. James End, in Duston and Dallington parishes: Devonshire Street, unmade, undrained, swampy from slops thrown from the houses; miserable fragments only of footway. Here are seen two parallel streets, standing about 100 feet apart, of small two-storied houses, each 10 or 11 feet broad; in the open space between the backs of the houses are little gardens, with midden-privies and pigsties; and now irregular groups of cottages being built up here, with the result of moving privies closer to the houses, and of seriously overcrowding an area that before was not at all too extensive. In the same neighbourhood a little row of houses faces the high road; new cottages are being built on the edge of the road, 12 feet in front of the others... On the opposite side of the high road the cottages of St. James's Row are seen without any back openings whatever. This row obtains its water – 'very good water' – from a well 20 feet off a pigsty and privy-pit. The soil is gravel, and the water in it stands about 3 ½ feet from the surface. In St. James's Square there are two pumps, one out of order – the other giving water too bad to be used. Some parts of St. James's End take their water from the Northampton Company. In this suburb there is an absence of any regulations about new buildings. Houses 12 feet wide, with party walls half a brick thick, are seen in course of erection, the space behind them, containing the dustbin and privy, being scarcely larger than the area on which the house stands. Elsewhere the window of a living-room has, at about 8 feet distance, a direct prospect of a midden-heap 10 feet long and 4 high.'

Dr. Buchanan's Report on the Sanitary State of Northampton, 1871, (Medical Dept. of the Privy Council)

The report also describes the suburbs of Cotton End, Far Cotton and Kingsthorpe Bottom, all of which were condemned as unhygienic. It is notable that as far as the NTCFLS is concerned, much effort was put into creating hygienic surroundings in the first place before houses were erected. For instance, when Cotton End was being developed in the 1860s, part of the plan was to cement up all the cesspools. The Inspector was to inform the Society of all cases where the builders failed to comply, and proceedings would then be taken against them.

In the early part of the 19th century, before the new building regulations came into force, a typical house consisted of just two rooms, one above the other, with a back room and privy built on and almost covering the small backyard. Other houses might be built in courts, without any backyards and even without any back windows. In 1871 it was reported that the new type of cottage had a 15 foot frontage, 2 or 3 storeys, with 2 rooms on each floor, and a basement used as a coal-cellar. The privy was outside the house in a fairly sizeable backyard.

Despite the new building regulations and efforts to improve sanitation, as late as 1889 the Medical Officer of Health for the town was still reporting on the deplorable state of some of the older houses still standing:

'There are houses, at the present time, standing in the older courts so palpably insanitary, that not only are they in every respect unfitted for human beings to live in, but even the brute beast could not, and would not, thrive in such places. It is in these haunts of filthiness and unwholesomeness – the quarters of the poorest of the poor, that physical life if not subjected to actual devastation, is irreparably damaged by the unwholesome and unhealthy influences to which the occupants are perpetually exposed. Misery and abject wretchedness reign supreme in such places.'

Lee F. Cogan, Medical Officer of Health, Northampton Borough Council, *Report of the Health of Northampton during the Year 1889*

It is against this background that the founding of the first building societies must be seen in order to appreciate the almost revolutionary fervour which inspired the men involved. One of the founders was Joseph Gurney who later became a close friend of Thomas Adams. Joseph was a tailor and it was in his shop in Gold Street, Northampton, that a group of men held the meeting to found what would one day become Britain's largest building society.

Joseph Gurney was very radical in his political views and very self-disciplined, being a strict tee-totaller. He belonged to the Chartist movement, a largely working class democratic movement of the 1840s, one of whose aims was universal manhood suffrage. Gurney was described as 'a stronger Chartist than the Chartists, a greater Radical than the Radicals, and a more advanced Socialist than the Socialists'. His pioneering spirit led him to address meetings of working men and explain to them that with every pint of beer they drank, they lost a foot of ground. (At that time plots of land could be bought from the NTCFLS for 2 ½ d a foot - the price of a pint of beer.)

(Until 1887 a restrictive covenant prohibited the use of houses for the sale of intoxicating liquor on the estates the Building Society was developing - although the reason would seem to be fear of lowering the tone of an estate rather than an objection to alcohol as such.)

The Freehold Land movement was founded in Birmingham by James Taylor for the social and political enfranchisement of the people – to enable them to become 40/- freeholders and thereby have voting powers. When the Northampton Society was founded it was modelled on the Birmingham plan. At

Land for the People!

> ***Working men of Northampton! – of England! to you the Committee appeal. Your own enfranchisement is within your reach. Be independent and noble minded. The British legislature, by a great majority, told Joseph Hume, Esq. M.P., that you were unworthy of a "vote", and denied you the right to possess it! Cease to ask for that which you can, by your frugality, obtain! To the cause of your own freedom you are invited, to the brilliant deed of your own political redemption you are now challenged!***
>
> Rules of the NTCFLS adopted 1848

first the NTCFLS bought plots of land worth a minimum of 45/- (£2.25) with a view to distributing them as allotments. They soon realised that it would be a good idea to set up a building department and started developing a small estate on Primrose Hill, on the Kingsthorpe Road just north of the Roman Catholic cathedral. The Society then became known as the Northampton Town and County Freehold Land and Building Society. In the early days there were only 4,000 houses in Northampton to accommodate a population of 25,000. By the 1920s the population had grown to 100,000 and the number of houses, to 20,000. 5,000 of these houses had been built by the Northampton Town and County Building Society on an area of about 300 acres over a period of 50 years.

The political spirit of the founders can be seen in their adoption of two slogans – 'Land for the People!' and 'Get the 40s of Freehold!'. Primrose Hill, bought in 1850, was divided up into streets with such names as Freehold Street, Elysium Terrace and St. George's Street. 'Elysium' means 'the abode of bliss' and thus the Englishman's ideal for home, while St. George, the patron saint of England, embodies knightly chivalry and its conquest of evil. The ideals of the Society were thus reflected in their choice of street names. Joseph Gurney himself bought one of the houses on Freehold Street and called it Elysium Cottage.

The estates were carefully planned and laid out with sewers and good conditions for road-making, the houses being provided with up-to-date sanitation and long gardens that could serve as allotments. The meeting to take official possession of the two estates on the Kingsthorpe Road took place on January 18th

Land for the People!

1851, and it is interesting to note that despite its radical roots there was clearly some hostility to the movement among some of the members of the working class at the meeting:

'On Monday all the members of the above Society held a public soirée and meeting at the New Hall, Newland. The object was to celebrate the purchase and take possession of the two estates on the Kingsthorpe Road. Between 2 and 3 o'clock the members and their friends had assembled in pursuance of public notice, and at 3 o'clock a procession left the hall and headed by an excellent band processed to the Kingsthorpe Road. A considerable crowd accompanied the procession, some of the subjects of which behaved very disgracefully, pelting the members with matters more tangible than their foul language.'

N.M. 18.1.1851

The meeting which followed the open-air procession was enlivened by many political speeches. Mr. Willis of Luton, for example, proclaimed:

'The object of James Taylor and the Freehold Land movement is to rescue the representation from the two great aristocratic parties who now divide it between them, to extend the franchise, and elevate the condition of the working man. And its progress is emphatically proclaimed by the fact that there are now 30,000 members having £170,000 invested in freehold land.' (op.cit.)

The Times was quoted, as a sign of the significance of the freehold land movement's achievement:

'We really think there is a vast deal to be said for the movement. Considering how many worthless fellows there are who possess a vote, and that in a constituency not of 3000 or 30,000, but of 300 or 150, when a vote becomes something more than a name, no reasonable person can grudge the right to a man who earns it by his own industry and frugality, and who probably brings to it some improvement, both of morals and of condition. Nor can it too be denied that the accumulation of land into fewer and still fewer hands, which has been going on for centuries and goes on still, has sensibly diminished the number of British freeholders deriving their votes from land... The commercial or rather social side of the question, is quite as much in favour of this movement. Everybody interested in the welfare of the working classes laments the almost utter want of safe and beneficial investments suited to their opportunities and means. Under existing circumstances, an industrious and skilful work-man has no alternative but to throw away his hundred pounds as soon as he has earned it, and to begin another as fast and as cheerfully as he can... When such is the case, it is impossible not to start with a strong prepossession in favour of a scheme which provides not only an estate and a political rank to be won by the weekly

Land for the People!

NORTHAMPTON TOWN AND COUNTY FREEHOLD LAND ASSOCIATION

Among the many noble institutions of the present day which tend to promote the social and political welfare of the working classes, it is to be regretted that there are none whose object is the purchase of Freehold Land for themselves and heirs for ever, and in the immediate vicinity of their residence.

To remedy this deficiency, it has been determined to establish a FREEHOLD LAND SOCIETY to enable every Mechanic or Working Man, by small weekly contributions to purchase a piece of land, on which he may erect a cottage, cultivate a garden etc. etc. - either occupy it himself or let it to others - so that he may possess a 'stake in the Country, and a voice in the election of Members of Parliament'.

The principal feature of such a Society is that by the purchase of Land in large quantities, it is able to supply each member with a small allotment at a cost very considerably less than he would have to pay in the Retail Land Market; - thus for the payment of 1s 6d *per week* it is calculated that in five years, and in some cases much less than that period, every member will be in the full possession of a plot of 'FREEHOLD LAND' worth at least 45s per annum.

N.M. 9.12.1848

investment of one shilling and sixpence for four or five years, but a bit of terra firma, to be cultivated and improved and built upon, and converted into the home, perhaps of a prosperous family.'

N.M. 18.1.1851

The recent nature of the Enclosure Acts of the late 18th century was clearly seen as part of the background to the freehold land movement. At the meeting the Rev. W. Robinson of Kettering observed that his ancestors *'had always been in favour of small allotments, and opposed to Enclosure Acts. It was because he inherited this feeling that he felt deeply anxious for the success of the Freehold Land Societies, by which the good of small allotments would, he thought, be brought back improved.'*

The moral virtue bound up with the possession of freehold land was further expanded on by the Rev. Robinson when he described the good citizenship engendered by the possession of personal property. His flowery language evokes the hope and idealism of the period:

'He had seen a man driving a pig - a string attached to one of its legs. Imagination followed the pig to the humble house - traced it to its sty - saw it become a part of the daily care and economy of the cottage - the wash regularly provided - the inferior potatoes selected and given to it, and all its wants assiduously attended to. Fancy indulged in a further flight, and saw the grand day - the day of killing the pig, and all the hearty feasting such a day brings with it. Finally the substantial parts are seen salted, and hung up, and the main want of many a future day provided for. That man, rely upon it, is a good citizen. (Great cheering)... When depredation or outrage occurs, no suspicion will alight on him.'

(op.cit.)

Thomas Adams joined the NTCFLS in its early days when he was still a journeyman baker. It was perhaps because of this that he was eventually able to buy his own bakehouse. He became Cash Steward of the Society in 1880, a post which involved receiving the savings of members at an appointed time every fortnight, called 'a subscription night'. The Cash Steward would normally take in subscriptions in his own private home, and when Thomas moved into his house on Colwyn Road, he had a little office built out into his garden where he could carry out his duties.

The very first Secretary was Frederick Parker of Wood Street at whose house subscriptions were to be paid, unless another suitable place was designated. The only proviso was that alcohol must not be sold on the premises. The rules stated that the Cash Steward had to keep books and that they must correspond to the Secretary's. He had to make good any shortfall and had to attend the subscription nights punctually or forfeit one shilling.

Land for the People!

> ***Subscriptions to be paid fortnightly, by 3s a payment. The first Subscription night is fixed for the 16th day of January next, from 6 to 7 o'clock in the evening, at the house of the Secretary in Wood Street, Northampton, where the Cash and Check-Stewards, and Sub-Treasurer will be in attendance...***
>
> ***Any communication addressed to the Secretary, Post paid and inclosing stamps for answers, will be attended to.***
>
> ***Entrance-fee, One Shilling per Share.***
>
> ***December 21st, 1848***
>
> NM 13.1.1849

The Rules of the NTCFLS were adopted on the 12th December 1848 and make fascinating reading for they not only evoke the spirit of the time, but explain how the system actually worked. They open with the following words:

'*The grand objects of this Society are – to improve the Social, promote the Moral, and exalt the Political Condition of the unenfranchised millions.*

Solemnly impressed with the necessity and the importance of giving to working men the Suffrage, and extensively, if not universally, enabling them to obtain it by their own unaided industry and frugality, the Committee now issue the Third Edition of the Prospectus, with a sincere hope, that thousands will, in this Town alone, join this Institution, and independently work out their own political emancipation.'

Rules of the NTCFLS adopted 12.12.1848

A man who saved 1s 6d (15p) per week for 5 years could be assured of attaining the Freehold Qualification to vote. By putting together the contributions of the members the Society was able to purchase large tracts of eligible building land and retail the same to the members at the wholesale price, in lots available for building purposes which the members could let off or use themselves.

If members fell on hard times, they could suspend their subscriptions without incurring fines or withdraw altogether. No one could buy more than six shares. When an estate was purchased, it was divided into suitable lots which would then be offered to the members according to seniority of membership.

Land for the People!

The 1881 directors of the Northampton Town and County Building and Freehold Land Society: (back l-r) C.Lea, R.Roe, H.Martin, E.Draper, H.J.Wilson, T.Adams and (front l-r) W.Lightwood, T.Purser, J.Gurney(Secretary), J.M.Vernon (President), H. Holding, S.Clarke and J.Allen

Each member's name would be written on a piece of paper specifying whether he was drawing one or more lots of land. Names would then be drawn out of a bag or box, and the land distributed accordingly. A small sum was charged as a premium for a prior advance, but the contributions paid before purchasing an allotment could continue at the same amount until the total owing was paid. With the consent of their parents or guardian, even children could buy land by this method, so a young man of 17 could become a Freeholder at the age of 21.

Thomas Adams' grandson, Percy, remembered how when he was about 8 (in 1889) he had to deliver the Society's circular to shareholders every Saturday. He was given a shilling a week for doing this, which he used to invest in the Society. By saving up in this way he was able to buy a plot in Cedar Road on the new estate north of Abington Park. Percy recalled that he was still a boy when he sold it to Sharman, the builder, for £50.

One of the more lasting reminders of this stage in the town's development is the numerous street names which commemorate important members of the Society. For instance, Henry Billington Whitworth, was for many years Chairman of the Northamptonshire Union Bank at the top of the Drapery (where the NatWest Bank is now situated). The Society initially carried out all its operations through this bank and the Chairman has no less than three adjacent streets named after him – Henry Street, Billington Street and Whitworth Road.

One of the first areas to be developed was land between the Wellingborough and Billing Roads, an estate to be known as New Town – hence Newtown Road. Upper and Lower Thrift Street were names as reminders of the Society's founding principles.

The estate between the Wellingborough and Kettering Roads has a particularly large number of street names commemorating trustees of the Society – Adnitt Road, for instance, was named after Frederick George Adnitt, President of the Society and twice mayor of the town. Frederick Bostock, Frederick Stimpson, Pickering Phipps Perry, Richard Turner, Robert Derby, Philip Manfield, C. Lea, R. Roe, T. Purser, J.M. Vernon, S. Clarke, J. Allen – they were all trustees who had streets named after them. Thomas Adams was also commemorated in this fashion, Adams Avenue being named after him, for he became Secretary of the Society in 1889. He had in fact been carrying on the Secretary's duties since about 1885 to help out his friend, Joseph Gurney, who had been Secretary since 1856 and whose eyesight had begun to fail.

Although Thomas had been a shareholder since the early days, it was not until 1873 that he was elected Director. He was also appointed on the Finance Committee and the Survey Committee, which gave him a great deal of experience in valuation. Thomas' obituary in the Northampton Mercury relates the important work he did as an officer of the Society, saying that he had done incalculable service in promoting the spirit of self-help among young people.

'Hundreds of young men and women have had to thank him for the start he has given them in life. No trouble was too great if he could only give young people a lift. He was always accessible, and would put himself about in order to do anyone a service... His sympathy with every form of thrift was warm. His desire to make the Society a means of doing good to the community, by encouraging young men and women to acquire their own houses, and so helping them to become good and happy citizens was very great.'

N.M. 15.2.1890

Thomas had a lot to do with the management of what were called the 1st and 2nd Kettering Road estates and the East Park and Kingsley Park estates. As the map shows, the Society was mostly concerned with the area expanding east of the town. Being on high ground, unlike Far Cotton and St. James End, this was the more healthy area and consequently more valuable land. The fact that the land being developed was situated high up was often quoted in the literature.

Land for the People!

Estates within the Borough of Northampton
Developed by the Society

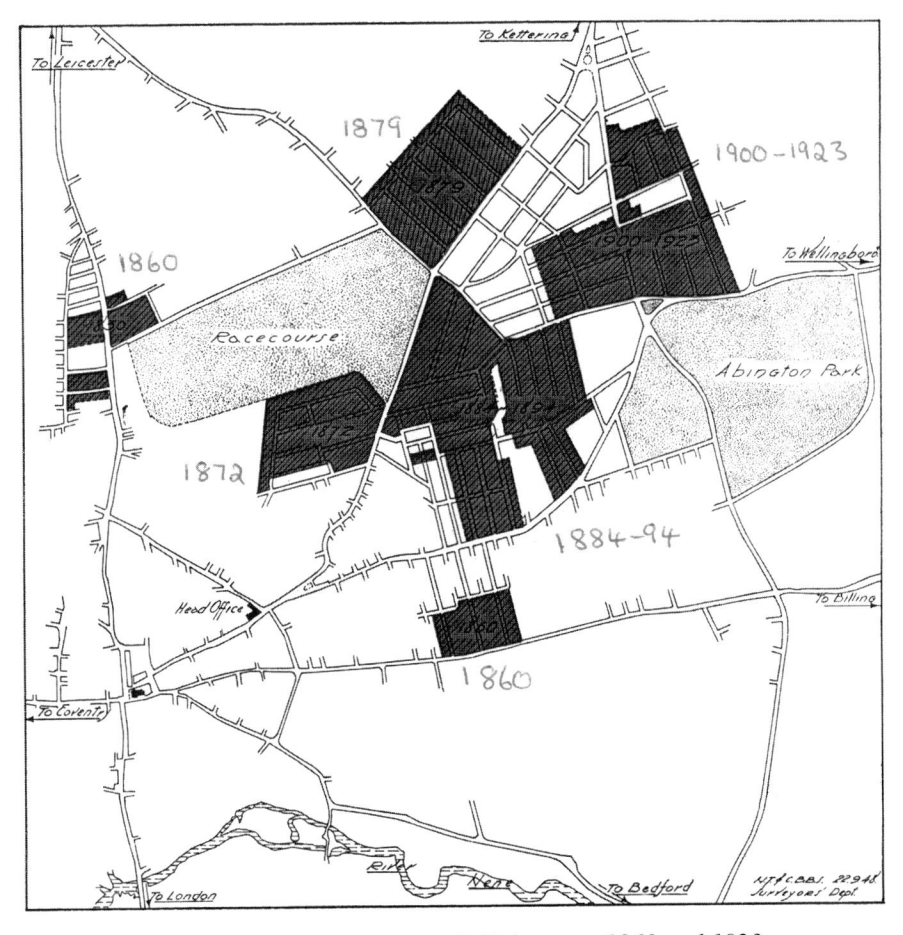

The Building Society estates built between 1860 and 1923

Land for the People!

Thomas became a Director shortly after a Kettering Road estate was purchased in 1870 – this is the estate to the west of the Racecourse, fronting on to the Kettering Road and having Clare Street as its western boundary.

The street pattern is typical of the estates that were developed on the edge of town. The land had been enclosed in the 18th century to form fields (as opposed to strips and commons). Round the fields had been planted hedges, and as each field of land was developed, it was common practice to lay the street along the line of the hedge. Hence the occasionally surprising nature of the street patterns in this area.

The organisation of the Northampton Town and County Freehold Land and Building Society was still very similar to how it was in the beginning. Admission cost only one shilling, which bought part of a share worth a maximum of £40. Three shillings must be paid in every fortnight. Every investor (or lender, as they were called), received an interest rate of 4%. When a lender became a borrower they paid 5% interest plus 6d a quarter to pay the management expenses. In 1886 the Secretary received £340 and the Stewards £86 a year, but the Trustees and Directors worked without being paid. When a lender wanted to build, the Society would lend two thirds of the value of the building. During the first 22 years of its existence it had received and expended over £40,000, about ¾ of which had been subscribed by the working classes.

The quasi-religious fervour still existed among the members. At the meeting held to celebrate the purchase of the Kingsley estate, the Rev. Iden Payne made a long eloquent speech in which he called attention to the problem of drunkenness, and proclaimed:

'A society, like this, by helping to make every man his own landlord, and by encouraging a spirit of self-respect and independence, would do much to prevent a man forgetting his manhood by indulgence in strong drink. He could not help looking at the work in which the society was engaged as a religious one. He could not help feeling that every institution of our land that tended to elevate the masses, that tended to inculcate self-respect, and to make a man honest and industrious, was religious in its objects and aims.'

N.M. 1870

The fact that only ¾ of the investment in the Society had been subscribed by working class people is interesting when one considers how it was set up for the purpose of helping the working class obtain the right to vote. The middle class entrepreneurs, such as Thomas Adams himself, were clearly making use of the opportunity to obtain a safe investment for their savings. It is quite remarkable how several plots and houses were bought by one individual – men such as Thomas Adams in fact. On the Kingsley estate opposite St. Matthew's church Thomas owned at one time nos. 260 and 261 Byron Street, 524 Shelley Street, 456 Kingsley Road and 511 Kingsley Park Terrace. Of course the 1867

Reform Act had extended the vote from male house owners to adult males who rented their home, so the initial impetus of the building society movement was lost.

The other aspect of the building society – that of building homes of a decent standard for the working classes may also have been lost sight of by this time.

In 1885 the government passed an Act to allow the Local Government Board to supersede local corporations to carry out necessary improvements to local dwellings and hand the bill to the corporation. This was a result of a widespread neglect of duty by Councils. The Northampton socialist newspaper, 'The Ratepayer', made scathing attacks on Northampton town council, and printed a typically angry outburst in February 1886:

'There are 500 houses in Northampton unfit for human habitations, notwithstanding this disgraceful state of affairs, the majority in the Council turn a deaf ear to all propositions of amelioration. We hope this will open the eyes of the most purblind elector in the town, that they never can get justice from men who have sprung from the ranks of labour. It is an acknowledged fact that the parvenue is the most selfish tyrant when he gets place and power... How can you expect men who have a lot of house property, who are living off their rents, ever to assist you in getting a house at cost price?'

The Ratepayer, Feb. 1886, p.3

The attack was directed at men such as Thomas Adams. He was one of many directors of the building society who were also councillors. There was bound to be a conflict of interest on occasion and the Ratepayer never missed an opportunity to expose the situation. Questions, for instance, were asked as to why so much attention was paid to improving the Racecourse, when nothing was being done to improve areas near the river Nene, such as Cow Meadow (later known as Becket's Park). The answer proposed was that the councillors had a vested interest in the area around the Racecourse, and consequently no concern for the needy areas to the south of the town.

'How comes it that the attention of our Town Council has never been directed towards this dismal swamp, at certain times of year? Are they waiting till the Freehold Land Society buys an estate within a stone's throw of its pestilential influence, before they carry out this most important improvement?'

In 1884 one working class member of the Radical party, Edward Powell, voiced the objection held by a minority within the party that 'only one man in twenty got a house through a building society'. His socialist colleague, Robert Reid, went so far as to accuse the local party of neglect:

'Self-made men, adhering to the doctrine of self-help, the Northampton Radicals never tried to force the implementation of artisans' dwelling legislation.'

Land for the People!

The inference in this case was that councillors who were also directors of the building society were only concerned with the houses which they were renting out on the building society's new estates, and not with the really needy areas of town.

In 1884 less than 5% of housing in Northampton was owner-occupied, the majority of it by tradesmen, white-collar workers and skilled footwear or building workers. In 1925 the figure was 21.75%, but even in the municipal wards comprising the majority of the building society's housing – Kingsley, Abington and St. Michael – working class owner-occupiers accounted for only 21-28% of the total. This would belie the familiar boast that:

'Northampton is an excellent example of a property-owning democracy.'
L.W. Dickens in the Chronicle and Echo 3.9.1965

Whatever the motives behind the practice of purchasing several building society plots, one may only suppose that there were enough plots available to supply the middle classes as well as the working classes, and that the working classes had not proved as ready to save up for a house as had been hoped.

Thomas had a lot to do with managing the Whitworth estate to the south of the Kettering Road, an area which was to play an important part in the future of his bakery business when it was carried on by his sons. This is the estate containing many streets named after prominent building society directors. It was at the foot of Adams Avenue that Thomas' sons, Frank and Wallace, set up a large bakehouse in 1896. On the estate had previously been situated the last windmill in Northampton. Nowadays the expanse of housing can obliterate the high sloping nature of the site which would have been ideal for a windmill. The press also report that the site had seen the last yoke of oxen used for agricultural purposes in the borough area. At the top (near Abington Avenue) there must also have been a spring, for a small reservoir was sited here in the early days of the development, between Stimpson Avenue and Lea Road, behind the Crockett and Jones shoe factory.

Thomas' oldest son, Walter, would also build a bakehouse on the estate, in 1887, on the corner of Derby Road and Kettering Road.

Just beyond the Whitworth estate were the lands belonging to Monks Hall Park and Lady Wantage of Abington, who now lived at Overstone Hall. In 1897 Lady Wantage, the owner of Abington Manor, gave her house and much of her land to the Borough of Northampton as a public park. She also began selling other areas of adjacent land to the building society for housing development. Monks Hall Park (the area to the north of Wellingborough Road and east of Stimpson Avenue) was another old estate which was sold off to the Society for building. Here, Edgar Adams, Thomas 4th son, built another bakehouse to cater for the growing number of people now living on this eastern edge of town. His

Land for the People!

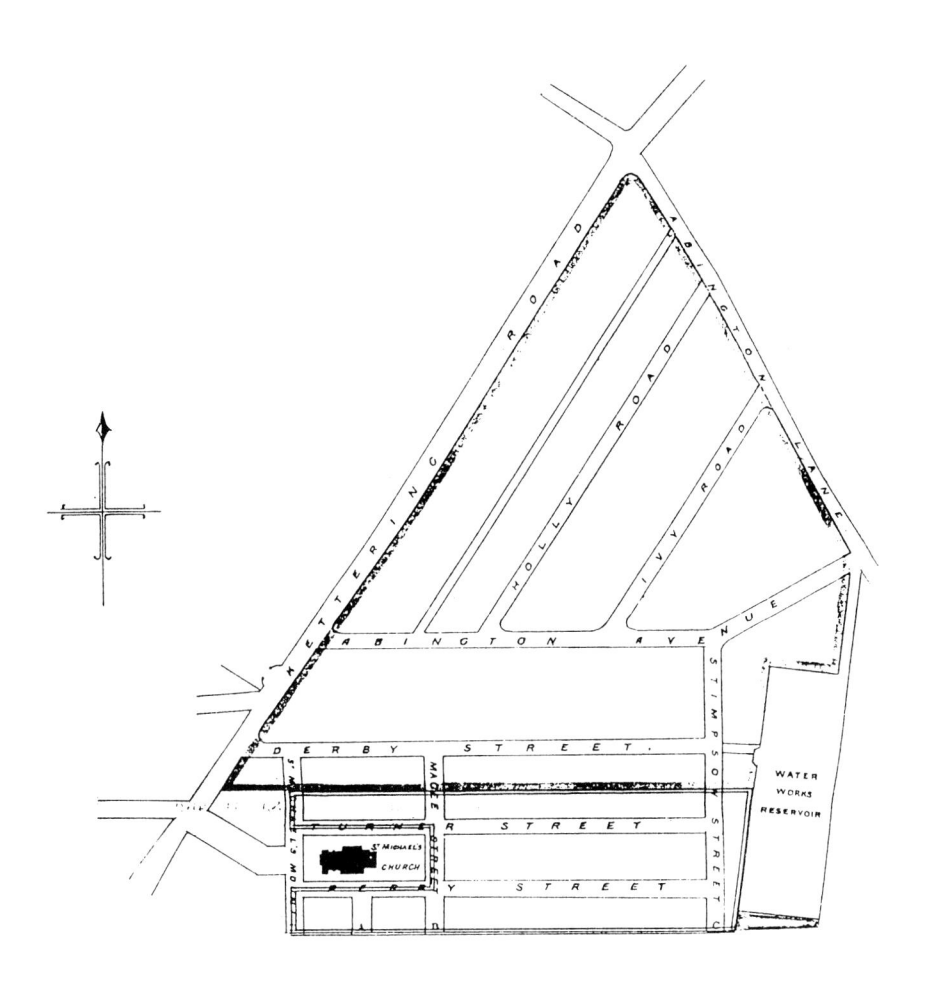

Plan of the East Park estate between Kettering Road, Abington Lane (now Grove) and Stimpson Street (now Avenue), 1884

Land for the People!

bakery stood at the corner of Allen Road and Wellingborough Road and can still be seen today, as in fact can Walter's, and Frank and Wallace's, although they are no longer used as bakehouses.

In the middle of the 20th century one of the houses on the Whitworth estate was bought by Jess Lay, who took a great interest in local history, in particular that of his house. Through his research into the deeds of his property came to light some of the original plans for the estate. The name, Frank Adams, occurs frequently. Thomas' son had bought no less than eight plots of land, had houses built on them and then sold them to the Borough Council. Mr. Lay's house was one of them. It is interesting to note how, on a smaller scale, this process is really the same as the massive process of development carried out by the Northampton Development Corporation in the 1970s, which provided private and council housing for the town.

The papers unearthed by Mr. Lay explain how the Whitworth estate was originally part of the parish of St. Giles and formed part of an allotment of land awarded to Robert Peach on the enclosure of the open and common fields of Northampton in the 18th century. Charles Whitworth bought the land and passed it on to his son, Henry Billington, the banker. When widowed, Henry's wife, Anne, sold the estate to the builder, Henry Martin, in 1881. Within a few months Martin sold the land to the Northampton Land Investment and Advance Company. In June 1882 the estate was finally bought by the building society – the transaction actually naming Pickering Phipps Perry (merchant), J.M. Vernon, Richard Turner (gentleman) and Frederick Stimpson (gentleman). These four were Trustees acting on behalf of the Society.

The system for the Society's purchasing arrangement seems strange to us now. In 1885 Perry was actually able to sell his interest in the estate to Turner and Stimpson.

> *No lime kiln, brick kiln or place for the manufacture of lime, bricks, tiles, or any other similar articles shall be permitted upon any part of the Estate. Nor shall any slaughter-house, Knacker's Yard, Gut Manufactory, Tallow Melting Works, Smelting House, Ironfoundry, Braziery – or any noisome or offensive trade or business be carried on on any part of the Estate.*
>
> Building Society plans (Adams papers, no. 78)

Land for the People!

*The Society's earlier headquarters at 11 Abington Square,
acquired in 1897*

Land for the People!

Mr. Lay's papers illustrate further the way in which the system of development worked. Plots were staked out and eight were sold to Frank Adams on Perry Street and Derby Road in June 1885. In 1891 Frank is also known to have bought six other houses on the Whitworth estate – nos. 43, 45, 109, 111 Adams Avenue and nos. 166 and 167 Bostock Avenue. Frank obtained a mortgage from the Society for £930 and had the plots on Perry Street and Derby Road developed. In 1887 he was able to sell them to the Borough Council with the proviso that he or his executors could buy them back. (After Frank's death his executors sold the house that would eventually be owned by Mr. Lay, to James Marriott, the milliner of 13 Abington Square.)

By 1923 an Act had been passed to take away the building societies' powers to buy and sell land, but before that date two final purchases of land were made – Gallows Close and the Wantage estate, both north of the Wellingborough Road and adjacent to Phippsville (the estate built to the south and east of St. Matthew's church). Thomas Adams was no longer alive at this time (1899), but his sons, Walter, Frank and Wallace, had all become directors of the Northampton Town and County Building Society, as it was now called, and were involved in its last decades of building.

The size of plots varied considerably now, and the plans included plots labelled from A to F. 'A' denoted the smallest plot worth one share, and 'F' the largest, worth six shares. Stumps with numbers on were placed in the centre of each plot, so that prospective buyers could visit the site to see the position of their future home. About 60 years since the development of the first estate on Primrose Hill, the style of house had of course changed somewhat – spacious semi-detached houses and large elegant terraces being included alongside the terraces built on the smaller plots.

In 1897 a new head office was built on Abington Square to replace the small office at no. 68 Abington Street. No longer was there the need to strive to encourage the working classes to gain the right to vote, yet the aura surrounding the Society was still one of democratic zeal. In the Northampton Independent dated 11th August 1923 it is stated that:

'the greatest of all factors in the wonderful development of Northampton has been the Northampton Town and County Benefit Building Society who have laid out no fewer than 14 estates with 5,000 houses.'

On the occasion of the Society's 80th anniversary dinner in 1928, one of the official speeches described the various estates as:

'the outcome of the judgement of men of experience and practical genius, who understood the needs of their time. These men were the pioneers of housing and town planning, and did a noble work without State subsidies, and without State control or interference.'

N.I. 3.3.1928

Land for the People!

*The new head office on Abington Square acquired in 1923
(Sketch probably dating from 1930s)*

Their contribution to town planning was more similar to the present day than would at first appear, for they did not only concern themselves with houses. The Whitworth estate is a prime example of a healthy mix of factories, workshops and housing for the workers in this area. Around St. Michael's church the small side streets still thrive with the various businesses being carried on in the old Victorian buildings.

Thomas Adams would find it difficult to recognise the present building society which has developed from the early days back in 1848 and that first meeting in Joseph Gurney's tailor shop.. The quasi-religious fervour of the early days and the zeal of the early 20th century belong to the past now. It was a rewarding and exciting occupation for a man such as Thomas, who had risen from a relatively poor village background to become a middle class entrepreneur able to devote much of his energies towards helping other members of the working class improve their situation in life.

Land for the People!

Linked with Thomas' zeal for the building society movement was his zeal for radical politics and work in local government. As he became increasingly interested in Radicalism, he was to find that Northampton was an unusually exciting place to be living at that time, for the town was about to embark on its long struggle with Parliament. Charles Bradlaugh, the elected Radical M.P. for Northampton, was denied five times the right to take his seat in the House of Commons.

The story of Thomas' friendship with and support for Bradlaugh is the subject of the next chapter – a story even more dramatic than that of the early days of the building society movement.

Chapter 5

THE RADICAL REBELLION

In the middle of Abington Square, high on a plinth stands the statue of a man looking down on the surrounding scene and pointing a finger as if in warning. The man is Charles Bradlaugh, one of the most dominant local figures in Northamptonshire politics in the second half of the 19th century.

On a shelf in the home of Thomas Adams' great-great-grandson stands an ornately carved clock given to Thomas by Bradlaugh as a token of appreciation for all the work Thomas had done to support him in his parliamentary campaign. The clock's inscription runs: 'To Councillor Thomas Adams, From Charles Bradlaugh, In remembrance of loyal friendship and devoted service. April 2 1880'. The M.P. wrote a letter to Thomas' eldest son on the occasion of Thomas' death, speaking of Thomas as *'the truest friend a man could have'*.

N.M. 15.2.1890

Charles Bradlaugh was one of the most radical M.P.s ever to represent Northampton – notorious for his free thought and agnosticism and famous most of all for refusing to take the oath on the Bible when taking his seat in the House of Commons.

In the early years of his adult life, Thomas Adams had been very religious, serving as a Sunday School teacher at his local Congregational church. In 1867, at the age of 37 he heard Bradlaugh speak for the first time in Northampton and was overwhelmed by the power of Bradlaugh's convictions. The occasion was a turning point in his life. Harry Snell, a working class agitator, described the occasion when he himself first listened to Bradlaugh speak:

'I have never been so influenced by a human personality as I was by Charles Bradlaugh ... as man, as orator, as leader of unpopular causes and as an incorruptible public figure he was the most inspiring human being that I have ever known.'

Fergus D'Arcy, *Charles Bradlaugh and the World of Popular Radicalism 1833-1891* (PhD Thesis Hull University, 1978)

The Radical Rebellion

*Clock given by Charles Bradlaugh to Thomas Adams
in token of his gratitude for Thomas' support*

Thomas became Bradlaugh's political agent and often had him to stay at no. 77 Colwyn Road on Bradlaugh's briefer visits to Northampton. Percy Adams, Thomas' grandson, recalled how courteous and kind Bradlaugh was:
'All my family had a great affection for Bradlaugh, who was always considerate and sympathetic.'

C & E 3.9.1965

Bradlaugh did not persuade Thomas totally to turn against his faith. He did not deny the existence of God *'because to deny that which was unknown was as absurd as to affirm it'*. He was an agnostic rather than an atheist and greatly admired the 18th century rationalist philosopher, Spinoza, who believed in a guiding and creative spirit rather than the traditional God of the Bible. In 1863 Bradlaugh said:
'I have deemed that I attacked theology best in asserting most the fullness of humanity.'

F.D'Arcy (op. cit.)

When Thomas followed Bradlaugh, he abandoned his Congregational upbringing and became a Secularist or Free Thinker – what we would now call Humanist. His children were still too young to appreciate or be shocked by the radical change which had occurred in their father's thinking. Having been a Sunday School teacher at Doddridge chapel, Thomas was now to find himself in opposition to one of the chapel's notable ministers, Thomas Arnold, when the

The Statue of Charles Bradlaugh on Abington Square

debate developed about Charles Bradlaugh's standing as parliamentary candidate for Northampton.

Secularism was founded in 1846 by the Holyoake brothers. Its central idea is *'free thought, not lawless thought. It advocates liberty of action without injury to others. Its standard is utilitarian. It is the religion of the present life only. It teaches men to seek morality in nature and happiness in duty. It repudiates Atheism.'*

N.I. 10.1984

Thomas' Secularist views and position in Northampton society led to his occasionally being asked to conduct Secularist funerals, such as John Bates' of West Street, popularly known as Gentleman John. The Secularist burial service emphasised the positive aspect of death – the reminder that we must love the living while we are still able, and work to improve the conditions of our fellowmen while we are still alive. At the ceremony in the Billing Road cemetery, which was built to accommodate Non-Conformist burials, Thomas concluded the service with his own words:

'Believing as we do that our friend has done his best in life, it is a lesson for us to do likewise; he having done his duty, let us also do ours.'

N.M. 28.4.1888

Although a Radical, Bradlaugh was not a Socialist. In fact he opposed it, because he said it destroyed a man's independence. He wanted to see working men secure better opportunities for themselves, as individualists.

The Radicals became an active force in politics in the 1860s and were connected with the Chartist movement, which sought to widen the suffrage and introduce a secret ballot. Radicalism was essentially a challenge to mainstream Liberalism, or 'Whiggery', from a small group of independent artisans and shopkeepers whose own Liberalism was more radical than the majority of Liberals and was often combined with Free Thought, rather than the usual Non-Conformity. They were led in Northampton by Joseph Gurney, the master tailor mentioned in chapter 4, and by John Bates, a basket-maker. Gurney became one of Thomas Adams' closest friends. As with the building society movement, the Radicals' policies sought to achieve a wider representation of the working class in government.

A SECULARIST FUNERAL
INTERNMENT OF "GENTLEMAN JOHN"

Alderman Adams proceeded to read, with due solemnity, the burial service of the fraternity, which runs as follows: 'Friends ... it were heartless to deny the sadness and the gloom-shadow cast by death, and the tears that drop into the open grave are tears that sully no courage, nor have to manhood aught of shame. Yet since Death must come to all to whom Life has come, while it were cruelty not to sorrow, it were cowardice to break into despairing and useless repining. While we give tears to the dead, let us from the grave turn back to life, life which still has its duties, if for awhile it has lost its glory and its joy. The message which comes from this open grave is one of Love and Work. Of Love, in that our dead remind us that when the grave opens, Love's work is closed, and bids us be gentle to the living, that we need drop no tear of remorse over the dead. Love should be the draught offered to the lips of the living, not only the libation poured out on the corpse in the tomb. Of Work, in that he recalls to us that life is uncertain and brief at its longest; that all we can do to help and improve our generation must be done now, while this priceless treasure of life is ours, and that when Death's night overshadows us, our work is done for ever for either good or ill. We leave our dead to his rest. We give him back to that great mother who bears and destroys, evolves and recalls, builds up and pulls down - to Nature, the One and the All, the Eternal Life and Death, with whom Death is but the first stage of a new life. For us, we turn back to our work, while conscious Life remains to us, to do our best until our turn to sleep shall come. Hope and work belong to the living; sleep and rest to the dead. We leave him to eternal rest, and bid him tenderly our last farewell.'

N.M. 28.4.1888

The Radical Rebellion

In 1866 the Northampton Mercury reported on a demonstration held on the Market Square to support the Reform Bill introduced into Parliament by Gladstone. The description of how on a wet October Monday morning the Square filled with brass bands and political groups from all over the county, how the demonstration was seen as a physical threat with the potential for violence, how the procession marched all over the town from Abington Street to the Mounts to Marefair and Bridge Street, paints a picture of a town much more politically active and inspired than it is today.

In the 1950s there were still people alive who could remember the excitement of Bradlaugh's campaign. On the occasion of a memorial service at the statue of Bradlaugh in Abington Square, the Northampton Independent quoted the words of Mr. Bullard, then in his nineties:

'how he cycled the 14 miles from his home in Newport Pagnell on a penny farthing to join in the election battles that raged round Bradlaugh, and was nearly mobbed in the back streets round the Horsemarket. "Those", he declared, with the emotion creeping into his still virile voice, "were exciting times... Someone even caused a sermon to be preached against me." '

N.I. 8.5.1953

The Victorian era was a time of great political and social reforms, and it would seem natural for a man such as Thomas Adams to have been fired with the reforming zeal which was so much in evidence around him.

By 1868 he had been selected by the Northampton Radical Association to stand in the municipal elections for the West Ward as 'the working man's candidate' to oppose Mr. Dennis, put up by the United Liberal Association without consulting 'the working men'. The Liberal vote was thus about to be split and weakened by the Radicals, who drew their support from former Liberals. In the 1868 municipal elections Thomas Adams came last out of four candidates. The Radical vote was not yet making its mark, and in fact the Liberals were making great strides against the Tories in Northampton.

One of the disagreements between the Radicals and the Liberals was the Radicals' support for Charles Bradlaugh. In 1868 Thomas and Joseph Gurney nominated Bradlaugh as the Radical parliamentary candidate for Northampton. Two years later Thomas became the registration agent for the Northampton Radical Association and thus embarked on a ten year struggle to get Bradlaugh elected as M.P. for Northampton, followed by a further six year struggle to have him permitted to take his seat in the House of Commons.

It is enlightening to read one of Bradlaugh's speeches, made at the 1866 demonstration in favour of the new Reform Bill. His words convey the eloquence and power to inspire which elicited the fervent support evident in men such as Thomas Adams:

The Radical Rebellion

Charles Bradlaugh

'I hope that you will be determined to assist in winning that battle which the Reformers are now fighting. I am not a good lawyer, and therefore cannot pretend to argue the question legally, but I am a man, and from that manhood I declare it is a right none can withhold from you – a right which is illegally withheld from you – a right which it is a usurpation of power to pretend to withhold from you – a right which you hope to possess, and a right, until you attain the possession of which you will not be doing your duty. You have been told that the Reform Bill does not intend to attack this and to attack that. Let it be my purpose for a moment to tell you what it does attack. It intends to attack the sham of class distinction in reference to electoral right. It declares that Government should be the best contrivance of human wisdom to provide for human want; and it declares that every man in the State should have a voice in the making of the laws which he is compelled to obey. And it does attack the few who are wicked and weak enough to think that they can have an interest apart from and independent of the people.

The people make the nation, and not the few. The people dig and delve and work at the loom, work mid the din and whirr of machinery, and go down into the bowels of the earth to bring up its riches. It is the labour of the people that make the greatness of the country; it is the labour of the people which achieves the means for the best expenditure by the Government; it is the labour of the people that achieves the great wealth of the nation.

If asked whether wealth should be represented, we answer that the riches of the poorest man are as important as the thousands of the rich man. We declare that each man that is kept without the suffrage is kept from the fullness of his citizenship. We declare that every man has a right to political life, and we declare that we are mere dead machines for digging and delving, for winning gold for others, so long as we have no voice in the manufacture of that Government which taxes our earnings and uses our money for governing.'

N.M. 27.10.1866

The Reform Act was in fact passed in 1867 and widened the suffrage to male householders and lodgers in towns, and to certain types of householder in

The Radical Rebellion

the counties (i.e. rural areas). 17 years later agricultural labourers were also included in the suffrage. The Radicals had partly achieved one of their goals, but until 1884 Bradlaugh still campaigned for the franchise to be extended to the agricultural labourers in the counties –

'a body of men who have been demoralised generation after generation by the injustice of our laws. Go back a century or two, and the heart and life and strength and soul of England was in its yeomen, the tillers of its soil.'

N.M. 5.1880

Thomas Adams, Joseph Gurney and all the other Radicals who chose to support Bradlaugh's candidacy had a difficult struggle ahead of them in 1868. The existing M.P.s were two Liberals, Lord Henley and Charles Gilpin. Henley was becoming less popular with local Liberals, so Bradlaugh's supporters felt they had some hope of getting Bradlaugh elected. Charles Gilpin, however, was a Quaker and President of the NFLBS – a pillar of society who was unlikely to lose his support.

The central theme of Bradlaugh's campaign was his attack on the aristocracy:

'The future welfare and happiness of this country depends upon the union between the middle classes of England and what are called the lower classes. The upper classes are going.' F. D'Arcy (op.cit.)

This stand was likely to be well received in a constituency such as Northampton, based on small manufacturers and artisans and where the majority of church-goers were Non-Conformists. (Non-Conformists tended to be anti the aristocracy, who were Church of England.) The self-made Radical manufacturers and entrepreneurs of Northampton, of whom Thomas Adams was but one example, liked Bradlaugh's desire to fuse the middle and working classes.

Other popular issues for which Bradlaugh stood were a compulsory national education system and the separation of Church and State.

The Liberals in Northampton continued to oppose the Radicals, and the division led to a split in the anti-Tory vote and a consequent loss of Liberal seats both in the local Council and the House of Commons. For instance, the Liberal M.P. Lord Henley lost his seat to the Conservative, Pickering Phipps.

Bradlaugh's proportion of the vote was steadily growing in the three elections between 1868 and 1874. However, the Liberal/Radical division meant that Northampton now found itself with *two* Tory M.P.s.

The drastic situation led to the '1874 Compact' whereby the Liberals and Radicals agreed to co-operate and not oppose one another. The Compact was probably the reason why Thomas Adams won the next municipal election and was able to take his seat in Council for the West Ward. He was to represent this ward for the next twelve years, until 1886. Fred Covington was the other Radical who won in 1874. Prior to that there had only been two Radicals in the Council –

Joseph Gurney (1814-93)

Tebbutt, who had won a seat in 1871 and Joseph Gurney, who had been the sole representative of the Radical cause for the previous thirteen years.

The Radical cause gained in status when Gurney was elected Mayor in 1875 – a quite remarkable feat considering the strong opposition of the Non-Conformist Liberals to the agnosticism of the Radicals.

The 1874 Compact came under particular pressure when Bradlaugh and Annie Besant caused a furore by taking a stand in defence of contraception. They spoke out in favour of a book by Charles Knowlton called 'Fruits of Philosophy'. Bradlaugh and Besant were in fact put on trial for their views and found guilty, but the judgement was reversed on a technicality. The notorious case damaged Bradlaugh's support in Northampton and turned the Liberals even more against the idea of co-operating with the Radicals. Thomas Adams was one of the four Radicals who attended a meeting with the Liberals in an attempt to save the 1874 Compact, but to no avail.

The 1880 parliamentary election saw Bradlaugh introduce three new pledges – to campaign for women's suffrage, to oppose any further extension of the Empire, and to campaign for new peerages being non-hereditary. In an amazing reversal of fortune, 'old' Liberals such as Philip Manfield and Vernon, now decided to serve the Radical cause by accusing the *old* Liberals (as opposed to the new Liberals or Radicals) of splitting the Liberal vote. All Liberals were asked to co-operate with the Radicals. The result was a Radical victory, with Bradlaugh coming second in the election after Labouchère. It was on this occasion that Bradlaugh presented Thomas Adams with the engraved clock as a token of his appreciation for his work as his election agent.

The Radicals' struggle to gain power in Northampton now became a battle with the Houses of Parliament. Bradlaugh wanted to affirm his allegiance to the crown on taking his seat in Parliament, rather than take the oath on the Bible. He thought that the new legal reform allowing affirmation in court meant that he could also affirm in Parliament. There had already been accommodation made in Parliament for Roman Catholics, Quakers and Jews: in 1830 Roman

Catholics had been allowed to take a Catholic oath; in 1833 Quakers had been allowed to affirm, and in 1866 for the sake of the Jews the oath had been made theistic.

Contrary to popular belief Bradlaugh did not persist in refusing to take the oath. He did in fact offer to take it when he knew that was the only way he would be allowed to take his seat. However, Parliament refused to allow him to do so, stating that *'it had been found that the oath would have no binding effect on his conscience'*.

F. D'Arcy (op. cit.)

To defend Bradlaugh there was founded the League for the Defence of Constitutional Right, and in retaliation to this was set up the Anti-Atheistic Committee. Meetings of both groups became violent, and at one point police had to help stop Bradlaugh from entering the Houses of Parliament. No less than ten constables had difficulty forcing him back down the stairs. Thousands of staunch followers from all over the country would have stormed the House if required, but Bradlaugh was a pacifist and wanted no violent resistance. It was fortunate that he had such principles because in the early 1880s there were huge meetings of 70-80,000 people in Trafalgar Square that could easily have got out of control. During this time, as religion became associated with bigotry, Free Thought, or Humanism, was increasing in popularity.

It was not only in Northampton and the rest of Britain that Bradlaugh's fight evoked strong feeling. When speaking to the Northampton Town Council in 1884 Bradlaugh described how he had met with overwhelming support wherever he had travelled, at home and abroad. The slightest reference to his campaign *'had been received with uproarious cheers...*

'Northampton's right, and Northampton's vindication! ... I happened to be in France last week and I went to the Chamber of Deputies on the special invitation of the President, sent to me because I was your member, and being in Paris he desired, on behalf of the Deputies of France, to add his testimony and theirs of sympathy to Northampton in their struggle.'

(F. D'Arcy, op. cit.)

In those days it was not unusual for opponents at a large political meeting to sprinkle pepper on the floor, which then rose in a cloud when the audience stamped its feet to express their approval. Bradlaugh would stop speaking, hold up his hand and say, *'But I weary you'*, and the crowd would roar *'Go on, Charlie, go on!'*

In the midst of all this overwhelming support Bradlaugh objected to the House of Commons that they ought either to declare his seat vacant or take some course of action to permit his sitting. He lost no support from his constituency in Northampton, which resolutely re-elected him in the subsequent five elections – three bye-elections in 1881, 1882 and 1884, and two general elections, in 1885 and 1886. Finally Parliament gave in and allowed him to take his seat. Within two years he had had passed the Affirmation Act which gave the same legal rights to Free Thinkers as those enjoyed by religious believers. Unfortunately the six years' struggle of fighting against the House of Commons took its toll on Bradlaugh's health, and he died in 1891 after only five years representing fully his constituency. Northampton, on the other hand, had achieved a great victory in its refusal to give up the right to choose its representative in Parliament, regardless of his beliefs.

Self-made men such as Thomas Adams, with their roots in Non-Conformity, owing no allegiance to the established Church, and perhaps having turned against religion altogether, were the backbone of the Radical Party in Northampton, but although 1880 saw their greatest victory in electing an M.P. of such notoriety as Bradlaugh, the following decade was to witness a change in their fortunes as a new force emerged in British politics – Socialism.

In 1887 the Great Strike and Lock-Out in the footwear industry took place, lasting for about six months, and from then on a distinct 'labour consciousness' began to grow in Northampton. Before the dispute the rivetters and finishers in the shoe industry had 3 - 400 members of the trade unionised. Afterwards the number rose to 3000. It was not surprising that the working class should start to turn against the leaders of the Radicals. These leaders were self-made men – employers who had been born in Northamptonshire with nothing and had worked their way to wealth and municipal honours in the years after 1850. They no longer had the same interests at heart as the working class.

Some historians such as Fergus D'Arcy in his thesis 'Charles Bradlaugh and the World of Popular Radicalism 1833-1891', have criticised the Northampton Radicals for not showing the slightest evidence of social concern:

'Their motivating force was the desire for power – power for the honour it conveyed.'

On the other hand, the Radicals' belief in self-help was a valid political philosophy, leading to their support for building societies rather than social legislation to improve the dwellings of the working class.

In 1884 the revolutionary socialist, Robert Reid, brought a charge of neglect on this issue of self-help in the Northampton Liberal and Radical Union (NLRU) and he was answered by Stephen Clark with the words:

'The existing building societies afford a better mode for working men to acquire houses.'

(F. D'Arcy, op. cit.)

Trade union members posed a problem for the Radicals in 1888 when they decided to run their own candidates for the municipal election. In the East Ward Daniel Stanton was a member of the NLRU and was nominated by his union at a public ward meeting. The NLRU had already selected its official

The Radical Rebellion

candidates, and to avoid conflict had to give one up in order to accommodate Stanton. This in turn led to conflict within the NLRU executive where Thomas Adams denounced the action taken:

'The fact of selecting Mr. Stanton was tantamount to a declaration of war against every Liberal and Radical shoe manufacturer in the East Ward.'

F. D'Arcy (op. cit.)

With great political astuteness Thomas succeeded in persuading the NLRU to withdraw from the East Ward – a victory for Stanton could not then be interpreted as a victory of Labour over Radicalism.

A similar conflict took place in the West Ward with the Radical shoe manufacturer, Charles Tebbutt, who had been a councillor for many years, being rejected in favour of Frederick Inwood, a shoe laster and trade unionist.

The consequence was a split vote and the Radicals did worse and worse in the municipal elections through the 1880s.

Joseph Gurney, the popular Radical councillor of long standing, could not understand the growing rift between the working class and their employers. He declared:

'Did a man cease to be a working man when he ceased to be a journeyman? He had been a working man all his life...'

F. D'Arcy (op. cit.)

Despite the sensitivity of the issue a clear statement was needed to set at rest the minds of the working class members of the NLRU, and in 1888 a resolution was passed recognising Labour's right to representation.

---

20 Circus Road,
St. John's Wood,
London N.W.
Feb.10, 1890

Dear Mr. Adams,
If I do not write to your mother, it is only because I cannot. All I can do is to ask to be permitted to share your great grief, and to tender to you my sincerest sympathy. My loss is not as great as yours, but I lose the truest friend a man could have.
Yours very sincerely,
C.BRADLAUGH

N.M. 15.2.1890

The Radical Rebellion

Thomas Adams died in 1890, a year before Charles Bradlaugh. Both their deaths coincided with what may be seen as an end to the Radical era, so it is fitting to bring the Bradlaugh story to its conclusion. In actual fact Thomas' son, Frank, carried on Thomas' work for a few years after Bradlaugh's death, helping to set up the Bradlaugh Radical Association. The Liberal element of the NLRU was still so strong that when Bradlaugh died, it was said by his former supporters that the Radical fight which began in 1868 would have to be recommenced. It seems amazing today to see how determined Bradlaugh's supporters were to split the Liberal vote. The event that precipitated their action was the selection for the second time of Philip Manfield, the Liberal shoe manufacturer, as Bradlaugh's successor. The Radicals thought that Manfield, as a Liberal, was not entitled to a second term in office.

As might be expected with such a conflict of interests and groupings, the 1892 municipal elections were characterised by a plethora of candidates – Tories, Liberals, Radicals, Bradlaugh Radicals and Socialists. The majority of votes went to the Tories, so the balance of power in Council was once again Conservative. The power which Charles Bradlaugh and Thomas Adams had worked so hard to achieve for the Radical cause in Northampton had rapidly disintegrated. Even if Bradlaugh had lived, the rise of Socialism would have forced the Radical element of the NLRU to align itself either with the Liberals again or with the new Socialists, if they had wanted to wield any real influence.

Fergus D'Arcy summarises Bradlaugh's contribution to Northampton politics:

'He did not provide a uniquely novel political programme. Rather, he himself became the programme around which the forces of Northampton Radicalism gathered. Before he came to the town, its Radicals were unorganised and powerless. From the time of his arrival they went from strength to strength. Within a year of his death they were divided, disorganised and facing the rivalry of organised Labour and Socialism. Just as they had wrested concessions and a share of power from the previously dominant Whig-Liberals, they too now had to make the concessions and share the power.'

F. D'Arcy (op. cit.)

Bradlaugh's physical and moral courage in organising resistance to an exclusive government was what brought him popularity and influence in the world of the working class in Victorian Britain. He was most widely known for what he stood against – the State, Church and society in general. He wanted to remove restrictions, destroy prejudices and resist encroachments of State power.

By the 1880s the working class could no longer be comfortably represented by the Radicals - a party of labour, manufacture and commerce. In that decade manufacturers and trades people were increasingly coming to see eye to eye with the people of privilege and landed property.

Although Thomas Adams' death was untimely, at the age of 59, his life ended just when the political era of the self-made man was coming to an end, at least in Northampton.

The Free-thinking or Non-Conformist Radicalism of men like Thomas Adams had, as it were, come to the end of the road. They had set up building societies to help the working class gain the right to representation in Parliament. They had campaigned for and achieved a wider suffrage. The working class now had the right to choose their own representatives and they no longer chose businessmen, even if these men had themselves risen from the ranks of the working class. Labour and Socialism did not need the support of the Radicals, and the Liberal element of politics was once more reverting to the more traditional way of thinking.

It is not known whether Thomas was fully aware of the change that was taking place in the political world around him. However, even if he did see the writing on the wall, he could look back with satisfaction on what he had helped achieve in his home town – not only regarding the campaigns of Charles Bradlaugh, but also the more mundane work he had undertaken as a town councillor, and later as Mayor of Northampton.

Chapter 6

ON COUNCIL BUSINESS

Thomas' story now reaches the point where the similarity to the tale of Dick Whittington, mentioned earlier, becomes so striking. By 1884 Thomas had gained so much respect for his hard work and public service, both in the Council and the Building Society, that he was nominated as Mayor of Northampton. Forty years previously he had walked into Northampton in search of work, a poor lad with all his worldly goods slung over his shoulder.

His reputation as a Radical, however, made his nomination a very unpopular one among the Conservatives, and the Council meeting to elect the Mayor for 1885 saw some rowdy behaviour by both parties. The Conservatives refused to second the nomination, which would have been the normal procedure for the election of the non-political post of Mayor.

Thomas had been proposed by Robert Derby, who spoke about Thomas' being 'the most industrious, persevering and successful tradesman in the town'. Dr. Buzzard, for the Conservatives, stood up amid a storm of hisses and hooting to accuse Thomas of being unsuited to the office of Mayor.

'He was an extreme party partisan of an extreme party. As such he had always with boldness and great plainness of speech been true to his professed character... but the Mayor of a town ought not in their opinion to be solely the leader of a party. He ought to be the mouthpiece and representative of the townsfolk at large.'

N.M. 15.11.1884

Dr. Buzzard went on to nominate the Conservative, William Mills, and in dwelling on Mr. Mills' qualities, indirectly insulted Thomas Adams. Mr. Mills *'was not given to the use of intemperate language for the promotion of party aims... Mr. Mills would promote, by his example, and in other ways those social, religious and general principles which hitherto had been the first care of the mayors to promote.'*

Thomas finally succeeded in winning the election, but by only 11 votes to 10, and he made an honest speech in reply to the Conservative opposition:

On Council Business

'The hackneyed phrase had been used that the Mayor should efface himself politically. Knowing his strong political feeling, if he were to say that he would be absolutely unpolitical, persons before him would say that he was a hypocrite, and if there was one thing he hated more than another it was hypocrisy. Although he might seem at times to work with his party, yet having been placed in the chair, he would act without fear or favour, and would never swerve from what he thought was the right course.'

N.M. 15.11.1884

The celebration dinner given at the Town Hall was an occasion for speeches which set Thomas' election in a wider context – as a victory for civil and religious equality. Referring to Thomas' secular views, Mr. Cleaver declared that 50 years ago an agnostic such as Thomas would not have been tolerated as Mayor. Continuing on this theme, he referred to Bradlaugh's exclusion from Parliament as being a trampling underfoot of civil and religious equality; Northampton was said to be envied for the determined spirit which it had shown in defence of its M.P.

Thomas' own speech did not refer to his remarkable rise from the relative poverty and obscurity of his father's home in Drayton to the high office of Mayor of Northampton, but this must have been in his thoughts. Instead he dwelt on the influence which he believed that he and his fellow councillors had over the life of their town:

'Just in proportion as the representatives were public spirited and broad in their views, so would a town prosper. While if the public men were miserable and petty, the town would be characterised by the same things.'

N.M. 15.11.1884

Finally, he explained the three important aspects of local government in which he was particularly interested – improvement in the parks and recreational facilities such as the Racecourse, the public purchase of the private monopolies of the Waterworks and Gas Works, and the unification of local government so that the Board of Guardians, the School Board and Town Council could work together as one body.

During Thomas' time as Mayor much work was done on the first of these plans. The minutes of the Council meetings reveal the minor concerns with which Thomas and his fellow councillors were occupied. However trivial, they are worth mentioning here. The trivial and less trivial activities of the Council can paint a more vivid picture of what Northampton life was like in the 1880s than any history textbook. First-hand reports are always valuable in bringing history to life.

For instance, cattle were allowed to graze on the Racecourse, and their access to water from the spring was to be made easier. St. Georges Avenue was

On Council Business

The Racecourse, ca. 1896
(The spire of St. Matthew's church is in the background on the right)

declared a new road and opened to the public. Byelaws were passed in order to govern conduct in parks:

'No person shall drive or bring or cause to be driven or brought into the parks or grounds, any bull, ox, cow, heifer, steer, calf, sheep, lamb, hog, pig or sow unless in pursuance of an agreement with the Corporation.

No person shall in any part of the parks or grounds, beat, shake, sweep, brush or cleanse any carpet, drugget, rug or mat or any other fabric retaining dust or dirt, except the Corporation set out a place for such purposes.'

Corporation of Northampton Minute Book 1880-1885

It must be remembered that at this time Abington Park, now the largest of Northampton's parks, was still in private hands, so the Racecourse was considered an important amenity to the new residents in the growing suburbs to the east of town. Horse racing did in fact continue until 1904 when it was condemned as dangerous on account of the sharp bends and numerous public footpaths across the track. Crowd violence and drunkenness were cited as another reason for banning racing. Interestingly, by 1914 the railings, put up during Thomas Adams' mayoralty, were being condemned as unsightly and their removal was called for.

The other recreational area with which the Council was concerned was the meadowland along the banks of the River Nene. The path across Cow Meadow to the locks (now Becket's Park) was to be repaired. Stone was to be broken for that purpose by the unemployed, who were often given such work by the Board of Guardians. The new walk was to be continued to Nunn Mill (near the present site of Avon Cosmetics). The banks were to be protected by a brick wall and the gravel path from the locks to the north end of the meadow was to be widened to ten feet and planted with trees. These improvements to Cow Meadow were to be completed in commemoration of the 50th anniversary of Queen Victoria's accession, and the meadow was to be called Jubilee Park.

The land along the river eastwards from Cow Meadow was called New Commons and Peach's Meadow, and they also were described as part of the Public Parks, Walks and Recreation Grounds of the town.

Further west, along the banks of a tributary of the River Nene just north of Castle Station, on land called Miller's Meadow, a bathing place was to be provided for the free use of females. There was already a bathing pool at Midsummer Meadow, but it was in a dilapidated state. The river bank at Miller's Meadow was to be raised above flood level and the land planted with trees and fenced with an iron railing.

Baulmesholme was the riverside area around the existing Gas Works. (Part of the land had been sold to the gas company at about this time.) A fence was to be erected to prevent cattle trespassing on the ozier beds. The land next door to Baulmesholme was called Foot Meadow. In both areas young boys were often found chasing the cattle grazing there, so more superintendance was required by the police constables. A similar problem existed on the Racecourse, where it was suggested that a constable be appointed permanently during the summer months.

Apart from these recreational facilities, the Council Minutes show that much time was devoted to improving the town's water supply, which was becoming more and more inadequate as the population grew.

In 1884 the Northampton Waterworks Act had authorised the building of a reservoir at Ravensthorpe. At this time Northampton had five pure water wells and one for street watering. The main well pumped 300,000 gallons per day and the others, 200,000 altogether. With a population of 65,000 this only allowed 7g per head per day. A major manufacturing town would expect to supply 25g per head per day. In those days of poor sanitation, pollution of the water supply was always a danger, and in 1885 the Scarletwell pump near the site of the old castle had to be closed and the water condemned. The Water Company was finally purchased by the Corporation and the new reservoir created to cater for the town's needs.

Improvement of the town's streets also featured frequently on the Council's agenda, with central streets such as Mercers Row being 'flagged', and Wood Hill and Dychurch Lane being 'paved with wood'. Marefair (the road leading down to Castle Station) was to be widened because of the dangerous corner - an indication of the hazard presented by horses and carriages even in

The River Nene at the site of Becket's Park, ca. 1880

those days before the advent of the motor car. The market square must have been gated, for the wooden gates at the principal entrance were 'to be replaced by iron gates'. Streets in the new residential areas were frequently mentioned as 'ready to be public streets', such as the streets behind the Mounts and the Avenue off Cliftonville. Cliftonville was clearly the new élite area for the shoe manufacturers to build their homes. Robert Derby, Moses Philip Manfield and William Coulson all lived there. Today it is still possible to imagine the elegant houses as homes, some still surrounded by their spacious gardens.

Even the minor matter of erecting street lamps in the new suburban roads and elsewhere had to be agreed upon in Council – 'four lamps in Ivy Road and six lamps in Holly Road'. Appeals were being made at this time for electric lighting to benefit street lighting, encourage commerce in the town and improve the lighting in workshops. The Ratepayer newspaper made a strong case for electric lighting rather than gas:

'The incandescent lamp could be introduced into every house in the town, with the best sanitary results. Look at the pale faces of the workmen who issue from our workshops in winter, all caused by the air they breathe being poisoned by the gas. Look how it blackens our walls... We have just had several serious explosions of late, blowing fronts of houses into the street.'

The Ratepayer, June 1886

However, despite the Council's efforts the Minister of Health still found cause to complain to the Urban Sanitary Authority of the County Borough of Northampton:

'Every observant frequenter of Northampton thoroughfares, both pedestrians and those travelling in vehicles, knew that its streets are badly made and insufficiently cleansed and watered.... It is common knowledge that in driving through many of the Northampton thoroughfares, passengers are exposed to discomfort and dangers, owing to the bad state of the roadways. That the streets, more or less, are found in a condition of filthiness is notorious, and I have frequently seen many of the back streets bearing the aspect of 'garbage grounds'... The gullies are oftentimes a source of nuisance owing to insufficient cleansing, masses of putrefying and stinking filth being retained in the gully pits for considerable periods.'

Extracts from Annual Reports of the Medical Officer of Health, to the Urban Sanitary Authority of Northampton, (ca. 1900)

The smells of the streets did not only come from the poor sewerage system. Thomas Adams himself made demands for more public conveniences at Abington Square, Regent Square and West Bridge. He cited an occasion at 11pm on a Saturday night when along the main streets could be seen *'many men facing the wall, as if they were earnestly engaged in making out the owner on the door-plate'.*

Corporation of Northampton Minute Book 1880–1885

Another sight which would surprise people today, is conjured up by the Council's demands for a prison van for the removal of prisoners *'so they do not have to be chained together when paraded through the streets – the rich prisoners can have their cab'.*

(op. cit.)

Matters connected with the police, fire and ambulance services are also of interest for the light they throw on what life was like in the mid 1880s. Violence must have been an ever present threat at election time. At the parliamentary election in 1885 fifty constables were brought in from the County to aid the Borough to keep the peace. The Borough was to be responsible if any of these constables were hurt.

Violence was not of course restricted to political events. Vandalism occurred –

'There was wholesale wilful breaking of the new street lamps.'

(op. cit.)

The question was discussed of electric bells on each fireman's house to summon them to a fire, but the proposal was eventually rejected.

On Council Business

NORTHAMPTON ASSOCIATION
For Apprehending & Prosecuting Robbers, Thieves, &c.

£1 REWARD

Whereas some evil-disposed Person or Persons have lately from time to time Wilfully and Feloniously

MILKED THE COWS

GRAZING IN THE

Midsummer Meadow in the town of Northampton,

AND HAVE

TAKEN AWAY THE MILK,

(Belonging to Mrs. CHECKLEY a Member of this Association.)

And whereas much wilful damage and loss of Milk has been caused by Persons driving and running about the said Cows.

Whoever will give such information to the said Mrs. CHECKLEY or to Messrs. SCRIVEN & TERRY, Solicitors to the said Association, as may lead to the Apprehension and Conviction of the Person or Persons who committed either of the above offences, shall be entitled to receive the above Reward from the said Mrs. CHECKLEY; but in case the said Reward shall be claimed by more than one Person, the same shall be paid to or divided amongst such Person or Persons, and in such share or shares as the Sub-Committee appointed by the said Association for that purpose shall decide, and whose decision, or that of a majority of them, shall be final.

NORTHAMPTON, 25th JULY, 1885.

STANTON & SON, PRINTERS, NORTHAMPTON.

Crime on Midsummer Meadow, 1885

The lack of a proper ambulance service led to the proposal being made that the police and fire brigade should receive instruction in first aid. The ambulance was to be equipped with a small handbook, an extra strong stretcher *'suitable for conveying the most violent intoxicated man'*, and *'an ambulance hamper'*.

(op. cit.)

As far as housing is concerned, it was recognised that *'the town compares favourably in the matter of the housing of the working classes, with others of similar size'*, but even so, poor sanitation was an ever present problem:

'Water closets of cottage properties (should) be provided with proper flushing apparatus. Often lack of regular flushing causes a nuisance, and drains and sewers become excessively foul.'

(op. cit.)

As elementary education became compulsory and more and more female teachers were being employed in this profession, the School Board decided to pass a resolution to compel those women teachers who got married to give in their resignation. Mr. Randall justified the resolution as *'protecting the teachers from designing young men who are always looking after girls with good earnings'*.

(op. cit.)

Such then were the issues with which Thomas would have been dealing during his time as Mayor. He was re-elected for a second year – a very unusual occurrence, but this was not so much a sign of his popularity as another reflection of the notoriety of his political views: The Town Council needed more magistrates, and in 1884 sent a requisition to the Lord Chancellor. On the list were Thomas Adams and Philip Manfield, said to be the two most popular names. By 'backstairs influence' on account of their political Radicalism these two names were excluded from the subsequent appointments.

When Thomas was re-elected as Mayor (an honour which automatically made him Chief Magistrate) there was an implied threat that unless he and Manfield were appointed magistrates, they would always be voted Mayor and Deputy Mayor and thereby have their seats on the Bench.

When the Conservatives were voted out of power in a general election and replaced by Gladstone's Liberal government, Lord Henschell became Lord Chancellor and soon appointed Thomas and Manfield as magistrates.

Thomas had encountered a similar problem when he tried in 1881 to become elected as overseer for the parish of St. Sepulchre (a post which was connected with the work of the magistrates). Other magistrates refused to sanction his appointment because he was 'a political agent'. (This was just after Thomas had helped secure Bradlaugh's victory in the parliamentary election.)

Fellow Radical, Joseph Gurney, protested on Thomas' behalf and succeeded in gaining approval for him to take up the position of overseer. On moving to Colwyn Road, Thomas transferred his services to the parish of St. Andrew's. This work involved assessment of property and matters of parochial law.

After completing two terms as Mayor, Thomas was made an Alderman and so continued his council work, being on the Water Committee, Vice-Chairman of the Estate and Corporation Act Committee, and trustee of various town charities such as 'Sir Thomas White's Loan'.

His energy seemed to know no bounds, for even in 1890, the year of his death, Thomas was re-elected as President of the Liberal and Radical Association. It was in fact his attendance at the meeting to re-elect him as President that precipitated the deterioration in his health. Influenza developed into bronchitis, and he died about a week later.

In the obituary and description of his funeral, which has already been quoted in chapter 1, the flowery Victorian language does not hide the fact that Thomas must have been a very well-known and much loved local figure.

'It seems but as yesterday that he was amongst us in the heyday of lusty life, with cheery word and hearty greeting... He had a rugged honesty which always commanded respect and admiration, even when his views did not find universal assent... He would fight hard for the cause he espoused, and knew how to hit out straight and effectively; but with true English spirit he was ready to shake hands with his opponents when the fight was over.'

N.M. 15.2.1890

He is an interesting figure from any point of view – for being the epitome of the self-made man, for his devotion to the puritan views of the Congregational Church and his subsequent conversion to humanism, and for his involvement in the early crusading days of the building society movement. As regards Northampton's history, he was a significant figure in the Radical movement and the support given to the somewhat notorious M.P., Charles Bradlaugh. More particularly, he was the founder of a bakery business which went through all the hardships and exciting developments that characterised the Victorian era. His story continues in the lives of his children, grandchildren and great grandchildren who took the small business through the 20th century and brought it safely into the 21st.

Ten years before Thomas died he handed his bakery business over to his eldest son, Walter. It is to Walter's diaries and other reminiscences of the Edwardian era that the story now turns.

Chapter 7

BRANCHING OUT

'12 January 1883
  Bread sunk from 6d (2½p) to 5½d today ...
24 February 1884
  Have sunk the bread to 4d on account of so much underselling...
13 April 1885
  Rose the bread to 4½d...
10 September 1886
  Refused to serve Mrs. Revitt at 3½d per loaf. Am not to call again.'

These extracts come from Walter's diaries, and illustrate the constant battle which the bakers had to wage in order to meet the demands of competition and still make a profit on their bread.

At the Northampton and District Master Bakers' Association dinner in 1889 the main topic of discussion was still on the theme discussed at the dinner ten years previously, mentioned in chapter 3 - the need for bakers to unite to exert greater influence on the pricing of bread. Underselling was still forcing many bakeries to run at a loss.

Walter had been in his father Thomas' business since he had left school and had taken over at the age of 22, in 1880. The struggle to unite local bakers had been so hard that the Northampton Bakers' Association eventually closed in the early years of the 20th century. It was revived in 1907 and Walter was elected President. In an interesting interview with the Northampton Independent he discussed the need for united action and referred to a system that had proved successful in Wales:

'In Wales the bakers are more united because they have a sale note that binds them together, and the millers join hands with them by refusing to supply flour to those bakers who try to undersell others. Some years ago we tried the same principle ourselves, and worked together at first very well indeed, but in the end we found it impossible to keep up the arrangement. The public gain in the long run by getting their bread far cheaper than the cost of flour and other working expenses warrants.'

N.I. 1.6.1907

British School
Northampton

Midsummer 1869

My dear Father and Mother
    I hope you will be pleased, when you receive this letter from me, to see how much I have improved in my writing during the past year. The subjects we learn are Reading, Writing, Arithmetic, Dictation, Geography, Grammar, History and Texts of Scripture, a knowledge of which will be of great service to me, when I leave school.
    Thanking you for keeping me at school where I shall be able to improve my mind, and fit myself for the business of life.
    I remain
        Your Affectionate Son
            Walter Adams

Letter from Walter to Thomas and Elizabeth found in his school textbook

Branching Out

When considering later developments during the 1960s and 70s, it will be worth remembering this illustration of the way in which the power of the millers is closely bound up with the success of the bakers. The link has already been noted in the earlier history of the late 18th and 19th centuries.

Another important baker in Northampton, Mr. Linnell, pointed out in the same article that there was no need for the public to feel cheated by the town's bakers:

'For the past six years bread has been below its proper price in Northampton - that is if people have been getting anything like weight. We are noted as a town of cheap bread.' (op.cit.)

Mr. Gandy of Hunter Street, another well-known baker, explained that:

'The baking trade in Northampton has been in a shocking state for the last two years. The public have been getting bread far too cheaply, and the poor baker has to suffer. Why, in Wellingborough and Bedford bread has been 5d a loaf for a long time whilst it has remained at 4d here, and baking hasn't been a living. For 200 loaves, to sell which we call on an average at 100 houses, we have received 8s 4d more than the cost of the flour. Out of that we have had to pay our men, rent, rates and taxes, keep a horse and cart, and live ourselves. And then you have to stand and be shot at by your customers...

Ten years ago we were getting double the profit we are now, and a man who was doing ten or fifteen sacks a week considered himself well off. Now we work like niggers and hardly make a living.' (op.cit.)

So how had Walter benefited in the 'good old days' of the 1890s to which Mr. Gandy alluded? Both Walter and the two next oldest sons, Frank and Wallace, had achieved great success in that period - to such an extent that Walter had built a modern new bakery and house on the corner of Kettering Road and Derby Road in 1887 when he was only 29, and Frank and Wallace reached even greater heights in 1896 when they joined forces and opened the first steam bakery in the town, on the corner of Wellingborough Road and Adams Avenue.

Frank had served his apprenticeship at several establishments in Northampton, unlike his older brother who had been fortunate in inheriting his father's business. At the young age of 19 Frank had set up on his own in a small bakehouse behind the Swan Inn, on what used to be called Cow Lane (later Swan Street, now situated behind the Derngate theatre). Frank's experience illustrates the ease with which one could set up a bakery business. His grandson, Philip, explains:

'All you had to do was get a tenancy of an outdoor beerhouse with a bakehouse behind. If you'd got enough money to buy a sack of flour, you were in business...

Walter Quincey Adams

'You'd go to the brewer to collect the yeast - 2 or 3 gallons of brewer's yeast in a bucket.'

In 1888 Frank moved into bigger premises on the new estate between Billing Road and Wellingborough Road, on the corner of Palmerston Road and Woodford Street. As his brother Walter had done a year previously, he was moving into the heart of the growing suburbs to the east of the town.

Apart from selling directly from his bakery, Frank had probably started off at Cow Lane with a small round when he would sell his wares from a basket or a handcart as he walked the town centre streets. In general bakers sold far more bread through their bread rounds than they did from the shop: if a shop sold a hundred loaves, the delivery round would sell about four hundred.

A set of portable bread scales were always taken on the delivery round in case the customers required their bread weighing on the doorstep, or the police used their powers to stop the round and check the weight of the bread. The portable scales were a legal requirement. There was fierce competition to build up a bread round - some of the larger bakeries sent men round giving away free bread as samples in an attempt to wean customers away from other bakers, but despite this, most customers remained loyal.

Frank's experience not only illustrates the ease with which a man could set up as a baker, but also the success which was possible to those with a good business sense. As the Northampton Independent reporter wrote, who interviewed Walter in 1907:

'There was a time when everybody considered baking a royal road to fortune, for you frequently saw a man start in the trade with a hand truck, and before many weeks were out he had a horse and cart and "pulled down his barns to build greater". But times have changed, and profits too, and now the baking trade, so far from being a royal road to fortune, is often a steep decline down which the man who is always loafing but far from a loafer rushes headlong, until he falls into the arms of the Official Receiver.'

N.I. 1.6.1907

Fortunately, Thomas' sons did not find themselves in that position.

Branching Out

When Frank moved out of Cow Lane, his brother Wallace took over, staying there until going into partnership with Frank in 1896 at Adams Avenue. Similarly, when Walter moved out of Mount Street to his new premises on Kettering Road opposite the Racecourse, the fourth son, Edgar, took over, this time running Mount Street as a confectionery bakery selling fancy cakes and biscuits.

Within about 15 years Edgar had also moved on to greater things. He bought from the building society two plots of land on Wellingborough Road at the foot of Allen Road. The corner property was built as a bakehouse, and next door was his own residence. The bakery is still a baker's shop and an estate agent's now occupies the front room of Edgar's old home.

The only sons who did not start out as bakers were Arthur and Herbert, although even they returned to the trade eventually. They both earned their living as shoemakers, until Arthur decided to take over Wallace's bakehouse in Cow Lane in 1896. He then moved to a bakery in Augustin Street before finally leaving Northampton. Herbert tried being a country baker before joining Edgar at Mount Street, and finally running a bakery on Whitworth Road at the corner of Billington Street.

Branching Out

The first major business move made by Thomas' sons was Walter's building a new house and bakery on Kettering Road. His father would still have been alive to see it, and was then living not far away on Colwyn Road. Walter's great nephew, Philip, can remember the interior of the old bakery at Mount Street. It was still quite new when Walter moved out, having been built in the 1880s in the traditional design of a side flue oven, fired with coal, and using peels to place the bread in the oven.

A double deck oven

Branching Out

The new bakery on Derby Road was so modern that it merited an article in the Northampton Mercury. The ovens, of which there were two, were called John Jennison's 'Smokeless Deckers'. Instead of having a fire inside the oven in the morning, the small furnace beneath the ovens was set going overnight so that all the baker had to do in the morning was put his bread in. A pyrometer ascertained when the required heat was reached, at which point the damper was put in and the fire allowed to go out. The flues ran all over and round the ovens so that the heat remained equable and baked all the items thoroughly and evenly. When a good solid heat had been obtained, many batches could be baked in succession without any of the bother of making fresh fires. The new bakehouse had a domestic advantage because it provided a continual supply of hot water, with the water pipes running along through the flues and then on to various parts of the house.

Walter's granddaughter, Pam Cooper, can still recall the family and the interior of Walter's fine new home. He had married Elizabeth Lea, the daughter of a strict Baptist farmer in Cransley. When she moved to Northampton she became an active member of Mount Pleasant Baptist Chapel (on Kettering Road). Pam remembers her as being 'the more vigorous one of the marriage'. Elizabeth had a brother George who had a farm near Kettering and to whom the younger grandchildren would go for their holidays. Pam remembers those days with great pleasure despite Great Uncle George's strict ways:

'We had to go to chapel in the morning, Sunday School in the afternoon, and chapel again in the evening. And then he would get a girl called Mona to come and play hymns around the piano.'

Pam's mother, Winifred, was one of Walter and Elizabeth's three children, the oldest being Percy, and the middle child, Cecily. Winifred married Frank Robinson who provides another interesting example of a self-made man - the kind of rise to fortune which seems to have been quite easy in the Victorian and Edwardian era:

'Father came from quite a poor home, left school at 14 and went to work on the railways. After a year he managed to get a job at Phipps & Son, a shoe mercer's on Guildhall Road. He started in the eyelets department and worked his way up, and eventually became manager of the export department and finally a director of the firm.'

It is interesting to hear Pam reminisce about her grandfather's time:

'Inside the shop was a stack of glass-topped tins full of all sorts of biscuits. You could lift the lid and take out what you wanted. At the back of the shop you could see Grandpa doing the books. Mother would regularly take me to the shop. Passing through the bakehouse you would hear the crickets sing and then you'd reach the stables.

Branching Out

  Grandpa's house was rather nice. It had bay windows with beautiful lace curtains. He used to sit there and watch people going by and the activities on the Racecourse. Kettering Road had a tram running up and down then. Every Sunday we used to go to dinner there. There was a chenille cloth on the table before the meal was set and a very beautiful mahogany sideboard with brass fittings. There was a middle room - a dining room - and a lovely old gramophone. We used to play Gilbert and Sullivan. Going through the passage to the kitchen, we'd have our supper there, and then came the scullery. Upstairs were the usual three bedrooms. The back room was full of interesting magazines like Punch. The bathroom had brass taps, a white bath, and always a cake of Pear's soap.'

  Some of the early entries in Walter's diaries before the move to Kettering Road conjure up a life that is now almost unimaginable to town dwellers today. Walter must have owned several plots of building society land in that area, for in 1885 he was writing with excitement of how he had harvested his own oats and tares at Holly Road. Then in 1886:

  'Took the cows to Whitehills and then went through the wood up to the fields where I helped Mr. S. stack barley.'

  In the early years of the 20th century Walter's wife learned to ride a bike and he writes with pleasure of the cycle rides which they could now enjoy together. Open countryside was of course not far from their house by the Racecourse. Such seemingly carefree days were not without mishap, as these two entries about his young children, Percy and Cecily, reveal:

'24 June 1887

  Poor Sissy knocked down and run over by a light cart and horse. Fortunately she is not hurt very much, her nose being the worst place…

1 April 1884

  Percy lost for half an hour!'

  For a long time Walter was a Sunday School teacher at Mount Pleasant chapel, taking classes in the morning as well as the afternoon. Although he was never as devoted to the Baptist cause as his wife, his diaries reveal a serious thoughtful side to him:

'5 January 1905

I have been too concerned with self reproach and must listen more to the voice of God.'

  When he retired in 1919, he left the business to his son, Percy. During these years he devoted more and more of his time to his work as a director of the Northampton Town and County Building Society (formerly the NTCFLS). He carried out much valuation work and was chairman of the Survey Committee for many years - a committee to which even in 1935 at the age of 77 he was re-

Branching Out

TELEPHONE 187.

W. Q. ADAMS,
212 Kettering Road.

Prize Medal
PORK PIES
THE BEST THAT MONEY CAN BUY.
......

All the ingredients used in our productions are guaranteed to be the best obtainable.

elected. In the 1920s he was involved with the building society's purchase of yet more land from Lady Wantage, the former owner of Abington Manor.

As far as his bakery business was concerned, in the early part of the 20th century this was proving to be very successful. Although he was in competition with Frank and Wallace, the arrangement was quite amicable, for there was plenty of custom to be shared. Walter and Frank even borrowed bread from one another if they were running low - sometimes even just one loaf, and Edgar only baked confectionery, supplying his brother Walter with that side of the trade.

Pork pies were a very popular item in Walter's shop, and according to an article in 'Where to Buy in Northampton' (1891) the quality of the bread was said to be *'highly esteemed in the neighbourhood for its nutritive qualities as well as for its sweetness and lightness.'*

Walter probably employed several men and boys to help him run his business. They may have started at 3am - a comparatively late start by the practice of the time, but in the 1930s it is known that the night's work began as early as 11pm. While still on Mount Street Walter's diaries already refer to three delivery rounds, which he calls the first, second and home rounds. Some bakers worked through the night on Friday to complete the large number of orders for Saturday.

Purchasing a new oven was of course a major event, and a baker had to get used to its way of working, almost like dealing with another person. On buying a new oven at Mount Street in 1885 Walter records in his diary *'first batch too cool and second too hot'*. A certain sense of pride is noted when he mentions his first takings at the new premises on 212 Kettering Road: *'Opened shop today - took 15s 8½d (80p)'*.

At the back of the new bakehouse there were stables built, and in fact horses and carts were used to deliver bread until the 1950s. Each delivery man had his own horse and a relationship would be built up over the years, with the delivery man able to walk up the street with his basket, make a clicking sound and have the horse follow on after him. Bert Masters, one of Adams' employees who started with them in the 1950s, recalls with delight the story of one delivery man who mistreated his horse and reaped the consequences:

'This guy was always whipping his horse and ill-treating it. The horse didn't like him. What used to happen regularly was that Ted would get to the last street, up on Spinney Hill, and his horse would know that it was the end of the round. As Ted went off with his basket, ready to call his horse up, the horse used to turn round and canter back down the hill. Into Derby Road would come the cart with no Ted on it!'

W.Q. Adams' cart

Walter's establishment on Kettering Road was no doubt one of the most modern and efficient in the town. As a comparison, it is interesting to note the reminiscences about the more old-fashioned country bakers of the same period. James Slarke and Harry Williams were two people whose reminiscences were fortunately captured for posterity in an oral history project in the 1980s. James recalled the difficulties of fuelling the bakehouse ovens when coal proved too expensive:

'Sturgess and Ward's (of Towcester) used to have these big wood faggots from Silverstone - about 6 ft long. There were special horse-drawn carts made just to carry them. They used to store them in the open buildings up the jitty behind the Saracen. Arthur Ward used to put three of these faggots in the oven and light them, and when they'd burnt right down to ashes, the hearth would be white hot.'

(Northamptonshire Libraries Oral History Project, tapes C14 and C65)

Both men recalled the practice of taking the Sunday dinner to the local baker's to be cooked. James remembered that Arthur Ward recognised every tin brought to him:

'There were probably about 50 or 60 or more because he only charged about a penny to do it. And if you came by there when he was drawing these dinners out, the smell used to be lovely... Some people used to take their joint

and instead of putting the Yorkshire (pudding mixture) in the tin, they'd take it in a jug, and when the meat was sufficiently cooked he would tip the Yorkshire into the tin, and you got the flavour of the nice meat into the Yorkshire.'

The communal baking must have added to the sense of the warm sociable atmosphere of a bakery. A former employee of Adams', Ann Frost, recalled what life was like for her father, who was a baker in a village near Towcester:

'My father's bakery was like a village meeting place, full of gossip. It was a lovely life, full of friendship and looking out for one another.'

However, it was a hard life as well, for it could be extremely cold delivering bread in the winter. From the age of 5 Ann would deliver bread in a basket; on cold winter mornings her mother, out delivering on the cart, would get 'all iced up' by the frost.

At times leaving the cooking to the baker brought with it certain hazards, as Harry Williams recalled:

'You'd take the dinners down before you went to Sunday School... We took it to old Joe Shackleton's and he had a little clay pipe, but he broke half the stem off. He used to set it down on the side of the oven, when he was putting the pudding in.

One Sunday morning when we'd fetched it, we sat round the dinner table. "I don't like the pudding", someone said. Then another one created and another one; "I don't like it! I can't eat it!" Mother said, "Get on with your pudding! There's nothing wrong with it. Let me try it." Then she found the pipe - old Joe had dropped his clay pipe in it! She went out and took it all back.

... And another tale is - over at Sturgess' bakery a young chap dropped one of my mother's puddings. So he went in the kitchen and got a cup of water and topped it up. And mother said "It is a nice pudding today!" It was made with water, you see - that's absolutely true.' (op.cit.)

Such tales evoke a wry smile now about the casual standards of the old days, but already as long ago as the late 19th century government inspectors were regularly inspecting bakehouses to ensure their cleanliness and hygienic conditions. Ever since the first law regulating bakehouses in 1863 inspections were supposed to be carried out regularly. By 1891 bakehouses were covered by the Factory and Workshop Act. The Medical Officer of Health for each local authority was responsible for inspecting retail bakehouses.

The local reports for Northampton reveal that in 1892 there were no less than 101 bakehouses in the borough. This is a huge number for the small area, and demonstrates just how common baker's shops must have been. It also demonstrates how easy it was to set up a bakery. The Medical Office of Health (M.O.H.) in Northampton hardly had to take any action against a baker, although in 1903 he did state that the oldest parts of the town were the worst:

> '*A considerable amount of work has been carried out during the year in connection with bakehouses, especially as regards underground bakehouses. While Northampton cannot yet be said to have ideal bakehouses, yet I believe the standard aimed at is improving... Conditions in the oldest parts of the town are the worst - in approach, situation and surroundings. Often there is not enough air or light.*'
>
> Reports on the Health of Northampton by the M.O.H., N.B.C.

Underground bakehouses had to provide 500 cubic feet of air space per person (the equivalent of about 2.5 metres square of floor space), and above-ground bakehouses, 400 cubic feet.

In 1901 the M.O.H. wrote that although Northampton bakehouses were generally clean, reform was much needed in other areas. For example, local authorities should have the power to frame bye-laws to regulate the construction of bakehouses, the ventilation and lighting, and their management, including periodic cleansing of floors, utensils, placing all troughs on castors, and prohibiting the storage of coal and coke in the bakehouse.

It is interesting to read the description of one underground bakery in the town centre which was forced to close down in 1903:

> '*The walls are constructed of stone, they are damp, and in a state of decay, and there is evidence of sewage percolation from the house drains, which are defective. In a dark corner of this underground bakehouse there is a drain opening in the floor, untrapped, which discharges into a cesspool under the floor of the bakehouse; upon the removal of the slab cover of the cesspool the stench emitted was exceedingly bad.*'
>
> (op.cit.)

The hard working hours of a baker were another aspect of the trade which were still being debated as late as the 1930s. Headlines such as 'Abolish the Evil of Night Baking!' and 'Workers Who Hardly See the Sun Shine' introduced a report in the Northampton Independent on the occasion of the M.P. J. Banfield's raising the issue in Parliament.

Mr. Gandy, owner of one of the largest Northampton bakeries, was asked for his comments. He admitted that the prohibition of night working would bring with it many benefits, not least the better health of the workers themselves:

> '*A night baker's life is unnatural and upside down. He sleeps when others work and vice-versa. Owing to the curious way of living which his occupation forces him to adopt, he rarely sees his friends, he can never go to amusements, only at the expense of his health and consequently his job ... His health must inevitably decline owing to the sunshine he misses, and this factor in its turn has a harmful effect upon the production side of the industry, for unhappy and run-down workers cannot be expected to give of their best.*'
>
> N.I. 19.3.1937

He explained that the main reason for night working was the wish to keep the price of bread as low as possible in the face of competition. Night production meant that all the bread was ready for delivery in one batch first thing in the morning. If more than one delivery had to be made, the 4lb (2kg) loaf would cost an extra halfpenny (0.25p).

Mr. Gandy found it hard to understand the public's predictable objection to this minimal price rise, for he explained that bread was now a far smaller proportion of the family diet than it used to be, and a price rise would therefore not have such a dramatic effect on the family budget as it used to.

Despite the logical argument against night-working, there were still those who enjoyed the routine. One of Walter Adams' employees, Charles Mawby, actually had a whole article devoted to himself and his work in 1934 - in the same magazine, the Northampton Independent, which only a few years later was to publish an article criticising the practice.

In a series entitled 'All in the Day's Work' the headline was chosen 'He Likes Working at Night Time'. Charles Mawby would begin work at 11pm except Sundays, when he started at midnight, and finished at 7am. Saturday was his night off. He explained to the reporter how he first weighs out the ingredients, then has his breakfast at 3am, after which he mixes the doughs ready for baking.

'When he has finished his work, Mr. Mawby takes his recreation in his garden, for he is a keen gardener. After dinner at 12 o'clock he goes to bed in the afternoon until about 8 o'clock.

Night work suits him, for he keeps free of ills other than an attack of the common cold... For the summer he finds night work preferable to day work when the sun is pouring its rays on the bakehouse.'

N.I. 7.12.1934

Right from the turn of the century Walter's bakery on Kettering Road and later Frank and Wallace's steam bakery on Adams Avenue were examples of the most modern bakehouses, producing bread, pies and confectionery that were highly regarded in the town. Yet a significant change had occurred in bakery products which was not just to do with the improved ovens of the Edwardian era.

The bread made by men such as Walter and Frank was different from the bread made by their father, Thomas, in the middle of the 19th century, and the change had nothing to do with the way it was baked. The difference lay in the flour from which it was made.

In 1872 the first roller-mill was opened in Britain. Prior to this date, flour had had to be milled by wind- or water-mills, which used millstones to grind the grain. Roller-mills, an invention in the second half of the 19th century,

Branching Out

produced a different kind of flour. To understand the difference it is necessary to understand the structure of a grain of wheat.

The illustration shows that one grain contains the germ, the endosperm, and the protective casing called bran. The germ is what will sprout and grow into a new wheat plant. It represents only 2% of the grain, but is rich in protein, vitamins and oil.

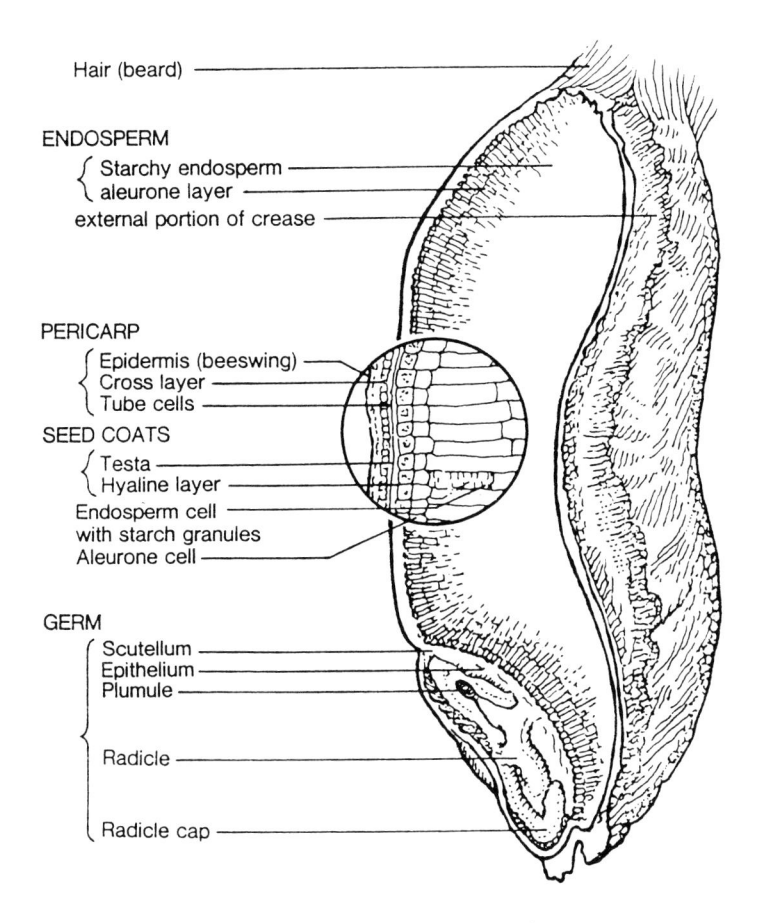

```
Hair (beard)

ENDOSPERM
    ⎰ Starchy endosperm
    ⎱ aleurone layer
    external portion of crease

PERICARP
    ⎧ Epidermis (beeswing)
    ⎨ Cross layer
    ⎩ Tube cells
SEED COATS
    ⎰ Testa
    ⎱ Hyaline layer
    Endosperm cell
    with starch granules
    Aleurone cell

GERM
    ⎧ Scutellum
    ⎪ Epithelium
    ⎪ Plumule
    ⎨
    ⎪ Radicle
    ⎪
    ⎩ Radicle cap
```

Cross-section of a Grain of Wheat

Next to the germ is the endosperm, which is the heart of the grain (85%) and the part which supplies the starch. All round the germ and the endosperm is the protective casing of bran, making up the remaining 13% of the grain's content. The bran consists of four main layers of skin, which not only provide important vitamins and minerals, but also the fibre so necessary in a healthy diet.

In stone-grinding the grain of wheat is crushed. The bran may be sifted out afterwards, but the germ is not removed or destroyed. In roller-milling the huge rollers shear open the grain, freeing the endosperm and separating it from the bran and the germ. What is left contains none of the goodness stored in the germ and bran, and is basically a granular semolina. Different kinds of flour have what are called different extraction rates, e.g. 75% or 95%, the number referring to the amount of the grain still left in the flour. Thus flour with an extraction rate of 95% is wholemeal, having lost only 5% of the bran. It was claimed that to produce massive quantities of flour by roller-milling, about 25% of the bran and the germ had to be extracted. This was not exactly true, but the roller-millers had ulterior motives in making the claim.

Firstly, a low extraction rate helps preserve the flour and bread, for the oil from the crushed germ inhibits the keeping quality. In the days before refrigerated cold stores millers would naturally have been in favour of any way in which their flour could be kept fresh.

Secondly, the new mechanised methods of dough-making were not suited to the flour containing particles of bran and wheatgerm. Low extraction rates were therefore favoured by the large baking concerns.

Artificial bleaching of the flour was also introduced at about this time, and it is another factor which produces flour better suited to high-speed mechanical dough-mixing. It is not carried out solely in order to obtain the whiter-than-white flour so long sought after over the centuries. It is also a method of instantly maturing the flour. Matured flour, if it has been deprived of its germ, was recognised as giving the most satisfactory performance for machine-made dough. (One of the bleaches widely used during the 1920s to 1940s was called Agene. It is now banned in England, being suspected of causing serious nervous disorders.)

Roller-milling, therefore, revolutionised flour production and consequently bread baking. By 1900 wind- and water-mills were an anachronism. Flour might no longer be being adulterated in the crude way that became common practice among the less scrupulous bakers of the 19th century, but it was still being altered, and in a way that nutritionists began to recognise as being detrimental to the health of the consumer.

By the early 20th century Walter and his brothers would have no doubt been benefiting from this new kind of flour with its good keeping qualities and

Branching Out

BRAX
BROWN BREAD

A scientifically prepared Brown Bread which contains all the valuable nutritive properties of the wheat with nothing removed except the husks, which are the irritating portions of the grain.

It is specially rich in *proteids* and this combined with the fact that it is non-irritant, renders it eminently suitable for children, elderly people and invalids, as well as for the general public.

It is *highly nutritious*, easily digested and yet sustaining, and can be eaten and *thoroughly enjoyed* at *every* meal.

BRAX BROWN BREAD is carefully baked and will keep fresh for several days, whilst it is never too moist, even when quite new.

BAKED DAILY, BY
ADAMS BROS,
22, MAREFAIR, 55, KETTERING ROAD,
209 & 211. WELLINGBORO' ROAD,
Bakery:—ADAMS' AVENUE.

HAZARD, Typ., 2*4. Westbourne Grove, London, W

its popularity among the public, who appreciated its lightness and white colour. Before the arrival of roller-milled flour Walter's diaries in the last two decades of the 19th century reveal how the quality of his flour could cause him quite a few problems:

'13 February 1883
2 bags of Castalian flour to come from Latimer and Crick to try at 35/- ... tried Castalian flour and find it very bad...
30 January 1886
I think Stops' flour is fusty...
18 August 1886
Tried Canadian flour but do not like it. Tried Stops, but find it coarse and bad colour...
23 February 1887
Bread goes off very bad.'

So however modern a baker's equipment, the flour could still cause problems, and Walter, along with his brothers, would have noticed an improvement in that respect as the availability of roller-milled flour became more widespread in the early years of the 20th century.

Even so, as the advert for Brax Bread demonstrates, bakers were aware of the demands for a healthier kind of loaf than the white. Frank and Wallace, as Adams Bros., were advertising Brax, and it would be interesting to know how popular it was among the general public. The advert suggests in fact that it was not, for it is praised as being 'suitable for children, elderly people and invalids'.

As the commercial bakers became more and more preoccupied with the volume and whiteness of a loaf, and with steam to enhance the bloom on new bread, so the traditions of domestic and professional baking began to diverge. Whereas for hundreds of years the housewife and baker had used essentially the same equipment and closely related methods, the development of ovens with steam injectors, of mechanical kneaders and dough dividers, rapidly made the commercially baked loaf something different from what might be baked at home.

It was Walter's brothers, Frank and Wallace, who introduced the first steam bakery to the town, and the story now turns to their experiences in the early decades of the 20th century and to the extraordinary story of Frank's son, Thomas Rigby - a story of misfortune and determination which bears a fascinating resemblance to that of his grandfather, the first Thomas Adams.

Chapter 8

TEA-ROOMS AND BAKERIES

When Frank and Wallace opened their new steam bakery in 1896, they must have felt an enormous sense of pride. Only five years previously Frank had moved to the comparatively small corner bakehouse on Palmerston Road, and Wallace to the bakery on the narrow backstreet of Cow Lane. Probably neither of them would have taken such a major step forward on their own, but together as Adams Bros. they felt able to undertake the rapid expansion of their business.

At the grand opening ceremony attended by the Mayor, Frank spoke of how the new system which had been installed combined 'the maximum of cleanliness and excellence with the greatest economy of labour'. As part of the celebration 300 loaves were given away to the poor.

The claims made in the name of progress are a telling indication of the hard work which was still expected of bakers' employees:

'The building is one of three storeys. At the top there is accommodation for a large quantity of flour. Here the flour is ranged in 10 stone sacks, a vast improvement on the customary 20 stone sacks, as the workmen can testify.' (20 stone is the equivalent of about 126 kg.)

N.M. 3.11.1896

The description of the new system continues:

'In this upper floor there is a hopper fitted with a sieve. The flour is emptied into the hopper, and the sieve set in motion, facilitating the departure of the flour into the dough mixer on the floor below where it is allowed to ferment. After fermentation the dough is put through a chute into the bakery on the ground floor. Here it is prepared for the oven and baked. The kneading formerly done by hand, with almost painful slowness, is done within the revolving machine, the interior of which is fitted up with blades that serve the purpose of hands, without ever getting tired.'

(op.cit.)

Frank and his family were able to enjoy the new domestic accommodation above the shop, which fronted on to the Wellingborough Road

*Frank's parents-in-law,
Daniel and Elizabeth Rigby*

and still exists today. Frank had married Sarah Rigby of Pitsford in 1879, when he was only 19 and Sarah 7 years older. Within nine years they had six children - four daughters (one of whom died as a baby) and two sons - Ada, Elizabeth, Sarah, Thomas Rigby and Frank. The reminiscences of Frank's granddaughter, Edna Bodily (daughter of Elizabeth), provide a vivid picture of life at that time. The lives of the five children illustrate most evocatively what life was like for young middle class people in the Edwardian era.

In 1900 Frank and Wallace decided to invest in the now popular tea-rooms. As mentioned in chapter 3, cafés had begun to be introduced more widely in the late 19th century and there was clearly an increase in their popularity. Adams Bros. opened a tea-room at no. 55 Kettering Road on the bend near Abington Square, and also at no. 22 Marefair, on the site of the new cinema and leisure complex. In fact in 1901 Frank and his family moved into the flat above the tea-room on Marefair, enabling Wallace to move into the premises at Adams Avenue.

Wallace had two children, Oliver and Ethel. Ethel later married Mr. R. Haywood, the Northampton cricketer, and Oliver was to grow up to play an important part in the growth of the business - not least in giving it his name when a new one was sought in the latter half of the century.

A letter remains in existence that proved to be the last one written by Frank to his son, Thomas Rigby. It reveals a very serious nature and approach to life, a quality which is also evident in Walter's diaries. The excerpt printed covers the advice he gave to his son who was just about to complete his training as a baker at the London Polytechnic. It is sound advice, but given in a ponderous, very 'Victorian' manner.

The café on Marefair had four storeys - the family lived on the third floor and the staff right at the top. It proved to be a flourishing business because it was the last café for people departing by train from Castle Station, and the first one for people arriving.

Tea-rooms and Bakeries

*Frank and his family: (standing) Ada and Elizabeth
(sitting) his wife Sarah, daughter Sarah, Tom and Frank*

The Races held on the Racecourse were a major event for the town, and Edna Bodily remembers the tales her mother Elizabeth used to tell of those occasions:
'They had to be very careful at the Races because they'd have some of these posh gentlemen come in and have a meal. They'd say "We'll have it in the upstairs room". They'd ask the girls if they'd fetch them something and when the girls had gone down, they'd go up on the next floor where the family lived and pinch all the best silver and things. So Frank had to learn to be very astute about that.'

The area opposite the tea-room was dominated by the medieval church of St. Peter's and by the 17th century Hazelrigg House. Edna remembers her mother's description of the beautiful residential area which then existed sloping down to the river Nene. One of Frank's daughters, Sarah, eventually married Hugh Latimer (of Latimer and Crick corn merchants), and Hugh's family had a house on Green Street, where lawns sloped down to the river.

Nearby Gold Street was a high class shopping street in the early 1900s, which added to the attractiveness of the area around St. Peter's Church, but already new and better residential estates were being built. The Latimer family moved to Billing Road at this time. Edna remembers it as being 'the place to

Tea-rooms and Bakeries

> 22 Marefair
> Northampton
> Mar. 28th 1906

Dear Tom,

We had hoped to have seen you on Saturday next, and are disappointed as the change is made, but never mind we hope to have the pleasure of seeing you in a fortnight's time.

We have got the Mare in again and she is coming round very nicely. She came home very poor. I hope your Grandmother and Aunt are better in health and that you get on alright without a maid. I think we shall have a busy time for you on Good Friday.

Now as your time is drawing to a close at the School I trust it may be some service to you in after life. It will have brought you in contact with fresh School-mates, perhaps some of them may remain friends for life.

Now there are one or two things I should like to particularly draw your attention to for after life.

I expect your Teachers have given you instructions in keeping all your Utensils clean, and as a Confectioner's Bakehouse is very liable to become dirty, that you should pay attention to.

The first duty of a business man is to be <u>always</u> clean in himself, and never in such a condition as to be unfit to see your best customer. Do not forget that all the customers are your customers and you should give <u>everyone</u> as far as possible your personal attention, as a very little thing sometimes loses you a customer, and there are plenty of Tradespeople on the look out.

The first thing when you open your Shop is to see that the front is nice and clean and if any swilling is necessary get it done early, then it will be dry for customers, and will many times save your Shop from becoming dirty…

Of course you will meet a great variety of characters in your class, so you will in every grade of society. If ever it should be your duty to have the control of men, I trust you will be as forbearing as possible and use no irritation, always avoid bad language and never allow it to be used in your presence.

Then again there is the question of sending goods home, a very important one. Always be in time, and do not disappoint anyone you have promised with regard to bread.

I think you know my view on that, viz:- the Baker should be at the customer's door every day at the same time; you then, many times save your customers the necessity of coming from the top of the house to attend to you…

I must now close. Your mother and Grandmother join me in wishing you every success at your School and in after life.

Trusting this will find you all quite well, and that we shall see you shortly,
Believe me to be your
          Affectionate
            Father.

Frank's last letter to Tom

Tea-rooms and Bakeries

live'. The Victorian terraces and villas on Billing Road are still attractive a century later, although most of them are now offices.

Ada and Sarah had both been made to work in the confectionery shop which was part of the tea-room, but the other daughter, Elizabeth, rebelled and determined to become a teacher. With the introduction of compulsory education this was a profession that must have been growing in popularity among young women.

Frank was a Congregationalist and attended the Doddridge chapel, which his father had attended on first arriving in Northampton. Edna remembers her mother's stories about how she, Elizabeth, refused to attend the family's place of worship:

'It was a very well attended church, but mother liked the new, absolutely full Princes Street Baptist chapel, and she went there and was married there in 1908 at the age of 26. She wouldn't get married till she had earned her maximum rate at teaching - 25s a week. It must have been terrible for a girl who been brought up in a business house in a town with gas and everything - going into a little cottage in the country with only coal fires and oil lamps. It must have been terrible for her.'

Billing Road from the General Hospital, ca. 1900

Tea-rooms and Bakeries

Elizabeth's 'cottage in the country' was in Cogenhoe, for her husband was one of the Mann brothers whose father owned the shoe factory in the village. The factory was built behind the pub and had a row of houses close by for the shoe workers. The site is now occupied by the Yorks bus depot. Edna recalls:

'My great-grandfather and my grandfather and my great uncle built three different houses in the village - three Edwardian villas. Great-grandfather always believed that when he died we should move up into his house and that would go on forever, but there were no sons to carry on.'

Some of Edna's stories sound like the plot of a 19th century novel - she can remember the marriage schemes of her father's mother:

'The Manns put an advertisement in - they wanted three girls in the closing room. Well, these three girls knew that there were a lot of Mann brothers that were single, so they made up their minds that they would apply for the jobs and marry them. And they did. My grandmother was one of them!'

The Mann family was Non-Conformist like the Adams, and it is interesting to hear the comments of a local J.P., Mr. Brook-Taylor, when he talked to Edna about her grandfather Mann being a magistrate in the early years of the 20th century:

'Your grandfather must have been the most extraordinary man, if he was a Non-Conformist. In those days it was definitely only landed gentry and Tories who were magistrates. To be a Non-Conformist and a <u>businessman</u> - my goodness he was outstanding. It was almost closed shop for the gentry.'

These comments are interesting also in connection with the experiences of Edna's other great-grandfather, Thomas Adams, and serve to explain the difficulties and antagonism described in chapter 6 when Thomas was trying to be accepted as a magistrate.

The divide between Church of England people and Non-Conformists did not just affect the appointment of men in positions of political power. There was a deep social divide which now seems quite remarkable. As Edna relates:

'There was a big divide - mother says that her mother, Mrs. Frank Adams, told her that in her young days the people who were Church of England and lived along Billing Road, would walk on one side of the road to go to All Saints' or St. Giles', and the Non-Conformists who went to College Street and Doddridge, walked on the other side, and never the twain should meet. Mother often told me that.

In the old days (of my parents and grandparents) you never went to anybody who wasn't Non-Conformist. For instance, you would have your coal from Wiggins' because they were Baptist. You would go for a solicitor to Hensman, Jackson and Chamberlain because they were Non-Conformist. You'd go to Higgins' along the Parade because they were Baptists. You'd only go with your own sort. You'd never go to a store that wasn't "your own".

Colours

Prussian Blue:
The best and most essential is Prussian blue, which may be bought from the druggist in a powder that is perfectly soluble in water without any acid.
Ordinarily Prussian Blue will not dissolve in water unless a small quantity of oxalic acid (a powerful poison) is added, but the pure soluble Prussian Blue which is a preparation of iron which is perfectly harmless, may be added to water to produce any depth of colour. 1½ grams to 3oz water would be sufficient.

Cochineal and Carmine:
Cochineal is prepared from the cochineal insects which are mostly obtained from some of the Spanish Islands. The insect is very small and has a silvery appearance. The colour is extracted from these by the acid and alkaline solution in reaction. A good red colour may be obtained by taking ¼oz of powdered cochineal, ¼oz of ground alum, ¼oz of caltartar, ¹⁄₂₀oz of cream of tartar. Mix all these ingredients well together with 6oz warm water and 4oz spirits of wine. Allow solution to stand 24 hours, then filter and bottle ready for use...

Yellow:
To one ounce of saffron add 2oz each of alcohol and water and allow to stand for several hours. The liquid thus prepared is of a deep orange colour and when diluted or used in small quantities will impart a beautiful yellow shade to all forms of sugar.

Green:
How to extract green colour from spinach: Wash thoroughly 1 peck of spinach and put it dripping wet into a mortar to be thoroughly pounded into a pulp. Put this into a strong cloth and wring out all the juice possible on a dish. Pour this into an untinned copper pan. Place it over a fire and stir it with a silver spoon until it begins to curdle, then pour it upon a fine air sieve to drain off all excessive moisture that comes off. Afterwards add to the green colouring that comes off from the spinach an equal quantity of sugar, a tablespoonful of spirits of wine and a pinch of powdered alum. Bottle ready for use.

Extracts from Thomas Rigby Adams' college recipe book (ca. 1900)

Cake Making

To make rich or plain fruit cakes best butter should be used out of which all salt and water has been worked. Otherwise the salt will cause the cake to have a dried speckled appearance. The water, if not worked out will cause much trouble by curdling the mixing, which in turn will spoil the texture of the cake causing it to be rough and uneven.

The sugar used should be caster sugar for a small or large madeira and rich Genoa cakes, and fine grained, which may be tested by holding up a handful. This, if fine grained, will run down between the fingers like sand.

In using eggs these should be of a good quality with strong whites and yolks of a good colour, remembering that rich cakes depend upon the whites of eggs for aerating and yolks for adding flavour.

After the butter and sugar is thoroughly beaten up, the eggs should be added - for a 2lb mixing not more than 2 at a time, as the adding of the eggs too quickly will cause them to curdle. When all the eggs are beaten into a mixing, the flour should be stirred in very lightly, but thoroughly to give a clear and smooth batter. Beating cake mixings up after flour is added will cause the cakes to come up in the oven with a pitched appearance and eat tough.

Eggs

...Irish or Italian eggs are preferable to most of the other kinds. French, Danish and Hungarian contain good whites, but have very little colour. Russian eggs are mostly small and inclined to be weak...

Extracts from Thomas Rigby Adams' college recipe book (ca. 1900)

Tea-rooms and Bakeries

When the Adnitt brothers started in business, (the department store now occupied by Debenham's on the Drapery), *they discussed this, and one decided to go to All Saints' and one to College Street, or they wouldn't have got the trade.'*

Like Sarah, the eldest daughter, Ada, married into another eminent Non-Conformist business family of the town - the Hawtins, who owned a building business. Ada's husband, Frederick, was the son of the founder. In 1910 they had a son, Alfred, who carried on the business and was responsible for building the Westone Hotel. Alfred grew up to follow the family tradition of becoming a director of the Northampton Town and County Building Society and also of being a loyal Non-Conformist worker - this time at Mount Pleasant Baptist church.

Frank had a big family, and as has been seen in the chapter on the early days of the building society, he was keen to enhance his income by buying some of the plots of land that were becoming available through the building society. He eventually owned many houses off Kettering and Wellingborough Road and four old cottages at the bottom of St. John's Street, near Cow Lane. Edna remembers his plans:

'Frank used to buy the building society properties for £150 and rent them out, and in no time they'd be his. He had this wonderful plan that by the age of 55 they'd all be his.'

Along with his interest in property Frank, like his father and brothers, was also very involved with local politics and the building society,. He carried on his father's support for the Bradlaugh cause during the 1890s when the new party called the 'Bradlaugh Radicals' was created in opposition to the Liberals and Conservatives.

1892 was the first year he stood for election to the town council, but it was not until 1897 that he won a seat. Significantly, this was the year when the Liberal and Radical Union party agreed not to stand against the Bradlaugh Radicals. The following year Frank was elected to the Board of Guardians where he served until his death. His work involved assessing applicants for relief, and he was said to be eager to change the traditional way of dealing with the needs of the poor. Instead of putting the unemployed to work breaking up stone, he supported a scheme to establish a kind of farm colony where the unemployed could work on the land. However, his ideas were not supported by the majority of the Board of Guardians.

His work for the building society made him eminently suitable when the Council decided to re-assess the rateable values of the Borough properties. The task was carried out in 1900, the year when the borough boundaries were extended and the tramways were electrified.

Tea-rooms and Bakeries

Despite his hard work on the various council committees, Frank was said to be a poor public speaker and for this reason perhaps, he lost his seat in 1900. His council work carried on, however, as he was then made an Alderman.

As far as the building society was concerned, he had been made a director back in 1891 and stood unsuccessfully for election to be Secretary in 1902. His other area of voluntary work was in the National Association of Master Bakers and Confectioners, where he was several times Vice-President and had to travel widely as a judge in baking competitions.

So much time did he spend on these various activities that his grandson, Philip, declares:

'Frank was a very far-seeing man. He was very well read, very fond of Shakespeare, but what he did - he spent too much time looking after the Council instead of his own business! I reckon his business suffered because of the time he devoted to his Council work.'

Thomas Rigby with his fellow students, ca. 1895
(Thomas is bottom left)

In any event, Frank did not have many years left to live in 1900. Six years later he died, at the young age of 47. Thomas Rigby was in Holland visiting a yeast factory with students from the Polytechnic, and returned early to arrive two hours before his father died. Frank's death precipitated a startling sequence of events which must have caused considerable dismay for the young man.

Thomas would naturally have expected to inherit his father's share in Adams Bros. However, in those days when one partner in a business died, the law gave the surviving partner the option of buying the other's share of the business. To Thomas' dismay that is what Wallace chose to do. Frank's widow, Elizabeth, inherited his estate, which included the shop at 22 Marefair, but in the meantime Thomas had to become an employee of Wallace at Adams Bros. When Elizabeth died, Frank's estate was divided among the children, so Thomas inherited the shop and the other children inherited the various properties and money which Frank had accumulated over the years.

Edna recalls the important effect of Frank's investments on her own education:

'Mother sold two of the houses that she'd inherited, and that's why she could afford to send us to the Girls' Grammar School. We always said it was the Adams money that sent us to that school.'

Thomas' brother, Frank, was working for J. & G. Higgins, a local shop, and did not seek involvement in the bakery business. When the First World War came, Frank joined up and trained with the 7th Northamptonshire Regiment, but while serving in Dorset he contracted tubercular meningitis and tragically died.

While Thomas went to work for his uncle he had to employ a manageress for the shop while living with one of his sisters at Primrose Hill on the Barrack Road. His consternation and dissatisfaction are not hard to imagine, as he found himself not only working for his uncle, but buying bakery goods from him to sell in his own shop.

However, Thomas Rigby had not only inherited a shop - he had inherited the same courage and determination which his grandfather had displayed about sixty years previously. Deciding to leave the employ of his uncle, he determined on setting up his own bakery and making his own goods to sell at Marefair. There was one drawback - he did not have a bakehouse or the money to build or buy one. He did however have a friend, a Mr. Marston, who owned a bakehouse in St. Andrews Road. Mr. Marston let him use the oven when it was finished with for the day. All that Thomas baked had to be put on a handcart and pushed about a quarter of a mile along the cobbled streets to Marefair. After a few months he managed to rent his own bakehouse in Narrow Lane, between Broad Street and St. Andrews Road. It was not even as big as an

Tea-rooms and Bakeries

WHERE NOW THE BAKERS' BOYS?

Time was, in the 1920s, when Northampton possessed no fewer than 132 bakehouses and of these, about 80 to 90 were in use. Today, how many bakers are there in Northampton? A score? I doubt if there are more, probably not as many.

What a common sight it was in the 1920s to see the two-wheeled, hooded, horse-drawn bakers' carts and horse-drawn vans. And the same can be said of seeing people take their Sunday dinners to the bakehouse and welcoming the bakers' boys crying their hot-cross buns at Easter...

In 1918, when I first started out to work at what was then Harris', at the corner of Oliver Street, a boy leaving school was then paid 6s and it meant for me a 7am start with a 7pm finish, and a 3pm finish on Saturdays, which was the half day...

Here are some of the bakehouses I can remember - Gray Street, Hood Street, Cowper Street, Carey Street, Hunter Street, Earl Street, Overstone Road, Great Russell Street, Clousham Street, Alcombe Road, Raglan Street, Portland Street, Dover Street, Market Street, Artizan Road, Billington Street, Adams Avenue, Adnitt Road (3), Roe Road, Abington Grove, Abington Avenue, Derby Road, Oliver Street, Milton Street, Shelley Street, Junction Road (2), Stanhope Road, Burleigh Road, Knightley Road, Alpha Street, Arthur Street, Semilong Road (at St. Paul's Road corner), Baker Street, St. Andrews Road (Cambridge Street corner), St. Andrews Road (Gordon Street corner), Gordon Street, Salisbury Street, Northcote Street, Lower Adelaide Street, Leslie road, Gladstone Terrace, Nelson Street (2), Louise Road, Lorne Road, Oak Street, Maple Street, Elm Street, Campbell Street (rear of Bull Hotel), Brook Street (1 - top and bottom), Upper Priory Street, Francis Street, Crane Hill (rear of Welcome Inn), Grafton Place, Grafton Street, Bellbarn Street (down a jetty), St. Andrews Street, Scarletwell Street (3), Bath Street, Bath Terrace (St. Andrew's Road corner), King Street, Windsor Terrace, Silver Street (rear of Bearward Arms), College Street (Jeyes' Jetty corner), St. Katherines Street, Horsemarket (no. 63), St. Marys Street, Marefair (no. 22), Marefair (no 56), Woolmonger Street, Green Street, Augustine Street, Bridge Street (no. 48), Collingwood Road, Birchfield Road East, Swan Street (rear of pub), St. Leonards Road, Southampton road, Main Road, Far Cotton, St. James Road (no. 63), Ambush Street, Althorp Road, Greenwood Road, St. James' Park Road, Argyle Street, Sandhill Road, The Riding, Dychurch Lane, St. Edmunds Road (2), Cyril Street, Palmerston Road, St. Edmunds Street (no. 59), West Street (2 - top and bottom), Vernon Street, Bouverie Street (no. 27), South Street, Melbourne Street, Barry Road, Wycliffe Road, Allen Road (2), King Edward Road, Thursby road, High Street, Kingsthorpe, Washington Street, Harborough road (no. 37), Sheep Street, The Drapery (ovens under the tram lines), Margaret street (2), Craven Street, Military Road corner, Poole Street, 58 Newland (now part of Lotus Ltd.), Kerr Street, 43 Ladys Lane, Wellington Street, 38 Upper Mounts, 54 Wellingborough road, 230 Wellingborough Road, 266 Wellingborough Road, Oakwood Road, 5 Regent Square, and one in Narrow Lane.

N.I. 3.4.1958

ordinary kitchen and the goods still had to be taken via a cart to the shop, but at least it was his own. His son, Philip, sees it as a momentous occasion:

'The lane is still there. I often go and have a look at it. The bakehouse building is still there.'

Happily for Thomas, in the midst of his struggle to keep his shop going he met and married his wife Gertrude Phillips from Brackley in 1913. Gertrude had been a shop assistant at Adnitt's department store, living in in the staff quarters on the top floor of the shop (now Debenham's). Gertrude was a forthright character and a good business woman and was able to look after the shop after their marriage. One of the former directors of Adams bakery, Iris Vickers, can remember Gertrude vividly:

'She was lovely and very outspoken. She ruled the shop girls with a rod of iron. If she walked into the shops and the biscuit tins were an eighth of an inch out of line, they would be told off.'

On marrying, Tom and Gertrude moved back to the flat above the shop and were all set to face the challenge and build up the business all over again. As Philip says:

'Thomas had to start from scratch. It must have been galling.'

Unfortunately it was not long before the outbreak of the First World War. As Tom was a confectioner rather than a bread baker, his was not a reserved occupation and he had to join the army, going to serve in France for two years as a signaller in the Garrison Artillery. It is not known exactly why, but he was quite poorly on his return after the war. At all events the bustle of life on Marefair in the heart of Northampton was no longer a prospect which Tom could face, and he finally decided to sell the business and buy a bakery at Helmdon, in the depths of the Northamptonshire countryside.

Philip can still remember the busy life around Marefair and the abrupt change on moving to the country:

'Back in Marefair it was all shops. There was King's the butcher, Latimer and Crick in the Horsemarket. Behind the bakehouse was Grose's garage - they ran their double decker buses from there. I can just remember a girl in the shop named Miss Wallace. I remember her taking me out into the street and holding me up to look at an airship that was coming over.'

Life in the country suited Philip and he traces his present love of country pursuits and hunting to those early years at Helmdon. It did not, however, suit his father. Edna Bodily remembers her uncle's difficulties:

Back in the 1920s, after seven years at Helmdon Tom and Gertrude decided that they would be able to run a far more successful business in the town. A small bakehouse came up for sale in Northampton on the corner of Wellingborough Road and West Street. By coincidence it was nearly opposite

Tea-rooms and Bakeries

the Adams Bros. bakery, but that was not to stop them. Tom's business was slightly different anyway as he was a confectioner rather than a bread baker.

Philip recalls the workings of his father's oven on West Street:
'There were two ovens - one on top of the other, and to get to the bottom oven the stock (on the oven door) was at floor level and you had to go down a pit. The oven was then waist-high. I worked in there. The coal used to go in the cellar and we carried it up each day, enough for the day's baking and that was put in a little bunker by the side of the oven. You see there were two fires, one for each oven. They had to be lit. You opened the dampers on the oven to create a draught. When the fires burned down and the oven was hot enough, you shut the dampers. We used to get a scuffle - that's a long pole with a sack on the end, dip it in water, put it in the oven and scuffle the ashes to the side, so that the oven floor was clean to put the bread in. By golly that was hard work. Then we put the bread in with the peel and fetched it out again after 45 minutes.

You let the fire down, but if you wanted another batch, when you'd drawn the first batch out, you'd open the dampers and the fire would burn up and give it another flush of heat.'

Thomas' bakery on West Street

In Wellingborough Road everyone lived 'over the shop'. It presented problems when Gertrude was trying to do two jobs at once - cook for her family and go to serve in the shop when required. Philip recalls often having burnt tomatoes for breakfast because his mother would have to leave off cooking when someone came into the shop.

Edna remembers how happy life was in the flat above the bakery: *'We used to sit up in the front room and watch the cycle parade go by. It was very much a little family shops area then. Wellingborough Road was much better than Kettering Road - it was all very nice family-owned shops.'*

(For anyone who has read the first book in this series, 'From Behind the Counter', it is amusing to see how Edna's image of Wellingborough Road compares to the image presented by the workers in Arthur Watts' furniture shop on Kettering Road. In contrast they described the Wellingborough Road as 'a

Tea-rooms and Bakeries

shocking street', being full of pubs and the rowdiness associated with closing time.)

Tom's business flourished on West Street, for there were a great many potential customers among all the workers in the nearby factories:

'In those days the Sears factory and Manfield's shoe factory were at their height, and on Friday pay-day all the girls had a cream cake when they went back at lunchtime. Another lady up the road - a Mrs. Kirby - she said there was a living in stockings from those girls. There were so many of them who worked at Manfield's. Aunty Gertie said there was almost a living in cream cakes from them.'

So during the 1920s there were no less than six bakery businesses owned by members of Thomas Adams' family - W.Q. Adams (now run by Percy), Adams Bros. (run by Oliver), Thomas Rigby's, Edgar's (still on the corner of Allen Road), Arthur's (on Augustin Street) and Herbert's (on Whitworth Road).

How these various businesses eventually all united again into just one Adams bakery forms the story of the final chapters. However, as the 1930s began to unfold, there was no sign of such a development.

Kettering Road from Abington Square end, ca. 1910

Tea-rooms and Bakeries

Edgar's bakery on the corner of Wellingborough Road and Allen Road

Tom went up in the world when he moved his business to Kingsthorpe in 1933, buying a bakehouse on Washington street, off the Harborough Road and next to the Cock Hotel.

Edgar opened a confectionery shop at 113 Bridge Street before finally retiring to Leighton Buzzard. By 1928 the bakery shop he had built at 337 Wellingborough Road had been bought by a relatively new bakery business that had opened up in town in 1908 - J.C. Stevens.

Arthur eventually left Northampton and Herbert retired from Whitworth Road, his son finally working for Tom in Kingsthorpe.

W.Q. Adams was going from strength to strength as Percy began to go into the restaurant trade as well, opening the Wedgwood Café in 1928.

Oliver also saw the potential in the café business and at the same time as Percy opened the Wedgwood, Oliver opened the Corner House on Wood Hill. He had already bought Tom's confectionery shop on Marefair and still ran the tea-room at 55 Kettering Road.

Tea-rooms and Bakeries

So the town seemed full of Adams shops and cafés. There was still a lot of competition from other bakeries, but the name of Adams was now a familiar one to the people of Northampton. The threat that was to come was not from other bakers in the town. It came from across the Atlantic, and was a very simple innovation that soon became enormously popular - sliced bread. The implications of this new idea will be explored in the next chapter, as Thomas and Percy both try to build up their businesses and grapple with the challenges that are presented by the phenomenon of 'the white sliced'.

Chapter 9

'THE BEST THING SINCE SLICED BREAD'

It is not known which enterprising baker in the United States first thought of slicing a loaf of bread before selling it. However it began, the practice soon spread, for it was found that bakers could sell more loaves that way.

When the idea reached England in the 1930s the bakers in the north were quicker to introduce it to their customers than those in the south. The northern bakers were generally more prosperous than the southern for they were usually wholesale bakers - that is, they sold their bread to corner shops. Bakers in the south, on the other hand, tended to deliver their bread from door to door. As a result, the northern bakeries were the firms who could afford to invest in the slicing and wrapping machinery that was now required.

The Second World War halted the spread of the new loaf - for the simple reason that the war led to restrictions on the use of paper, and sliced bread had to be wrapped. The huge amount of paper required would have had to be imported. As a result, Tom and Percy were able to postpone the day when they had to meet the new demand for the white sliced.

Nevertheless, new demands were still being made on bakers for the war brought new recommendations on the kind of bread to be baked - the new National loaf had to be made from flour with an extraction rate of 85%. This was rather like wheatmeal bread today, and was more nutritious than the normal 70% flour. An 85% extraction rate saved resources by enabling more of the wheat to be used for human food. It was not until the middle of 1941 that the National loaf was officially introduced - and its initial scarcity indicates the prevalence of white bread at that period. In response to local complaints that the National loaf was difficult to find, an article in the Northampton Independent declared:

'The situation was that some people tried to obtain the loaf immediately the Government had popularised it and before the necessary flour was available in the town... Leading bakeries in the town guarantee they can supply the loaf...

'The Best Thing since Sliced Bread'

USE NATIONAL MARK ALL-ENGLISH FLOUR AND WHOLEMEAL.

Milled entirely from home-grown wheat. Unbleached by artificial means, and free from all chemicals except self-raising materials.

NATIONAL MARK STRAIGHTS
(Blue label),
and
NATIONAL MARK PATENTS
(Green label), for biscuits, pastries, etc,

NATIONAL MARK SELF-RAISING
(Red label), for cakes, scones, buns, sponges, puddings, and general household purposes.

NATIONAL MARK WHOLEMEAL,
for digestive biscuits, brown scones, etc.

NATIONAL MARK (YEOMAN) STRAIGHTS
or
NATIONAL MARK (YEOMAN) PATENTS
for bread.

Support English wheat-growers by insisting on National Mark flour and bread made from that flour.

Look for the　　　　National Mark

on the Bag.

Issued by the Minister of Agriculture and Fisheries.

National Mark Flour advertisement, *c.* 1930.

'The Best Thing since Sliced Bread'

'A word to the prejudiced: The National loaf is ... far better than the standard loaf of the last war. The "dirty white loaf" as it came to be known in the last war was not popular. The National loaf today is different in many ways, even in colour. It is a brownish loaf.

Mr. W.Q. Adams told the Independent..."It is the best bread that can be eaten. It does not contain a lot of bran and is digestible." '

N.I. 16.5.1941

Tom Adams was also interviewed by the local press for his opinion on the National loaf -

'It is full of the body building vitamins so essential to health in war-time. By buying wheatmeal loaves you not only fortify yourself, but you are saving vital shipping space, so essential an economy in these days when the whole country is geared to the highest degree on war production, and space in ships can be used to more advantage.'

So the war postponed the need for Adams to face up to the question of how to compete with the big bakery firms who had begun supplying their bread neatly sliced and wrapped. Methods of baking and delivering continued much as they had done in the inter-war years.

Jess Lay, whose reminiscences were mentioned in chapter 4, recalls the scene on Derby Road where Percy's bakery produced a large amount of confectionery:

'I remember watching the men on the forecourt of W.Q. Adams - in about 1946. They would put long trestle tables outside, piled up with doughnuts they had just baked. They had a tin of jam and one man would split the doughnuts and one would dip his hands in the jam and squirt it into the doughnuts. He would never spill a drop.'

Richard Patching, who is still an employee of Adams, and Ted Frost, who worked for them until his death in 1999, can remember at first hand what it was like to work at Derby Road in the early 1950s.

'The Best Thing since Sliced Bread'

Eat *more* BREAD

It is cheap
It is nourishing!

Nowhere in the great wheat-producing countries of the world can you buy good, fresh, wholesome bread as *cheaply* as you can here in Great Britain.

It is baked in spotlessly clean bakeries by skilled bakers who know how to make bread light, delicious and nourishing. Eat more white or brown bread, it is all highly nutritious and recommended by the best medical authorities.

British

BREAD

Your best and cheapest food

**Give the children more bread—
it's good for them.**

Between the wars; Ministry of Agriculture, and Fisheries, *c.* 1930.

'The Best Thing since Sliced Bread'

Ted started at the bakery at the age of 15:

'For the whole of the first year I did nothing but clean tins - flat black sheet tins 18" by 30". On Saturday morning you couldn't see me because I used to do them all. I stood them on edge. You had to put them in the oven to warm them to make them easier to clean.'

In the 1950s W.Q. Adams concentrated on the confectionery side of the trade, but Ted remembers how they made a few 'cobs' (crusty rolls).

'They were all slipped. A slip is a long piece of thin wood about 6' long. We used to put all the cobs on it, put it in the oven and "slip it off". It used to line them up in the oven. If you got them wrong you were left with a big gap in the middle. You'd have a big shovel to pull them out. They were all done on the hearth, on the bottom. There was nothing on trays - they were all hearth-done.'

Meringues were made in the side-flue chamber of the oven.

'The actual fire would be in the side-flue chamber. We used to fire it, let it die, take the fire out and then put a hessian sack on a pole, wet it, swirl it round, get all the muck out, then bake the meringues. The main fire-chamber was at the back, heating the pipes and then the heat went forward. The side-flue was very very messy!'

Although W.Q. Adams' new ovens had made the papers in the early part of the century, the machinery available to the workers there in the 1950s seems quite basic:

'We used to have four mixers, belt-driven with a leather belt. If you wanted anything done, you had to have the donkey engine at the end going. You had to slip the belt on the machine and then carry on. It wouldn't mix very hard because it was belt-driven. That was about the only bit of machinery we really had.'

Before Ted had to join the army at the age of 18 he was 'promoted' to 'coke man'.

'I used to have to go in Sunday nights at 10 o'clock and work till 6. I had to get the ovens hot so that people in the daytime could come and work them. Then I got someone to help at 4 o'clock in the morning to do the rolls.

There was a lot to do at night. I had to light the fires. I had two in one oven and three in the other end. Then I had the water boiler, which was a pot-bellied stove. You had to keep them all going all night. We never actually started making anything till about 4 am. I used to weigh things up and get things ready. I did that six days a week.'

From coke-man Ted graduated to doing the doughnuts and sausage rolls: *'I used to do sausage rolls individually - little bits of pastry. I used to cut them out in squares and do them individually, not like they do now, in the machines. It was all hand-done. In the stable yard where they had used to keep*

'The Best Thing since Sliced Bread'

the horses we used to do doughnuts on a little gas-ring. We used to get a bit of dough and actually fold the jam into a doughnut. You might pipe it in with a grease-proof bag. Then you'd seal the end and let it come up. On the gas-ring was a pan with hot fat in it. You did a dozen at a time. You dropped them in the fat. That's why there was always fingerprints on the doughnuts - because you had to pick them up with your hands. There used to be two of us. There was no room to do it indoors.'

Richard Patching has vivid memories of making the crumpets, which were obviously very popular:

'Above the stables we used to hoist the flour in 140lb bags with a hook wound down to the back of the lorry. This hot plate I worked on was about 30' long and I can't imagine how they got it up there. It must have weighed about 5-6 tons. I used to work on that 12 hours a day. We used to have to walk across the roof to get to the area where we made the crumpets. In those days we did 24,000 a day!'

Like Ted, Richard also got involved with the job of firing the ovens, but in his case it meant using his lunch break to walk up the road to another bakehouse in Oliver Street where he would get the coke up from the cellar to fire the ovens.

'The minute you took a shovelful of coke out of the cellar, you had an avalanche. So we had to wear a mask.'

The Kingsthorpe bakery with Thomas Rigby in the foreground

'The Best Thing since Sliced Bread'

BREAD
INTO BATTLE

The housewife deserves a bouquet for the part she is playing in the War effort, but she is falling down on one thing—the daily waste of bread. Too many crusts are being thrown away, or put into the pig bin. Wheat takes the lion's share of our shipping space. And even if waste of bread is as little as half an ounce per head of the population each day this means eight families of four waste a loaf a day, a town of 12,000—the size of Horsham—a sack a day and the whole country a shipload every twelve days—thirty ships a year! A whole convoy! Bread into battle—YES INDEED!

HOW TO KEEP THE LOAF FRESH

Make sure the loaf is quite cold before putting it away. The best way to keep bread fresh is to wrap it in a clean, dry cloth and store in a well ventilated place in a cupboard. Remember, bread must have air. If you keep it in a bin, be sure the bin is well ventilated; even with ventilation holes, keep the lid tilted. Keep the bin scrupulously clean. Wipe it out every day. Wash it out once a week and dry it thoroughly.

TO AVOID DRY LOAF ENDS

When you get to the last three inches of your loaf, place it crumb side down on the bread board—

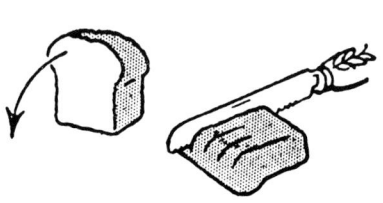

and cut this way. You'll eat the crust while it's fresh and you won't cut your fingers.

Wartime, 1939–45. Ministry of Food leaflet, 1944.
(Bread wasn't rationed until *after* the war.)

'The Best Thing since Sliced Bread'

Richard Patching's mention of a bakery in Oliver Street leads on to another side of Percy's business. He had not stood still as far as bakery shops were concerned, but had expanded during the 1930s so that by the time war broke out, he owned shops at 12 Kingsley Park Terrace (at the end of Oliver Street), 212 Kettering Road, 156 Beech Avenue, 1 Weedon Road, 28 Abington Street and 79 Abington Street (The Wedgwood Café) - each in a growing suburb of the town, with 28 Abington Street being a particularly important central location. By contrast his cousin Tom had to content himself with the West Street shop and his new bakery/shop on the Harborough Road at Kingsthorpe.

While the bakeries were carrying on as best they could during the war, the catering side of the business was growing. Oliver Adams' The Corner Shop Café and Percy's The Wedgwood were well-established popular cafés in the town now. Unfortunately for Percy, shortly after he had bought The Wedgwood in 1928, his son Norman died at the young age of 19. He had just completed his training at the London Polytechnic, but developed a skin eruption on his neck which finally led to blood poisoning from which he died. It was devastating for Percy to lose not only his son but also the heir to the family business. His daughter Barbara, however, who was 5 years younger than her brother, grew up to become a keen business woman and to display a great flair for catering. She was now heir to the business and when old enough, eagerly took over the running of The Wedgwood, even buying another restaurant in Towcester, called The Pickwick, in 1948.

It is said that Percy's sadness at losing his son led him to immerse himself in local politics. He was a Liberal councillor for St. Michael's Ward in 1932 and remained on the council for the next 24 years - following in the footsteps of his uncle and grandfather before him.

The loss of his son also led him to take a great interest in his nephew, Peter, who lived close by in Holly Road. Peter and his twin sister, Pam, were the children of Percy's sister, Winifred. Percy almost adopted Peter as a replacement son. Peter remembers helping in the office and the shop, alongside his mother. Percy's own wife, Nell, was of quite a weak disposition - every afternoon Percy would take her out for a ride in the country in his Armstrong-Siddeley.

The nearby Mount Pleasant Baptist chapel still played an important part in the lives of Percy and many of the Adams family - Percy was in fact made a deacon for life in 1924 until his death in 1969. In the history of the chapel it is interesting to note that Percy supported a proposal to create a Boys' Brigade in 1919, which was objected to by those who thought that it was too militaristic - it was of course very close to the end of the First World War.

The Mount Pleasant chapel made a particularly important contribution to the welfare of Northampton when the idea was conceived of providing long-

'The Best Thing since Sliced Bread'

term care for the elderly members of the Baptist and Congregational Churches of Northampton. This was the beginning of the foundation of the Bethany Homestead, which still flourishes today on Kingsley Road to the north of the Racecourse. The Hawtins (now related to the Adams by Frederick Hawtin's marriage to Frank's daughter Ada in 1907) were very involved with the project. Frederick's father gave the site and the foundation stone was laid in 1925. It was a sad loss to the church when Mr. Hawtin died in 1930, after over 30 years of service to the Baptist cause.

Frederick, Ada and their son, Alfred, contined to support Mount Pleasant, along with Ada's sister Elizabeth, Percy's sister Winifred, her children, and of course Percy and his family. So despite Thomas Adams' turning to secularism in the distant 1860s, many of his descendants still espoused the Non-Conformist cause, and in fact played a significant part in its work. Edna Bodily, one of Percy's cousins and another keen member of the Baptist church, is still a member of the management committee of the Bethany Homestead. Her sister Annie, who married the shoe manufacturer, Frank Webb, was also very involved with the management of the home, alongside her husband's family. It is such a family affair that Edna can comment with some amusement: *'When we sit round table in committee, we're all cousins or related in some way!'*

She is however concerned about the future, as the enthusiasm for the Baptist cause and for voluntary work in general wanes: *'I'm worried about who will come along to run it when the older generation is gone.'*

The Wedgwood Café, Abington Street, ca. 1956

'The Best Thing since Sliced Bread'

Meanwhile, as Percy strove to fill the void left by his son's death, he became fascinated by local history, and in particular the history of the site on which The Wedgwood was built, for when alterations were being made and the builders were working in the cellar, they found some very old stone walls three feet thick, a beautifully made stone well and a stone-built cistern, presumably for storing rain water.

Percy found that Speed's map of Northampton of 1610 shows the site to have been occupied by Gobion Manor and farm. In the early years of the 12th century Hugh Gobion, of Anglo-Saxon descent, had been granted considerable tracts of land in Northamptonshire (the village of Yardley Gobion, for example) and Hertfordshire. The land in Northamptonshire included a farm within the east wall of Northampton which became Gobion farm, and in about 1106 Hugh built himself a manor house there.

Percy visited nearby St. Giles' church and found a very old worn tomb where one of the early Gobions was buried. From 1160 - 1166 one of the Gobions was Sheriff of the town. Another story he discovered about the Gobion family in this period runs as follows:

'Earl Gobion, who lived in ye farmhouse in Abington Street of this town, killed a man in an election riot, but he got pardoned, and to quiet the town granted to the poor liberty to follow scythe and sickle in the fields of Northampton, called Gobion's farm to this day.'

In 1622 the farm and manor were sold to the Northampton Corporation who eventually sold off the land as plots for building. In 1925 the site was occupied by a fine house belonging to Mr. Lankester, a wine merchant, with two large bay windows and a picturesque doorway in the centre. Mr. A.R. Cleaver converted the house into three shops with flats above, so when Percy bought the property in 1928 there was not a great deal to be done. He let two shops on the left and changed the third shop into The Wedgwood shop and café. Upstairs were two large dining rooms, one of which Percy named 'The Gobion Room', and on the side there was also space for a Dance Room.

When further alterations were made in the 1950s Philip Adams, Tom's son, happened to be having a new house built at Kingsthorpe. He saw the builders drag a huge piece of beautiful white stone out of the Wedgwood cellar and asked them to take it up to his new house. A stone mason fitted it into the edge of his porch, and it can still be seen there today - one piece of stone, but behind it so many centuries of Northampton history stretching back to Domesday.

The Wedgwood was at one end of Abington Street. At the other end stood Oliver's Corner House Café. This too was very successful, and in fact Oliver's bakery business (still called Adams Bros) also grew quite considerably between the wars. He had bought back 22 Marefair from Tom; he opened shops

'The Best Thing since Sliced Bread'

The Corner House Café

at 28 Abington Grove, 27 St. Leonards Road (in Far Cotton), St. Michaels Road and 55 Harborough Road, thus covering a wide range of suburbs to the north-east and south of the town. Two of them (Harborough Road and St. Michaels Road) were rather close to his cousins', but there was of course a great demand still for corner bakeries. Not only had he acquired several new premises, he still had his two shops on the Kettering and Wellingborough Roads, all of them being supplied by the bakery at the foot of Adams Avenue.

Unfortunately for Oliver, his son, Michael, did not want to take over the business on returning from the army after the war, and so in 1946 Oliver sold the Oliver Adams business of The Corner House Café to James Oatley, and opened instead a country club and hotel at Cornhill, Pattishall, which also proved very successful.

It was Mr. Oatley who made the rather dramatic alteration to the café that is still remembered with affection by many Northamptonians today. His son, Kenneth, had been an RAF navigator in Bomber Command during the war and had the novel idea of making the basement look like the interior of a plane. The waitresses were to be dressed as air stewardesses in navy blue uniforms, the portholes would have paintings of aerial views by the famous local artist Osborne Robinson (who later also painted the murals outside Sainsbury's in the Grosvenor shopping centre), and the whole café was to be called The Clipper.

Forty grey aeroplane seats in groups of four with tables between them and luggage racks above were installed to create a very realistic atmosphere.

'The Best Thing since Sliced Bread'

Even the door to the kitchen was labelled 'Stewardesses' Pantry'; blinds could be pulled down over the painted windows, and the hum of the air-conditioning resembled the sound of aircraft engines. The name 'Clipper' referred to the huge Pan American Airways transatlantic flying boats.

It soon became a very popular dining place and was busy from 9am to 11pm, packed with a variety of people. Struggling young actors by the name of Frankie Howerd, Lionel Blair and Nigel Hawthorne used to go there for a meal. In those post-war days of austerity many ordinary Northampton people found it the nearest they would ever get to sitting in a real transatlantic airliner. Students and other young people used it as a meeting place - Anne Page of Wootton remembers her student days as a nurse when it was a monthly treat to go with her friend to The Clipper for tea *'and have one of their triple meringues filled with cream'*. The specialities of the house were an American-style lemon meringue pie and enormous knickerbocker glories costing half-a-crown (12.5p).

The present manager of The Corner House, Ann Reed, talked about her own memories of it in the 1940s:

'It was about the only place to go for young people - The Wedgwood was a bit posh. It was open in the evenings - never on Sundays, and on a Saturday you went to see a play and then came here for your sundae - and if there were some boys here as well, so much the better! There wasn't hardly anywhere else for young people to go to on a Saturday night.'

Catering was clearly a lucrative business in those days when the town possessed relatively few cafés. Both The Corner House, or The Clipper as it was later called, and The Wedgwood had become a welcome part of the local social scene.

One of Osborne Robinson's curved 'window' paintings in The Clipper (An Italian city - note the damage in the centre)

'The Best Thing since Sliced Bread'

*One of Osborne Robinson's 'window' paintings in The Clipper
(The New York skyline and the Queen Mary)*

With the war over, how were the bakery businesses faring? The arrival of sliced bread on the scene was a new phenomenon that had soon to be faced, although war-time restrictions on paper continued in force until 1950 and sliced wrapped bread was still not available. The grey-coloured National loaf was declining in popularity.

Philip, Tom's son, returned from the war in 1945 ready to take over his father's business on his retirement. He could see, as Tom and Percy knew only too well, that the war had been a struggle for the baking trade as with all businesses.

'After the war', he says, *'the bread business was in a terrible state. None of us could make any profit out of bread because it was subsidised during and after the war. Both flour and bread were subsidised by the government to keep the cost of a loaf down, for you see, bread was such an important part of the diet.*

In 1946 a tremendous lot of wheat was imported - from Canada and America or wherever the millers could get it. Exorbitant world prices were being charged and the flour mills had to be subsidised to keep the cost to the baker down. Then the bakeries were subsidised too so that the public didn't have to pay the true cost of a loaf of bread.

It was typical government accounting - with no profit margin hardly. One or two automatic bakeries had been set up in the country before the war and the government took <u>their</u> costings, which showed a profit, and applied that to the whole industry. So the small baker really was operating at a disadvantage. The large bread bakers and the Co-op had got automatic equipment - they could make a profit and we couldn't.'

'The Best Thing since Sliced Bread'

The Board of Directors: (left to right) Harry Edwards, Thomas Rigby Adams, F.Watts, Percy Adams, Harry Trusler, Barbara Adams, Philip Adams

It was fortunate for Percy's business, 'W.Q. Adams', that he still produced a lot of confectionery because the raw materials for that were rationed and Percy's products literally sold 'like hot cakes'. Philip realises that the confectionery side is what kept W.Q. Adams and T.R. Adams going. Having The Wedgwood also helped because again all the raw materials were rationed and Percy and Barbara could sell all the meals they could provide.

In the face of all the post-war problems it was not difficult to find a solution - both W.Q. Adams and T.R. Adams were going up the same roads delivering bread from their horses and carts. The two firms would just have to amalgamate, and this was done in July 1946. The seven directors were the four members of the Adams family - Percy, Thomas Rigby, Philip and Barbara, plus Harry Trusler, Harry Edwards and F. Watts.

Despite the economies made possible by the amalgamation bread sales still needed to be increased, but with the spread of new post-war housing estates this was not difficult. Delivery was modernised by replacing all the horses and carts with electric vans. It soon became clear that further changes were necessary in order to compete with the larger bakeries such as the Co-op. Adams would also have to invest in automated baking equipment.

'The Best Thing since Sliced Bread'

Percy and Tom had put the business, now called W.Q. & T.R. Adams, into a company but retained the freehold on the bakeries and the shops so that they could lease them back to the company. They were thus in a position to mortgage their various properties to raise money for the new baking plant.

The tremendous investment in an automated baking plant began with the business putting its name on a building plot in King's Heath, at the corner of Gladstone Road and Mill Lane. The land had previously been allotments and was now part of a brand new post-war suburb being designed and planned in the very latest style of cul-de-sacs and greenery.

'Both Percy and my father were wonderful really. In 1946 they were both getting to retirement age, and the thing to do in those days was either to sell the business or keep the property and live on the rents. When it got to amalgamating the businesses with a view to putting in an automatic bakery plant, both Percy and my father mortgaged all their properties to build the bakery at King's Heath. They were on the point of retiring. I thought that was wonderful. It was wonderful for my father too - from having the bakehouse in Marefair and pushing the goods on a truck to his shop, to see all this develop! It was a big risk. We all risked our shirts. I hadn't got any property then, but I borrowed from the bank too.'

Aerial view (looking west) of King's Heath in the early 1950s showing Adams' first automatic bakery plant (centre right) and the pork pie factory that later became their present premises (centre left)

'The Best Thing since Sliced Bread'

Philip, Tom and Percy chose their equipment from the most advanced bakery engineers of the time - Baker Perkins of Peterborough. Their Uniflow plant would bake six sacks (280lbs) of flour into bread within an hour, producing no less than 1200 loaves. Within 15 hours the new bakery plant could match the output that Adams had been achieving in a week. Unfortunately, shortage of materials meant that the delivery time for the plants was no less than four years. It was not even possible to obtain steel to erect a building quickly. Once delivery was agreed, Adams had then to raise the £30,000 needed for the equipment, plus another £30,000 for the main building.

'Towards the end of 1949 we were granted a license to put up a new bakery, and Henry Martin Ltd were engaged to build it with St. John Brown and Partners the architects. An exciting period followed, watching the new building grow.

It had a barrel vault roof in the upstairs dough room, which gave an open space with no internal supports so that the dough bowls could be moved about easily. The floor was covered with iron tiles as the twelve dough bowls were very heavy, each capable of holding 560lbs of flour and 140lbs of water.

The huge dough bowls in the new bakery plant (1950s)

'The Best Thing since Sliced Bread'

During the planning of the layout of the plant the question of heating and steam supply came up - we had not budgeted for heating the building as the bakeries we had experienced had always been small enough to be naturally heated by the ovens. So a boilerhouse was added and a Cocknam vertical boiler installed, fired by coal with an automatic stoker - another £7000 ! We were just glad that The Wedgwood and the shops were making useful profits.'

Just before building started in 1950 the government lifted the restriction on slicing bread - enough paper was now available for the wrapping. Philip and his family were not yet able to supply the public demand for the new loaf - despite the fact that they were shortly to be moving up to the new bakery at King's Heath. They could not help worrying. A lot of trade was being lost to the Co-op who had started slicing and wrapping their bread. Not only that, a firm in Coventry that was part of the Sunblest group had started coming into Northampton with the new bread and going round every little corner shop. On top of this, the government now lifted the subsidy on bread as well as the one on flour, and at the same time kept the price of bread quite low. Automatic bakeries with their large turnover were at an immediate advantage because they found it easier to make a profit.

Undaunted, Philip decided to buy a small second-hand hand-operated bread-slicing and wrapping machine. He and his men had to stand and slice the loaves by hand and wrap them in plain paper. He remembers very well the worry and fear for the future that he and his family felt at that time:

'We preserved a little bit of trade, but you can imagine, it was a tremendous worry when we'd risked all this money and could see our trade disappearing. Anyway we battled on. Added to that, the paper was all allocated to the people who'd been buying paper before the war, and we hadn't got an allocation. We managed to buy 1 ton of plain white poor quality paper which came in reels. The paper had to be cut into pieces just large enough to wrap one loaf. Then eventually with the automatic plant we got an automatic slicing and wrapping machine and an allocation of paper which was printed with our name.'

On July 21st 1951 the first loaf was baked at the new plant. The future suddenly became brighter. Once Adams could compete with the big bakeries such as the Co-op and Sunblest, their profits improved. As Philip says:

'Our trade simply rocketed. We could supply a lot of little shopkeepers in Northampton, and we gradually bought vans and widened our wholesale rounds to Wellingborough, Kettering, Rushden and so on. And the trade! We just couldn't keep up with it. It was unbelievable. The first new vans we bought were of one ton capacity and we soon discovered they were too small to carry a day's sale.

In the 1950s up to 1960 we were growing. That's when the small family baker started to go out of business. It's sad, but that's what happened.'

'The Best Thing since Sliced Bread'

The automatic bread slicing and wrapping machine (1950s)

Adams had of course been 'a small family baker' for nearly 100 years, and they were lucky - or perhaps brave enough - to invest in a major plant bakery that enabled them to compete with other large concerns keen to deliver their white sliced loaves to Northampton.

By November of 1951 they had at last managed to break even financially. By Christmas they were baking 500 sacks of flour into bread weekly and had begun to operate three shifts. They expanded their range of products when they bought a second oven which had a metal sole to enable them to bake Vienna bread and rolls and other small loaves. Capital allowances on new machinery and equipment was 100% to encourage industry to rebuild after the war, and so Adams did not have to pay tax and just re-invested their growing profits.

The Adams family could now enjoy their success and look back with nostalgia not only on a century of business but on the mayoralty of their founder, Thomas Adams, in 1884 and 1885, for seventy years later in 1952 Percy donned the chain of office like his grandfather. A study of Percy's year as mayor is a fascinating opportunity to reflect on the changes which the town, and society in general, had undergone since the late Victorian period.

Business however never stands still. Just when Adams thought they had survived the demise of the corner bakery, another threat appeared, in the form of the ever-powerful millers. Not only that, yet another phenomenon came along from America that would bring the whole food industry in turmoil. The story of these new developments belongs in the final two chapters.

Chapter 10

MAYOR OF NORTHAMPTON - 70 YEARS ON

When Thomas Adams was made Mayor the hall was thrown open to the public and the speeches were greeted by cheers, boos and hisses. At least no bottles or other missiles were hurled at the platform, although this had been known to happen in the past - the most notorious incident taking place in 1665 when the outgoing Mayor, Francis Pickmer, expressed his hatred for the newly elected Mayor, John Friend. (See illustration.) As society became more overtly respectable, such goings-on became unacceptable and the Mayor-making took place behind closed doors in the presence of ticket-holders only.

Percy was always a popular councillor. When he first won an election in the early 1930s he had captured a Conservative stronghold, St. Michael's ward. It was not perhaps so surprising, for his electorate already knew and trusted him as their local baker. He had demonstrated progressive ideas concerning education and the moral welfare of the town and had already been asked twice to be Mayor prior to his acceptance in 1952. The ill health of his wife, Nell, had prevented him from accepting, but when his daughter, Barbara, agreed to take over the duties of Mayoress there was no reason to refuse. His acceptance meant that there was no longer any Liberal voice on the Council. From the days in 1900 when the Liberal party had won all the seats in the town, Percy was now the only Liberal left.

He clearly felt the need to point out the spiritual dilemma facing the new post-war generation. His speech bears an interesting similarity to the words of the new Mayor in 1946, Fred Watts, who played an important part in the first book of this series, 'From Behind the Counter'.

Percy was a devout Baptist, just as Fred Watts had been a devout Methodist. He addressed his words to the young people of the town:

'Our ideas of truth, goodness, beauty and justice are based on the Sermon on the Mount. We have never questioned the authority of Jesus of Nazareth, but you are in a different age; you have to make a choice.

Will you follow the religion of Jesus, that of love, or the religion of Karl Marx as exemplified in Russian Communism, the religion of hatred?'

C & E 22.5.1952

When Bottles were thrown at Mayors

The outgoing Mayor, Francis Pickmer, had the Town Hall locked up, held the key himself and refused to allow the members of the Council to enter. They broke open the doors, however, and elected Friend. Then Pickmer had his revenge by concocting a plot charging Friend with treason against King Charles II, by having expressed disapproval of some of the doings of 'the Merry Monarch'.

This accusation led to a warrant being issued by the then Lord Lieutenant of Northamptonshire and Friend was arrested and taken to Lord Cockayne at Rushton Hall. The new Mayor's friends went in hot pursuit, however, procured his release on £1000 bail and brought him back in triumph to Northampton.

Then Pickmer refused to allow Friend to be sworn in as Mayor before him saying he was 'a fanatic and a traitor'. By this time the town was in a ferment through Pickmer setting it at defiance.

But there was one higher than the Mayor at that time and he was the Recorder Lord Manchester. He lost no time in responding to appeals to visit the town and was met at Billing Bridge by 300 Northampton men on horseback. On arrival in the town, the Recorder was assured that the wealth and might of the borough were with the new Mayor and consequently the Recorder allowed him to take the oaths of office before him.

But the stubborn Pickmer had not finished his opposition. His next step was resolutely to refuse to give up the Mace. All threats and appeals to him to surrender it to the Recorder were useless so the Recorder sent a message to Parliament, then sitting at Oxford because of the Plague. Parliament hastened to vindicate the majesty of the law. The Sergeant-at-Arms arrived in Northampton with a force to arrest Pickmer. He was locked up in Oxford gaol but it was a whole fortnight before he relented by begging forgiveness and confessing where he had hidden the Mace.

He was ordered to pay several hundreds of pounds for expenses, and was disfranchised, dismissed from the Corporation and rendered ever after incapable of accepting any public office.

(Meanwhile, Friend lived to be Mayor four times and when he died he left The Black Boy Hotel in Northampton and other properties for the benefit of Northampton's poor.)

N.I. 30.5.1952

He also referred to other differences in the society around him, comparing it to previous centuries such as the time when his grandfather had lived. The atmosphere of events such as the Mayor-making was certainly quieter and less rowdy, but there were other developments which he felt were far from being improvements:

'The Council has much less power and liberty than then. We have very largely to obey orders from the Government because they perhaps provide half of the money.'

Coupled with this loss of liberty was the loss of individual thought in Council meetings:

'The pre-arrangement of voting takes away the value and dignity of the Council meeting and renders it merely an exercise ground for public speakers and gives an air of unreality to the debates when, no matter what is said, each member knows from the beginning how he is going to vote...What a refreshing thing it would be if we had a Council meeting where every member spoke and voted as he himself actually thought.'

(op. cit.)

Percy's year as Mayor culminated in the town's preparations for the celebrations for the Coronation of Elizabeth II. It was an exciting time to bow out as Mayor - the preceding twelve months had been filled with all the usual events and dinners and speech-making which every Mayor experiences. As in the case of Thomas' two years as Mayor, a snapshot of items picked at random from the town's affairs creates a vivid picture of Northampton as it struggled to build itself up again after the Second World War.

Bad housing was still an issue, and suggestions were made to introduce a scheme for the Council to take over the 'down-town slums' and give them another 10 to 20 years' lease of life by installing internal water and additional lavatories. In fact 4 out of 10 British houses had no bath or hot water, most having been built as red brick terraces in the late Victorian and Edwardian eras.

Little value was place on Northampton's old buildings, although the widespread demolition of the 1960s was yet to take place. Hazelrigg House, one of the few buildings which survived the town fire of 1675, was threatened with being converted into shops, but was saved by being taken over by a Ladies' Club.

The Council took great pleasure in introducing some modern art into the town centre by placing the sculpture, 'Lady with a Fish', in Memorial Square by St. Katherine's church. (The church is now demolished and was situated between College Street and Gold Street. The sculpture has since been re-sited in Delapre Abbey gardens.) The changing times were also reflected in the Council's decision to extend car parking facilities by the Garden of Remembrance next to All Saints' church.

Mayor of Northampton - 70 Years on

Percy and Barbara Adams as Mayor and Mayoress

Just as Thomas had been involved with planning new reservoirs for the town's growing population, so Percy presided over the creation of Pitsford reservoir, said to be the fifth largest in the country. Digging began in about 1952 and the flooding of the valley was scheduled for 1955.

Yet another link with one of his grandfather's interests can be seen when Percy opened Delapre Abbey and Gardens to the public *'adding another piece of England's green and pleasant land to the Borough's notable open spaces'*. Other areas were also opened up for leisure use in this year - Franklin's Gardens was the new sports ground owned by the Express Lift Company (by the Weedon Road), and the Overstone Solarium to the east of town became very popular with its new open-air swimming pool. The countryside in general was also being more appreciated as a place for walking, and the now familiar complaints about obstacles in the way of public footpaths were being voiced as early as 1952. County Councils were told that they had to survey their footpaths and prepare draft maps with a view to restoring the footpath system.

The cleanliness of the streets may have improved since the late 19th century, but concern was expressed at an increase in 'public carelessness'. The Council voted to condemn *'the general deterioration in the cleanliness of the streets and to ask the Borough Engineer to ... restore the town to its former condition of cleanliness'*.

To the north of the Market Square the shops in the Emporium Arcade, a lovely example of Edwardian architecture, were flourishing, and a reporter in the Northampton Independent reflected with interest on how only 50 years previously it had been an orchard and garden for grazing sheep. Little did he guess that the Arcade was shortly to be demolished in the wave of new building that destroyed much of the heart of the town centre when the Grosvenor shopping centre was erected in the early 1970s.

Hindsight also renders poignant the centenary celebrations at the Town Hall of the Roman Catholic convent of Notre Dame - its beautiful façade on Abington Street is still remembered by many Northamptonians, and the whole building was swept away in the 1960s.

Although on a much smaller scale than the massive shopping centres of the 1970s, the building of a new 'shopping centre with a covered arcade' round a square at King's Heath aroused considerable interest in the press - King's Heath was one of the new model suburbs of the post-war era. Other suburbs were also spreading - some amid the fears of local residents who resented the encroachment on green fields, such as Sunnyside to the north of town near Boughton, and Eastfield north of the Headlands area.

There were signs of the times in the public concern about speeding motorbikes over the Easter bank holiday and the sad announcement of the last train trip on the Blisworth-Stratford railway line. The arrival of television was

Barbara Adams outside The Pickwick Café

often in the news. By 1952 it was available to more than two thirds of Britain. The Mayoress, Barbara Adams, made the local newspaper when she was shown the importance of having a suppressor fitted to a television set in order to avoid any interference from electrical appliances. However, the excitement over the new invention was even then being countered by the views of those who believed that *'Television is a waste of time. TV can become a narcotic for the masses. TV will stop people thinking for themselves.'*

The Borough Council caused a great deal of disagreement when they decided to refuse to allow a summer extension of the drinking licences. Town pubs would still have to close at 10pm, whereas pubs in the rest of the county could remain open until 10.30pm. A similar furore was caused when the Sunday Observance Act was debated in the House of Commons. Northampton Christian leaders were vocal in their opposition to any repeal of the Act. The Rev. J. Ashplant of the Central Methodist church in Gold Street declared:

'My own church is at the beginning of a year of evangelism, and one of the things we stand for is the Christian observance of Sunday. It is a day of re-creation not recreation. Future legislation affecting the observance of Sunday either nationally or locally should be based on the assumption that rest and spiritual re-creation must be observed.'

N.I. 23.1.1953

The Rev. Ashplant was not, however, blind to the reality of the situation and admitted that mere repression of other activities on Sunday would not solve the problem of empty churches. The Anglican minister, the Rev. J. Ashworth of Abington, took a more serious moral tone: the Bill to abolish the Sunday Observance Act was *'designed for the deeper desecration of the Lord's Day, already sufficiently secularised, and under the cover of liberating man's spirit, it could well mean its further enslavement.'*

(op. cit.)

Percy as a devout Baptist and supporter of church Sunday Schools would probably have taken a similar line against the move to secularise Sunday. At all events the Council did not totally ease restrictions on Sunday activities. Although tennis was at last to be allowed in the parks, the children's swings were still to be chained up. As with the debate in 1946 on whether cinemas should be opened on Sundays, the concern was still felt that children must not be distracted from attending church Sunday Schools.

Although the War had finished seven years ago, it still cast its shadow over the town and the town's activities - rationing meant that people were still being encouraged to grow their own food and have an allotment. A group of cadets from Northampton Boys Grammar School visited Germany, and their itinerary included a harrowing trip to Belsen, the former Nazi concentration camp.

Shortages were still common - there being a black market for eggs, and people were so remiss at returning milk bottles that the Ministry of Food made it an offence to keep milk bottles for more than a few days, with a maximum penalty of £500.

However, signs of change were visible as the years of hardship were gradually giving way to a growth in the economy. One of the most immediate effects on the town's population was that restrictions on building were lifted, and more building licences were granted. It was announced that 90 acres of land was available for building and could accommodate 1000 houses. After years of waiting, there were 948 people on the waiting list for building licences. The building trade was being cited as the job with the best prospects, much as computing is today.

Shop hours were now being extended after the restriction imposed during the war to enforce the black-out. The shop 'curfew' was continued in the winter months right up until 1952 in order to conserve fuel and electricity, but now the Home Secretary lifted the restrictions and the town began keenly to debate how the shop hours should be re-organised. Saturday shopping had become a difficult time, with the shops overflowing with customers who could not shop at any other time on account of 6 o'clock closing (7 o'clock on the late night and 1 pm on early closing day). Most people wanted a return to a pattern more like the pre-war hours of 8pm on weekdays and 9pm on Saturdays, with the exception of early closing day.

'For the average male or female worker in office or factory, shopping presents a problem which is nothing short of desperate. Tied to practically the same hours as those of the shops, he is left with but two alternative ways in which to make his purchases.

Either he must join the hordes of shoppers, who like himself, must cram all of their buying into Saturday - and that in a large proportion of cases means the afternoon only, for not all workers are on a five-day week - or he must hare around the town in his lunch hour, even then to find that most of the establishments are closed up and bear notices of one- or two-hour closures..'

N.I. 5.12.1952

On a different level from Council matters, winds of change were even blowing through Buckingham Palace now that George VI was no longer alive. The press reported that the Duke of Edinburgh wanted to remove the red tape and extravagance at the Palace - there were too many servants, he said, and extravagant habits such as placing a fresh bottle of whisky in the bedrooms each day.

Abington Street decorated for the Coronation of Elizabeth II

As far as Percy was concerned, the Coronation of the new Queen meant a great deal of planning, but it culminated in a highly successful occasion, the reports of which demonstrate a very lively spirit of communal celebration in the town.

The programme organised by the Council began with two hours of bell ringing all over town, followed by judging of the best decorated street in the Borough. At 10am there was divine service on the Market Square, and for the whole day the televised proceedings of the Coronation would be shown in the Town Hall to which only the elderly ticket-holders would be admitted. Sports dominated the afternoon's events with items ranging from a 'Motor Car and Motor Cycle Gymkhana' in Lower Abington Park to an exhibition tennis match by county players at Franklin's Gardens.

Bands played in four of the town parks in the evening - Abington Park, Dallington Park, Far Cotton Recreation Ground and Kingsthorpe Park, followed by various events in Becket's Park later on - a procession of decorated boats, folk dancing, signal bonfires, fireworks and finally dancing until midnight.

The televised Coronation was of course the most vital part of the whole day, and many of the town's few television owners kept open house for those in their street without a set, while lively street parties carried on all day.

'In most cases all wore gay paper hats and many of the women Union Jack aprons... The tea tables groaned with fare, and during the afternoon there were fancy dress parades, organised games and community singing, while bands, pianos and gramophones blared out popular song numbers and dance music, both for old-time and modern dancing.'

N.I. 5.6.1953

It must have been a very satisfying way for Percy and Barbara to finish their year as Mayor and Mayoress. As has been seen in the various debates and pre-occupations of the year in Council, the town had a lot to do to build itself up after the War, but at last restrictions were being lifted and progress was on the way.

It was quite fitting, therefore, that a few months before being made Mayor, Percy's family business of W.Q. & T.R. Adams was able to open its new bakery plant at King's Heath, a momentous occasion promising a chance for the family to keep pace with the changing world around them.

Chapter 11

THE BOOM YEARS

Just a few years later another new phenomenon from America arrived on the British scene, throwing the baking trade once more in turmoil. For the final years of the 1950s, however, Adams bakery grew and prospered - staff recalling with great affection this 'boom' and the lively spirit of co-operation it engendered.

'A few years after the war they were building up the business. Everybody had just come back from the forces and they had the most wonderful team because everybody had had all this discipline. Practically all of them were ex-servicemen.' (Iris Vickers)

Iris started to work for Adams in the early 1950s when she was employed in the accounts department, later becoming a director of the company until she retired in 1987. In the early days she literally saw the money as it rolled in. *'In the 50s we had 33 retail rounds and 50 odd wholesale rounds in seven counties. The four of us sat there and pounced on the books. We added them up and balanced them, and the money was counted. It was very exciting. We were all part of building up the business.'*

One of the deliverymen, Bert Masters, started working for Adams in 1957 when the trade had grown even more. *'My actual job was wholesale. In those days we had about 10 retail 'electrics' (vans) going from door to door, and we also had mobile shops which would go round the villages. My vehicle was a 3 ton truck. My daily trip was about 40 deliveries.'* It was a hard life, not only regarding the hours but also the primitive conditions in the lorry: *'Heaters weren't invented then and it was 4 o'clock in the morning. By the time I got to Thrapston I used to pull in the lay-by in the winter and run round the van to try to get myself warm because I was freezing in the cab even though I'd got an overcoat and gloves on. I always remember when we had the first van come in with a heater in - we could not believe it! It had got this little tin box with a fan behind it.'*

Sliced bread was enormously popular and it was up to Bert and the other delivery drivers to meet the growing demand as best they could. Their

The Boom Years

The horse-drawn cart and hand-cart from the Derby Road bakery entering the Northampton Carnival (1950s):
(Left to right) Eric Hillyer, Barbara Adams, Philip Vickers, Philip Adams and Alan Wykes (the Wedgwood chef)

commitment even meant that they ended up working through the night on occasion. *'I'd start at 4am on a normal Friday delivering as far afield as Peterborough and St. Ives, and finish at 1pm. I would load back up with 3-4 quartern of sliced bread and then go back and do it again. This was because when sliced bread took off, I couldn't fit on the lorry the number of loaves I needed for the Saturday morning. So I had to take half of Saturday's bread out on a Friday afternoon. Everybody wanted bread first thing, so I'd finish at 7pm on a Friday.*

And of course a holiday weekend created really big problems. If you were closed on Bank Holiday Monday, on Saturday you'd got to pull in Saturday, Sunday and Monday.

The slicing of the bread evolved over the years. Eventually the idea of 'toast bread' caught on - bakers found that by taking every other blade out of the machine they could have thick slices. Later medium sliced bread was introduced, although the idea was not necessarily greeted with enthusiasm by the bakery staff. Bert remembers: *'Everybody thought it was a waste of time, but it met public demand.'*

Baker customers ordering their bread from Adams still saw Adams as their rival and did not want to have the Adams name printed on the waxed paper.

The Boom Years

*The Adams carnival float (1956) showing
Iris Vickers (far left) and Philip Adams' daughter Juliet (sitting far right)*

They could not afford their own slicing machine, so Adams obligingly allowed them to have the loaves wrapped in plain paper. Bakers could then pass them off as their own. Bert recalls the excitement of the boom in trade: *'Once we started delivering sliced steamed loaves in a white wax wrapper, it took off. It just took off! I think some of the bakers saw it as a way of making life easier for them. They didn't really like us.'*

Whatever the rivalry, there was still quite a casual trusting atmosphere about deliveries in those days. In the early morning no-one was awake in the numerous little bakeries which bought Adams bread. Bert remembers letting himself into the various shops: *'They left notes out, or they'd leave it to me because I knew the order off by heart. In the winter I've stood there and my hands have been that cold that I couldn't even write the ticket out. You had to be tough to stick it, especially for 40 years!'*

The drivers were very helpful and supportive of one another. If Bert was running short of bread, he used to leave an empty bread tray beside a telegraph pole at a certain junction as a kind of message to the other drivers. They would then leave at Bert's last shop whatever loaves they had got left over. Similarly, if any delivery van broke down, a fellow driver was sure to be willing to help him out, even if it meant borrowing a chain from a nearby farmer and towing the van all the way back to Northampton.

The Boom Years

The delivery men found that most villages had a grocery shop as well as a bakery. If they were supplying the bakery, the baker would not want them to sell to the grocery as well. Bert and his colleagues always honoured that arrangement. It was not difficult when the bakers were so eager to buy Adams bread. As Bert says, *'It was a very easy selling job. Our name was very well-known and respected. I used to point out that the profit from the turnover six days a week could pay the assistant's wages and the electric light bill. It always worked every time.'*

One of the more unexpected difficulties came when Bert had to train some new staff. *'You'd get a guy who could drive a truck, but he was no good at arithmetic.'*

Delivering the bread wholesale was of course just one side of the business. Other members of staff such as Richard Patching and Ted Frost remember the hectic life in Adams' own shops and in the bakery itself.

Ted worked in the bakery making doughnuts, crumpets and pork pies.

'We used to do crumpets by hand - we had a big hotplate about the length of a cricket pitch. We had six loose rings across. The depositor put the mixture into the rings. The holes in the crumpets are made by the baking powder bubbling up. We used to mix the liquid in big tubs by hand. It was like wallpaper paste. There used to be four of us making crumpets all day.

One of the familiar Adams delivery vans at King's Heath (1950s)

I was the crumpet man for a bit and then the pork pie man. Making the pork pies was quite something. We used to boil up all the jelly, the bones, the gristle and the skin. I remember fetching whole sides of pork from the butcher and boning it. We used to take the jowls (cheeks) out and use that, even though it was fatty. You got a leg of pork and the meat on that was superb. Then we used to get the rind, put the bones in and the gelatine and make jelly for the next day. They wouldn't like that idea nowadays. They wouldn't let you use bones and rind with the BSE scare. In those days you didn't think about it.'

The Crumpet Machine (1960)

The art of fancy cake baking was more highly valued then than now. It was very labour intensive to make iced fancies. Ted commented somewhat sadly, *'Now they like to produce something, take it out of the oven and have it finished. In those days it didn't make any difference.'*

Doughnuts were considerably easier to make, as has already been described, and Richard Patching remembers how they were just piled up high in the shop window in a heap. Sales of doughnuts were especially brisk on a Saturday morning. *'We'd start at 5am and we'd still be frying at 1 o'clock on a Saturday afternoon. They'd sell about 2000 on a Saturday morning in one shop.'*

Business was in fact brisk for bread in general, with queues building up outside Adams' shops before they even opened on a Saturday. One of the biggest queues could be found outside the actual bakery in King's Heath when the novel idea of a Cash and Carry was introduced. Iris Vickers had seen an article about such an outlet in Bristol, and Philip agreed to give it a try. The idea was very popular, but when shortly after opening there was a bread strike, Iris remembers the huge increase in customers:

'They had to have the police out every Saturday morning to control the queues. They were waiting all the way down Gladstone Road. People came from everywhere for it and the sales figures soared. People would even shop for their neighbours in the villages.'

(Iris Vickers)

The Boom Years

To return to Ted Frost's reminiscences about baking fancy confectionery and how it seems a dying art: he felt that a bakery is more like a factory nowadays. *'If you asked some of the young bakers to mould up a good cottage loaf, they couldn't do it. Not many of them can do harvest sheaves now either, shaped like a sheaf of corn with a mouse running up the side.'*

Arthur Alibon was 'the bread man' at the Adams Avenue bakery and Ted remembers admiring his skill at doing plaits and twists. However, alongside these high standards of workmanship went a level of hygiene and safety which would be unacceptable today. Ted would see Arthur making notches in his bread as he moulded it - *'He had a razor blade in his mouth. It used to make me cringe. It made my legs go funny.'*

In the bakehouse everything was made of wood - a material which is now considered unhygienic. *'You're not allowed to have a bit of wood in the bakehouse nowadays. We had to scrape the surfaces to get them clean. We had to make a scraper with a wooden top on and we had to scrape the paving slabs down.'*

An elaborate iced cake made by Adams in 1960

The Boom Years

The bakery business may have been booming, but what was the bread actually like as far as quality was concerned? During the Second World War when there was a shortage of shipping space the Ministry of Food ruled that bread should contain a higher amount of bran and wheat germ, raising the extraction rate from 70% to 85%. This bread became known as the National loaf and was thus introduced to reduce the amount of flour imported. It had the added effect of improving the nutritional quality of bread. Ever since the advent of roller-milling the nutritional quality of flour had deteriorated, although the popularity of the 'whiter than whiteness' continued to grow.

'I've been giving them sliced bathroom sponge and they haven't noticed yet.'

Cartoon by Bryan McAllister, the Guardian, 3 Dec. 1974 on the occasion of the strike of workers in bread factories

The Boom Years

In 1953 a government flour order lifted the war-time restrictions and allowed millers to mill flour to any extraction rate they pleased, but with two provisos: flour below the 80% rate had to have synthetic vitamins and nutrients added, and the National loaf was still to be subsidised. (It appears that the public were quite willing to continue eating the greyish National loaf, as after two years white bread consumption was still no more than 0.8% of the total.) Eventually the government decided that the 1953 order was unenforceable. As long as all the prescribed nutrients of calcium, iron, nicotinic acid etc were added, the nation's health was thought to be safeguarded.

Although not introduced until the early 1960s, a new bakery method called the Chorleywood Process sounded another death knell for traditional flour and traditional baking. Both then and now Adams place great importance on the maturing of the dough which brings out the flavour of bread. With the new process the maturing of the dough was replaced by a few minutes of intense mechanical agitation in special high-speed mixers. One London consultant even wrote to the Daily Telegraph in 1973 to complain about the harm done by the new baking method: *'Not only does the white loaf do no good, it is actually harmful to the body. Every encouragement should be given to the abolition of this foul food... the white loaf is not even fit to be given away.'* His comments are strangely reminiscent of the reaction to the adulteration of bread in the 19th century.

The giant bakeries that used the CWP (Chorleywood Process) defended it. Firstly it enabled bakers to make use of flour milled with a substantial proportion of English wheat, thus saving on imports. Secondly, it saved money on labour, reducing the cost of production, and it gave more bread per sack of flour. An extra gallon of water could be absorbed for each 280lb of flour, and this increased the bulk of the dough and hence the number of loaves.

Adams continued to favour the slower fermentation process, taking nearly three hours, which ensured the bread would have more flavour. For a while, however, even this tradition was compromised when another startling business development took place in the 1960s, as shall be seen at the end of this chapter.

Yet in the mid 1950s business developments were moving in other directions - Adams increased their retail outlets dramatically by buying up rival bakeries. On a small scale they were just following the trend set by the giant bakeries.

The first purchase was the company that had originally been developed by Philip's grandfather and great-uncle, Frank and Wallace - Adams Bros. Wallace's son, Oliver, had also opened the Oliver Adams Company just for the business at the Corner House café on Wood Hill. These two companies had been sold to James Oatley when Oliver found that his son did not want to carry on the

The Boom Years

bakery business. Remembering how Philip's father, Tom, had been prevented from sharing in Adams Bros. on the death of his father, and had had to go back to renting a bakehouse and pushing his goods on a truck to the shop in Marefair, it was with a great sense of satisfaction that Adams Bros. now came under 'WQ & TR Adams'. (For some strange reason - perhaps because 'Oliver Adams' rolls off the tongue - it was this name that was chosen in later years when the Adams family were deciding on a name for their new larger company.)

About two years after acquiring Adams Bros. and Oliver Adams the firm bought another business that had previously been in the family. Edgar Adams, Philip's great-uncle, had sold his shop at the corner of Wellingborough and Allen Road to Mr. Burman, who then sold it to Mr. Stevens. By the 1950s Stevens also owned shops at 54 Kingsley Park Terrace and Mercers Row, so Philip took great pleasure in buying up yet another local business. The acquisition of Stevens' gave W.Q. & T.R. Adams three more retail outlets plus a small bakery, and buying Adams Bros. had brought in the Adams Avenue bakery plus shops at 209 Wellingborough Road, 55 Kettering Road, 27 St. Leonards Road (Far Cotton), 28 Abington Grove and 55 Harborough Road (Kingsthorpe). A picture of the extent of the Adams 'empire' can be built up when the number of already existing W.Q. & .T.R. Adams shops is counted - 212 Kettering Road, 170 Wellingborough Road, Weedon Road, Beech Avenue, 12 Kingsley Park Terrace and 28 Abington Street.

Theobald's, Kettering (1950s)

The family now began to think further afield, and shortly after buying Stevens' they bought Theobald's of Kettering who were just about to sell out to one of the giant bakeries. All these bakeries provided Adams with an important supply of retail outlets to take the increasing supply of bread being baked at King's Heath, with its capacity for large-scale production. The big investment embarked on by the family with such trepidation after the war was now bringing its reward.

The final local bakery business to be bought by Adams was the prestigious old established firm of Lawrence's on St. Giles Street. Philip believes that it was another example of how he has benefited from 'not what you know but who you know'. 'A local estate agent rang me up and said, "Do you want another shop in the town centre? I've got Lawrence's to sell." I said "All right, we'll have it." ' This was in 1965 and came at a particularly suitable time for Philip and his family because his son, Thomas, was completing his National Diploma in Bakery Management. It was an ideal opportunity for him to gain experience by letting him manage Lawrence's.

Thomas remembers how old-fashioned the business was, and the challenge he enjoyed of making it profitable again. The bakehouse was situated behind the shop, on the Riding. (The building is now The Blue Plate Café and the big old oven door is still to be seen in the wall.) John Lawrence and his wife had been running the shop. 84 year old Bert Lawrence was still making the pork pies for which Lawrence's was particularly famous. Thomas recalls: *'The next youngest person to me was John Lawrence who was in his early sixties. It was very genteel and a very happy little atmosphere. I soon realised it was not the most viable business because of the old-fashioned way of doing things. Eventually we went to see the accountant and he said "Well, you're doing better because you haven't lost so much money this six months as you lost the last six months!"*

One of Lawrence's customers was Earl Spencer, and I discovered that they were delivering one small brown loaf a day in a van all the way to Althorp. The aristocracy being the way they were, they were used to paying their bills about once a quarter, so the Althorp estate would owe Lawrence's for weeks and weeks and weeks. It bothered me a bit, so I said "We'll have to write and say that although the loaf is only 2/6d, we'll have to ask a delivery charge of about 5s a day". They quickly said, "No thank you very much". Well it cost more than 5s a day to pay the man to drive the van to Althorp and back. It was something Lawrence's had been doing for donkeys' years just because they'd always done it, but they never made money at it.'

The Lawrence business had started in 1858, almost the same time as Adams. It is interesting to compare the way the two bakeries had evolved. Before the war Lawrence's delivery men wore a uniform on the lines of a chauffeur, and they delivered to the big country houses around the county. Lawrence's had always concentrated more on high-class confectionery than on bread.
Ted Frost worked for a while at the Lawrence's premises in the 1960s and he remembers how at first they only baked about 70lb of flour a day. Both the bakehouse and warehouse for the bread used to be situated in the Riding.

'The bakehouse eventually became the back entrance to Jack Haddon's florist shop and later the Blue Plate Café. There used to be four or five overgrown back gardens between the bakehouse and the warehouse. We had a

Lawrence's, St. Giles Street, Northampton

blue three-wheeled truck and we employed someone specially to wheel the bread down. He was called the packer. He used to do the fire too in the daytime - the ovens were still coke-fired. We used to do a lot of cakes, iced buns and Chelseas. Everything was fresh. Nothing was kept overnight at Lawrence's.'

Next door to the bakery shop Lawrence's owned a small off-license which was for wines and not spirits. Barbara Adams, with her interest in catering, saw the potential for a tea-room there next door to the shop. She wanted to reduce her workload and had let The Wedgwood to Berni Inns. They, however, were anxious to make the restaurant fully licensed and it was difficult to obtain a full on-license in the 60s. Barbara agreed to give up Lawrence's off-license and this enabled the Berni Inn to obtain a full on-license at The Wedgwood. As a sign of the times Barbara's new café was not called a 'tea-room' but a 'coffee shop'.

Just down the road at The Corner House the Clipper had sadly had to be closed because of a fire in the mid 1950s. Stringent new fire regulations meant that it would cost a great deal of money to fit the basement out appropriately, and so the unusual café, so popular with young people, had closed down.

'Oliver Adams', as it was now called, still retained the old names of the bakeries which they had bought up - Stevens', Lawrence's, Theobald's - so few local people realised there had been a change of ownership. The firm's successful small retail outlets, however, were now spread throughout the town and parts of the county. Despite this prosperity, by the start of the 1960s Adams' large bakery itself was not as secure a business as might have been supposed.

Just as Adams had been buying up smaller bakeries, so had the giant bakery companies been buying up other businesses. It was a trend that grew steadily during the 1950s. Who were these giants and how had they acquired so much wealth? They were not just bakers who had been even more enterprising than the Adams family - they were in fact the tradespeople who had loomed so large in the history of early 19th century baking and who had exerted such an influence on the small bakers then as now - the millers.

During the 1950s the owner of the powerful milling and baking firm, Garfield Weston of Canada, started buying up the more vulnerable bakeries in Britain in order to acquire more outlets and more production facilities. (He had already begun this process just before the war.) In 1953, when the subsidy was taken off flour in Britain he approached several large millers and tried to negotiate a discount, based on the huge quantities of flour he was buying. The millers, however, refused to submit to his demands. They lived to regret it. Weston decided to stop buying some of his flour from British millers and instead imported it from his own mills in Canada. This was a serious blow to the British milling trade, but two of the most powerful millers in Britain - J. Rank Ltd and Spiller's Ltd - retaliated by establishing their own bakeries and thus maintaining assured outlets for their flour. In essence this was no different from the development mentioned in chapter 1 where millers became proprietors of baker's shops and employed journeymen as their agents, allowing them a small commission on any flour sold. Rank and Spiller's went on to buy minor bakeries and family businesses, and many smaller millers went out of business or were taken over.

By 1960 all three of these giant milling/baking concerns - Weston, Rank and Spiller's - set about ensuring that their products would be on sale in groceries throughout Britain. A housewife would no longer have to go to a bakery for her bread but could buy it nicely wrapped at the local corner shop.

Rank took over the old established firm of Hovis and also the millers, McDougall. They called their bread Mother's Pride, but despite the evocative name the bread was thought by many to be the antithesis of homely bread. *'If you like wrapped sliced bakery bread, you'll find it difficult to make something similar at home.'* Which, June 1975

The Chorleywood Process of bread-making brought in the decline of the traditional method of maturing the dough for a good flavour - a method with which the Adams family was so familiar and which they valued so highly. The miller/bakers claimed that the overwhelming majority wanted their bread made using the CWP - two out of three housewives bought it. Market research revealed

The Boom Years

that it was favoured for 'availability', 'convenience' (i.e. size and shape) and 'hygiene' (wrapping). No reference was made to whether people actually *liked* it.

The message was put across loud and clear that the majority wanted this new bread. However, whole food organisations and independent bakers were not wealthy enough to launch million pound advertising campaigns such as Weston, Rank and Spiller's could afford. Their small voice of protest could not be heard.

It is not surprising that the success of Adams' bakery was brought to the attention of the giant milling/baking concerns. By now Adams was buying 1500 sacks of flour per week and were delivering as far afield as King's Lynn in Norfolk. Philip remembers how he eventually succumbed to the pressure. *'In the mid 50s we refused to sell the business and eventually Spiller's asked us if we would sell them a percentage of the business. So we sold them 25% of the shares and Harry Colbourne joined the Board of Directors. Ronald Croft, who had started work at 14 in the Kingsthorpe bakery and become foreman and then production manager at King's Heath - he too was made a Director. We finally sold the whole business to Spiller's in 1963.'*

Adams had been buying flour from various local sources - Heygate's, Westley Bros., Whitworth's of Wellingborough and Rank. On being taken over they had to buy all their flour from Spiller's.

Selling the business founded over 100 years previously by great-grandfather Thomas was of course a difficult step for the family to take, but they can look back on it now and see that it was the right thing to do.

Philip reflects, *'I don't think we made a mistake. If we'd remained independent, we'd have had a job to have existed eventually.'*

The story of what lay in store for Adams after being taken over in 1963 belongs in the next and final chapter. With initiative and the good fortune of being in the right place at the right time, Adams saw how to turn the tables in their favour again.

However, first of all came the second new phenomenon from America to bring turmoil not just to the bakers, but the food world in general - the new style of shop called 'the supermarket'...

Chapter 12

FULL CIRCLE

In the early days of the supermarket the threat posed to the baking trade did not appear particularly grave. In 1961 Adams even supplied the first Sainsbury's store on Abington Street (situated opposite the public library), but the growing popularity of self-service and large stores meant that a supermarket would always have an edge.

Iris Vickers tells the amusing tale of one incident when Adams had negotiated to supply Sainsbury's with their bread and to print the Sainsbury's label on the wrapping. *'There was a little old lady in a great long queue and she'd got a Sainsbury's loaf in her basket. I said to her, "Do you really think it's worth queuing all this long time for just one small loaf?" "My dear," she said, "This is <u>Sainsbury's</u> bread. It's certainly worth queuing for." I couldn't put her right. It was secret.'*

At first supermarket bread was not cheaper than in a bakery, but the spread of the stores and of competitive chains meant that the price of bread began to go down. Supermarkets became very large purchasers and were able to negotiate national terms for the price of their bread. Large firms such as Rank, Spiller's and Weston would then supply them, and a smaller independent bakery had no chance of competing.

The giant bakeries had some cause to feel badly treated by their large supermarket customers - Tesco, for instance, might say to Weston's, 'We're going to put our bread down by 3p a loaf. We'll stand 1.5p and you have to stand 1.5p.' However, this was not in fact any different from the way in which Weston, himself, had treated the British millers previously, expecting them to give his bakeries a big discount because of his large orders.

The impact of supermarkets' cheap bread was not without drawbacks for the customer. As a reaction to the need to sell their bread to the supermarkets more cheaply, the millers/bakers reduced the quality of their flour. They put more water in the dough and baked it for a shorter period of time - anything to reduce the cost of a loaf. It was at this time that people started talking about 'cotton-wool' bread. It may not have been as harmful as some of the adulterated flour concocted in the 19th century, but it was certainly not traditional wholesome bread.

The delivery rounds were another feature of the traditional bakery business that suffered under the advent of the supermarket. Customers now wanted to get in their car and do a big shop at their local supermarket where bread was probably cheaper anyway. The baker's vans, along with the mobile shops, died a natural death. Adams fought hard to keep their vans going, but found that they had to make changes. In the end the deliverymen became owners of their own van and delivery round, but even this died out.

An interesting post-script to the story of the supermarkets is one case illustrating how even supermarkets are not invincible. Bert Masters used to deliver to the Co-op supermarket that was built in about 1990 on the London Road, Northampton. He watched it die within a comparatively short space of time, and the decline started long before a competitor, Morrison's, opened another supermarket a few hundred yards away. Bert contrasts the failure of the new Co-op with the success of the older Co-op on the corner of Wellingborough and Barry Roads, and he believes that the secret lies in good customer loyalty. The Barry Road Co-op may not be as modern as the London Road store, but after many years it has built up a strong base of loyal customers.

Even the giant miller/bakeries proved to have a weakness. Spiller's decided to call in the services of the troubleshooter, McKinsey's, as part of an efficiency drive. The three giant bakeries with their three rival brands - Mother's Pride, Sunblest and Fine Lady - were extremely competitive. Bert Masters, who by now had been promoted to key account executive, remembers vividly his first-hand experience of the competition: *'What you did, they'd go one better. It was war, absolute war.'* He recalls how it was not just possible to sell too little, he could get into deeper trouble by selling too much. *'I tried to get one Co-op supermarket to take our products, and by the end of my presentation the chief executive ended up not just giving me one supermarket - he gave me fourteen. I ran into big trouble when I came back because Spiller's couldn't cope. The order was too big. I ended up having a nervous breakdown.'*

McKinsey's initiated various changes. The confectionery department at King's Heath was closed. The delivery rounds were to be supplied by a bakery in Nottingham and the W.Q. & T.R. Adams shops by the smaller Adams bakeries. Later in 1968 McKinsey's were brought in again and their new plans required Philip to supervise three bakeries - Northampton, Leicester and Grimsby. Understandably he was not pleased at the prospect of all the travelling involved and the added pressure of the work. Almost with tongue in cheek he wrote to the managing director and made him a bold request concerning Spiller's small bakeries of Oliver Adams, Stevens' and Theobald's that were supplying the Northampton and Kettering shops with confectionery. He pointed out that in

Spiller's reorganisation the small bakeries did not fit into the picture at all, so would they sell them back to the family? To his surprise the managing director replied that they were agreeable to this as long as Philip continued to buy flour from Spiller's.

So the Adams business was almost back to the situation just after the Second World War, in the sense that it again comprised several small bakeries with their various retail outlets, but with no large bakery from which to supply the bread. On June 1st 1969 a holding company was formed called Northampton Bakeries Ltd (which still exists today).

The Directors were Barbara and Philip Adams, Philip's son Thomas, and Iris Vickers. The holding company controlled the smaller bakery and catering companies of Oliver Adams, Stevens Scotch Bakery, Theobald's, J. Lawrence & Co. and Adams of Northampton (comprising The Wedgwood and The Pickwick restaurants). Each business had its own management - Colin Cloreley at Oliver Adams, Mr. Morgan and later Richard Patching at Stevens', Arnold Bryant at Theobald's, and L.N.J. Smith at The Pickwick. The head office was situated at Lawrence's on St. Giles Street.

The family decided to concentrate on the retail side of the trade, and made the important decision to promote their image as a traditional bakery, selling no sliced bread but just bread baked in their own small bakeries.

A Northampton bus on Mercers Row, advertising the familiar 'Adams Bread' (the bus had the original 1947 livery)

During the 1970s, therefore, Adams felt themselves to be in something of a time warp, although their business prospered. Lawrence's bakery was re-equipped, Stevens' at Allen Road was modernised and virtually rebuilt. Theobald's installed new ovens, and Oliver Adams, the largest company, was soon outgrowing its bakery in Adams Avenue.

Thomas, was now also helping to manage the bakery and he remembers how he heard about a premises up for sale on King's Heath, ironically next door to the bakery his family had had built in 1952. He and his father knew that they would benefit from being able to operate from a large scale bakery again, and Thomas still recalls the excitement of looking round the building. (It had been Baxter's pork pie factory.) *'I rang up my father that night and came up here with a torch. I left the plans at my father's.'* The family knew the building would be ideal and bought it over the telephone.

Philip recalls: *'We bought the bakery Christmas 1979 and had the great pleasure of reorganising the building. It was full of old fridges - a real mess. Tom spent the next nine months organising the refurbishment and we went to France to buy an oven.'* The bakery started up in 1980 and only supplied the Oliver Adams shops, thus replacing the old bakery on Adams Avenue. Some years later the building was extended and became the bakery which can be seen today on Gladstone Road.

During the 1970s while building up the trade at Lawrence's on St. Giles Street, the firm had an idea for an experiment which was to have far-reaching results. In the face of the mass production of modern 'cotton-wool' loaves, why not bake old-fashioned crusty bread in the old oven at Lawrence's? *'It was just at the time when fortunately people were getting fed up with sliced bread because the quality had deteriorated. So we were absolutely on the ball for crusty bread. As soon as we had the experience, we encouraged Oliver Adams and Stevens' bakeries also to make crusty bread. We had to put better boilers in the oven to make steam to make the bread crusty. We had a mini-boom! People hadn't had any old-fashioned crusty bread since before the war. We had queues of people waiting for the hot loaves as they came out of the oven. It was extraordinary - like the experience with sliced bread.'*

Adams was not of course the only independent baker to have the idea at this time. The new type of bread caught on across the whole country until the supermarkets realised that they needed to match what was on offer in the little independent bakeries. In-house bakeries, producing hot crusty bread became a new feature of the supermarket.

The increase in the popularity of crusty bread may not just be a reaction to the rather tasteless sliced bread. The new package holidays meant that people were travelling abroad more and enjoying the different breads on the continent,

Full Circle

An Adams shop window displaying everything from baguettes to bloomers and cottage loaves

the French baguettes in particular, and they wanted to carry on eating it at home. Adams made not only French bread but Vienna rolls, and the success of the trade meant that within two years they were able to buy a new German oven especially designed to bake Vienna bread.

On a larger scale Adams' success also meant that they were able gradually to absorb their small bakeries - Stevens', Lawrence's and then Theobald's, so that the bakery at King's Heath was supplying the bread to all the various shops in the county. It even became possible to buy other retail outlets as far afield as Rugby, Leighton Buzzard and Towcester, and their delivery area now extended to Bedford, Buckingham, Banbury, Brackley and Daventry.

So by the 1990s Adams was well established again as a major independent bakery, operating from a large site that still followed the more traditional methods of baking. The competition from the supermarkets was still a threat. How could an independent bakery continue to survive into the 21st century?

The answer was found in yet another trend which had arrived from America - fast-food. It was Tom who realised the potential of the take-away trade. One of his managers, Colin Clorley, had already tried it successfully in the 1960s. He had seen in Liverpool a baker's shop that was selling hot sausage rolls

- at the time an unusual trade for a baker. Colin immediately put a gas oven into The Corner House bakery shop and started doing a roaring trade; he was baking sausage rolls by the thousands right up until half past five on a Saturday afternoon. People were flooding past on their way to catch their bus at the old Derngate bus station, and would be tempted by the sight and smell of a hot snack. When the bus station closed in the 1970s the trade suffered badly, but the idea of hot take-away food had taken root.

Tom saw that the pace of life was getting faster and faster and nobody was going home for lunch any more. When he had been a schoolboy at Kingsthorpe Grove School he used to hear the Barratt shoe factory hooter at midday and then see crowds of men riding up the hill on their bikes, going home for dinner. People are now prepared to go out to buy their lunch. Corner bakeries are a natural place to provide the various rolls and sandwiches that people require, whether they be lorry drivers or solicitors.

Tom Adams in the bakery (1981)

Full Circle

Tom recognises the value of the trade: *'We are most fortunate to be in an industry where although our traditional business of selling bread and cakes over the counter has been curtailed by the supermarkets to a great extent, we've been able to do something else to replace it. So if you look in any baker's shop that is doing well, a very large proportion of their business will be pies and hot food baked off in the shop, or sandwiches and filled rolls made up on the premises. So the queues of people are not in line for their hot crusty bread - they're there now for the take-away food.'*

It might be thought that American fast-food chains like MacDonald's offer stiff competition to the bakery take-aways, but this has not proved to be the case; *'Strangely enough, firms like MacDonald's coming into the country with fast-food have been an advantage. They've persuaded the public that it's quite OK to eat out of a bag while walking down the street or in your car or anywhere else. My grandmother would have been horrified if anyone had walked out of her shop eating what she'd just sold them! It was sold for them to take home, not eat straight away.'*

Adams now sell all kinds of lunchtime food ranging from hot pizzas to chilled pasta salads. One advantage of their rolls and sandwiches is that they are always fresh, unlike those in supermarket chains, which are about two days old before they arrive in the shops. Adams' take-away food is so successful that it now constitutes 40% of their turnover. A few years ago the soaring trade in sandwiches even made a story in The Times. It ran: *'Britons are spending more on sandwiches than they do on pizza, pasta and burgers put together. Outperforming growth in all other fast-food sectors, sandwich sales have grown by 45% over the past 5 years according to market researchers Mintel... Shorter lunch breaks, the trend towards eating on the move or at work, snacking and growing health concerns are all believed to have contributed to the sandwich's burgeoning popularity.'* Times 18.11.97

In about 1993 at Theobald's bakery in Kettering, the manager Richard Patching, a long-standing employee of the firm, was seeking another outlet for the business, just as Tom had done. He had a similar idea, but took it one step further. He puts it this way: *'The high street had moved not just to the supermarkets, but also to the edge of the motorway and to the garage forecourt.'* If he could make cakes with a long shelf-life and protect them in transparent wrappings, they could be sold in garages and motorway service areas as a sweet snack to motorists. The cakes which he started making were American-style muffins flavoured with chocolate chips or blueberries. He started in a small way using nothing but an ice-cream scoop, wrapping the muffins, and selling them to wholesalers who would deliver to motorway service stations and garages. Richard remembers the excitement of the early days when he was developing his new product; *'I got my first big order at a distributing company in Market*

Harborough. I took samples over and they said they'd give it a go. They ordered 300. I said, "300 units?" and they said "No, 300 boxes!" I started to panic and I remember stopping at the first telephone kiosk and ringing through. "Everybody stop working and concentrate on muffins. We've got an order for 300 boxes within the week." That's how it all started.'

The long shelf-life is now twelve weeks and depends on achieving the correct chemical balance to prevent mould forming - Richard now talks about the PH value and the ERH value (equilibrium relative humidity), which would have been unknown to the first Thomas Adams over one hundred years ago. The trade took off in such a phenomenal way that now Theobald's bakery does nothing but make muffins - about 300,000 a week, sending them all over the country from Scotland to the Channel Islands, and wrapping them not with the Adams label but with the distributor's name.

Just as in the 1950s the millers decided to start making their own bread in order to increase their profits, a similar situation occurred in the smaller world of the muffin. Richard found that once distributors saw how good the product was, they were liable to start making their own - provided they had their own bakery available. He lost two big orders under such circumstances, but battled on. Matters reached such a head at one point that when he won back one lost order, he received threats over the phone from the rival producer. *'The competition is like the ice-cream wars - you step on somebody's patch and they come gunning for you.'*

Theobald's have recently bought a new automatic oven from Australia. A visit to the bakery reveals a world totally different from that of the old bakehouse described in chapter one. The machinery is controlled by a computer which itself is connected to a computer in Australia. If a fault occurs, it can be identified thousands of miles away and the information relayed to the company's computer in Leicester. Their agent, based in Peterborough, will then visit Theobald's to make the necessary adjustments. The muffins are barely touched by hand - the depositor squirts the batter into baking cups via eight tubes, and compressed air is used to suck the baked muffins out of the baking trays from where they are dropped into wire baskets to be taken to be wrapped.

The quantities of ingredients that need to be stored to cope with demand, are staggering - huge cans of rapeseed oil, enormous tubs of liquid egg (four tons are used per week), and a silo containing up to nine tons of flour. To make one batch of blueberry muffins a large bucket of Canadian blueberries stands ready to be added at the last minute.

A similar situation can be found at the King's Heath bakery in Northampton, where the reliance on computers and the large quantities and scale of production seem quite amazing to an outsider. Flour is of course no longer stored in hessian sacks in a loft, but blown by compressed air from the flour tanker into the silos. Each silo rests on four load cells which measure the resistance and record how much flour is stored. Compressed air is also used to blow the flour into the mixers, where a computer controls the temperature of the flour, air, water and the final temperature required in the dough.

Despite all this computerised equipment Adams still include in the process the traditional stage of long fermentation which is so crucial in producing the good old-fashioned flavour of their bread. In this respect Tom's great-great-grandfather would not be so confused as he would be elsewhere in the bakery. A thin liquid ferment mix is made of yeast, water and flour, left to stand for 24 hours and then added to the dough. One hundred years ago the ferment mix would probably rest for 12 hours before being added: the baker would mix and knead his dough in the afternoon, remix and 'knock it back' at about 3am, leave it to prove before finally baking it.

An automatic 'travelling' oven at King's Heath bakery (1960)

Full Circle

Unlike the dingy bakehouses of Victorian times, the huge bakery is spotless and is regularly checked by the Pest Control Officer - each 'bait-station', or mouse-trap, having its own number. However, as far as weighing the loaves is concerned, one age-old practice is still in evidence for the law still requires loaves to be specific weights - nowadays, 400g, 800g or multiples of 800g. Only 10g leeway is allowed, so the bakers still periodically take a sample loaf and check it on the scales. It is a scene strangely reminiscent of the days when the Assize of bread was of such importance in the life of a baker (although the price of a loaf is of course no longer fixed).

In contrast to the 19th century the hours of work are no longer a cause of concern, with 8 hour shifts being the norm. Doughmakers start at 5pm and then workers involved in subsequent stages of the baking process have later staggered starting times. The night shift is a busy time, not just for baking the bread. This is the time when custard tarts and Danish pastries are baked and the doughnuts fried - their respective doughs having been prepared beforehand during the day, when the rates of pay are lower. The huge bakery does not now just accommodate bread baking but a large confectionery department as well.

Future developments might include baking more varieties of foreign products such as American bagels and Mediterranean types of bread.

The business continues to expand by opening more shops in more distant areas around Northampton, such as Rugby, Olney and Corby. Expansion of the retail side of the business is preferred to increasing the wholesale trade. The latter is not a reliable avenue of expansion with orders being won and then just as easily lost.

Nevertheless, reliance on the individual traditional style of their bread does not guarantee the success of a firm such as Adams.

Part of the difficulty for independent bakers is explained by Tom. For a long time, since about the 1930s in fact, there has been a cheap food policy in Britain. The Empire made it possible to import cheap food and people are now used to it and reluctant to pay more expensive prices. On the continent, on the other hand, there has always been more legislation about bread prices and working hours, which has kept high the price of production. The Germans and French accept this and still consume more bread than in Britain. Supermarkets in Britain trade on the British insistence on cheap food, so that although the real cost of a loaf may be 25p, it is sometimes sold for as little as 17p. Tom traces this process back to the time after the Second World War when the government subsidy was taken off bread.

In Britain, at least, the consumption of bread has declined since 1900. In fact, since 1946 the decline has been steady every year. As the country has become more prosperous, people's diet has changed and includes a greater variety of products. No longer is bread such an important basic staple food.

Full Circle

In 1900 an average of 1lb (500g) of bread was eaten per head per day in the UK. In about 1980 it was estimated that only 11 million large leaves were bought per day for a population of about 55 million, thus giving one fifth of a loaf per head.

Despite all the new trends and changes, in several ways Adams bakery has come full circle. After the introduction of the new style of wrapped sliced loaf, crusty bread was 're-invented' and is now back in fashion. After following the trend for soft white bread in the 1960s, Adams' speciality is now their traditional long fermentation process, so much a part of the bakeries of their ancestors.

The most important way in which Adams has come full circle is of course the fact that there is now just the one family running the business again - Tom and his father. After the one master baker, Thomas, in 1856, there grew up six sons, all of whom had bakery businesses. By the 1930s the number had fallen to three - Percy, Oliver and Thomas Rigby. By the 1950s there was just Philip and Barbara, and now, since the death of Barbara in 1985 it is all back in the hands of just one family, Philip and Tom. Not only that, but virtually all of the original businesses and shops are back in the hands of the Adams family, even after the traumatic take-over by Spiller's in the 1960s.

It is an amazing achievement. In some ways it is no less amazing that the business still prides itself on baking bread in the traditional way. The history of baking has been marked by major changes, from the industrial revolution and its roller-mills to the rapid process of maturing dough, invented at Chorleywood. Fortunately Adams has seen tradition as a way forward, so that they can now look back on a business that spans three centuries.

When Philip first had the idea of producing a history of his firm, he knew that his family included many colourful characters and that their lives were involved in many colourful events, ranging from the campaigns of Charles Bradlaugh to the mayoralty of the last Liberal in the Northampton Borough Council in 1952. The story has grown and will continue to grow, but it is still rooted in the life of the young man who walked the ten long miles from the village of Flore to make his fortune in the town of Northampton.

Thomas Adams knew he would have a story to tell his children and his grandchildren. He did not know that it would eventually be written down so that one day the whole town would be able to read … a baker's tale.

Bibliography

Acton, Eliza *The English Bread Book* (1857)
Acton Eliza *Modern Cookery* (1855 ed.)
Adams family papers (in Northamptonshire Record Office)
Banks, Charles Edward *Topographical Dictionary of 2,885 English Emigrants to New England 1620-1650* (1931)
Bateman, Michael & Maisner H. *The Sunday Times Book of Real Bread* (Aylesbury: Rodale Press, 1982)
Beeton Mrs. *Book of Household Management* (1861)
Boorde, Andrew *Dyetary of Health* (1542)
Bradlaugh, Bonner H. *Charles Bradlaugh, a Record of his Life and Work* (London: T.Fisher Unwin, 1894)
Buchanan Dr. *Report of the Sanitary State of Northampton* (Medical Dept of the Privy Council, 1871)
Camden Hotten, John (ed.) *State Papers Domestic in the PRO covering emigration from GB to the American Plantations from 1600-1700*
Capell Wykes, Margaret *A Tale of Two Families* (Footprints, Jan. 1985)
Chronicle & Echo various items
Cogan, Lee (Medical Officer of Health, NBC) *Report of the Health of Northampton during the year 1889* (1889)
Copley, Esther *The Complete Cottage Cookery* (1849)
Corporation of Northampton *Minutes 1880-1885*
Cox, Rev.Charles (ed.) *The Records of the Borough of Northampton, Vol.2* (Corp. of the County Borough of Northampton, 1898)
D'Arcy, Fergus *Charles Bradlaugh and the World of Popular Radicalism 1833-1891* (PhD thesis Hull Univ., July 1978)
Dare, Edwin *Thoughts of a Journeyman Baker* (History Workshop Issue 3, Spring 1977)
David, Elizabeth *English Bread and Yeast* (London: Allen Lesley, 1977)
Evans, George Ewart *Ask the Fellows who cut the Hay* (1956)
Francatelli, Charles *A Plain Cookery Book for the Working Classes* (1862)
Freehold Land Society *Minute Book 1862-1875*
Freehold Land Society *Rules* (1848)
Gardner, Bartlett J. *Henry Adams of Somersetshire, England and Braintree, Massachusetts: His English Ancestry and some of his Descendants* (New York, 1927)

Gascoigne, Rev. T. et al *A History of Castle Hill Church (now Doddridge) and its Pastorate 1674 - 1895*
Hatley, Victor *Self-help at Northampton, 1851* (Northamptonshire Past and Present Vol. V)
Hollingsorth Wharton, Anne *English Ancestral Homes of Noted Americans* (Philadelphia: J.P.Lippincott Co., 1915)
Joyce, H.S. *I was born in the Country* (1946)
Ketteridge, Charles & Mays, Spike *Five Miles from Bunkum* (1972)
Lester, Fred *Looking Back* (Mayfield: 1951)
Liber Custumarum of Northampton
Mattieu Williams, W. *The Chemistry of* Cookery (1885)
Mayhew, Henry *London Labour and the London Poor* (1851)
Mead, Edwin D. *The Old English Home of John Adams' Ancestors* (Boston Herald 12.9.1927)
Medical Officer of Health for Northampton *Extracts from the Annual Reports 1892-1902*
Northampton Independent *various items*
Northampton Mercury *various items*
Northampton Town & County Building Society *Ten Million Pounds, a history 1848-1945* (1945)
Northampton Town & County Building Society *A Century of Service* (1948)
Northamptonshire Libraries *Oral History Project, tapes C14 and C65*
Orbell, P. *Nationwide, 150 Years Putting Members First* (Nationwide, 1998)
Reprints of British Parliamentary Papers Vol.3,4 and 5 (*Industrial Revolution - Factories 1854-1869): Reports of evidence given by Commissioners on conditions in bakehouses* (Irish University Press, 1969)
Robinson, Maude *The Daily Bread of Old-Time Sussex* (Sussex County Magazine, Oct. 1940)
Sayer, Alexis *Shilling Cookery for the People* (1855)
Smith, John M. *The Amos Bakery, Sutton Street, Flore* (1998)
Smith, John M. *The Works of Daisy Smith in Flore* (rev. ed. 1977)
Smith, Margaret *Mount Pleasant Baptist Church 1873 - 1998* (1998)
The Ratepayer *various items*
The Times *(18.11.1997)*
Timbs, John (ed.) *Lady Bountiful's Legacy* (1865)
Where to Buy in Northampton (1891)
Whitehouse, Ruth *The Quaker Meeting Houses of Northamptonshire* (1977)
Wickenden *Emigration from Taunton to New England* (1931)

Index

Adams, Arthur 50, 118, 146
Adams, Barbara 167, 191
Adams, Edgar 58, 118, 146
Adams, Frank 50, 88, 116-7,
    131-2, 134, 139-41
Adams, Henry of Somerset
    37-9, 40-1
Adams, Herbert 58, 118, 146
Adams, John, 3rd President of USA
    32-4, 38-9, 42, 48
Adams, Oliver 146, 158, 183
Adams, Percy 79, 121, 146, 155,
    157, 161-2, 167-9
Adams, Philip 143-4, 157, 160,
    162, 164, 185, 190-2, 199
Adams, Thomas (1831-90) 1-7, 32,
    44-50, 58, 67-9, 77, 80, 82, 84,
    90-3, 95-6, 99, 102-5, 112-3
Adams, Thomas Rigby 132, 141,
    143, 146, 162
Adams, Tom 185, 191-5, 199
Adams, Wallace 58, 116, 118,
    131-2
Adams, Walter Quincey 48, 67,
    114, 119, 121-2
Adams, William (ca. 1800-50) 2,
    36, 42
Adams (16th - 17th century Quaker
    family in Flore) 34-6, 42-3
Amos bakery 3-4
Assize of Bread 1, 7-11, 12-6
Becket's Park 107-8
Blue Plate Café 185
Bodily, Edna 132-3, 136, 141, 144,
    156
Bradlaugh, Charles 91-104
Building Society (1st name:
    Northampton Town and County Freehold
    Land Association, later the Nationwide)
    69 - 90

Clipper, The 158-9
Cooper, Pam 120
Doddridge Chapel - 46-8
Drayton 2
Flore 3, 32-3
Frost, Ann 124
Frost, Ted 150, 152, 179-81
Gurney, Joseph 73, 94, 99, 102
Inspection of bakehouses (1863) -
    17-32
Lawrence's bakery 184-6
Lay, Jess 86, 88, 150
Loaves 60-66
Masters, Bert 123, 176-9, 190
Mawby, Charles 126
Millers 18, 187-8
Mount Pleasant Baptist Chapel
    121, 139, 155-6
Northampton Radical Assoc. 94,
    96, 98, 101
Ovens 51-7, 120, 123-4, 144, 196
Patching, Richard 150, 153, 180,
    195-6
Racecourse 106-7
Recipes 14, 15, 19, 65, 138
Reed, Ann 159
Robinson, Peter 155
Stevens' Scotch Bakery 184, 186
Theobald's bakery 184, 196
Vickers, Iris 176, 180, 189, 191
Wedgwood, The 157, 186
Weedon 3-4
Whittington, Richard, Lord Mayor
    of London 8